A Concise Companion to
Feminist Theory

Blackwell Concise Companions to Literature and Culture

General Editor: David Bradshaw, University of Oxford

The aim of this series is to provide accessible, innovative approaches to major areas of literary study. Ranging from ten to twelve newly commissioned chapters, the volumes provide an indispensable companion for anyone wishing to gain an authoritative understanding of a given period or movement's intellectual character and contexts. To acquire such knowledge at present involves reading a formidable number of full-length specialist studies and many articles. The chapters are about 8,000 words in length, no longer; and they conclude with a brief guide to further reading.

Published

Modernism	Edited by *David Bradshaw*
Feminist Theory	Edited by *Mary Eagleton*

Forthcoming

The Victorian Novel	Edited by *Francis O'Gorman*
Romanticism	Edited by *Jon Klancher*
Restoration and the Eighteenth Century	Edited by *Cynthia Wall*

A Concise Companion to
Feminist Theory

Edited by Mary Eagleton

UCD WOMEN'S CENTER

Blackwell
Publishing

350 Main Street, Malden, MA 02148-5018, USA
108 Cowley Road, Oxford OX4 1JF, UK
550 Swanston Street, Carlton South, Melbourne, Victoria 3053, Australia
Kurfürstendamm 57, 10707 Berlin, Germany

First published 2003 by Blackwell Publishing Ltd

Library of Congress Cataloging-in-Publication Data has been applied for.

ISBN 0-631-22402-5 (hardback); ISBN 0-631-22403-3 (paperback)

A catalogue record for this title is available from the British Library.

Set in 10 on 12.5 pt Meridien
by SNP Best-set Typesetter Ltd., Hong Kong
Printed and bound in the United Kingdom
by MPG Books Ltd, Bodmin, Cornwall

For further information on
Blackwell Publishing, visit our website:
http://www.blackwellpublishing.com

Contents

UCD WOMEN'S CENTER

Contents

Notes on Contributors

Sara Ahmed is Reader in the Institute for Women's Studies at Lancaster University, UK, and is currently Director of the Institute. Her publications include *Differences that Matter: Feminist Theory and Postmodernism* (1998) and *Strange Encounters: Embodied Others in Post-coloniality* (2000). She has co-edited *Transformations: Thinking Through Feminism* (2000) and *Thinking Through the Skin* (2001). She is at present working on a book entitled *The Cultural Politics of Emotion*.

Kum-Kum Bhavnani is Professor of Sociology at the University of California at Santa Barbara, USA, where she also chairs the programme in Women, Culture, Development. Most recently, she was founding editor of the journal *Meridians: Feminism, Race, Transnationalism*. Her edited collections include *Feminism and 'Race'* (2001) and, with John Foran and Priya Kurian, *Feminist Futures: Re-imagining Women, Culture and Development* (2002).

Rosi Braidotti is Professor of Women's Studies at Utrecht University in The Netherlands and Scientific Director of The Netherlands Research School of Women's Studies. She is also the Scientific Director of ATHENA, the Thematic Network of Women's Studies for the SOCRATES programme of the Commission of the European Union. Her publications include *Patterns of Dissonance* (1991), *Nomadic Subjects* (1994), *Women, the Environment and Sustainable Development* (together with Sabine Hausler, Ewa Pluta and Saskia Wieringa, 1994) and

Metamorphoses (2002). She serves as an adviser to the journals *Signs, Differences, Feminist Theory* and *The European Journal of Women's Studies.*

Rey Chow is Andrew W. Mellon Professor of the Humanities at Brown University, USA. She has published widely in the areas of modern literature, film, cultural theory and politics, often with a focus on China and Asia. Her publications in English have been translated into a number of Asian and European languages, including Chinese, Japanese, Korean, French, Spanish and German. Most recently, she is the author of *The Protestant Ethnic and the Spirit of Capitalism* (2002).

Meg Coulson has taught sociology and women's studies in Scotland, the north of England and, most recently, in Australia at the University of Wollongong. Her publications include *Approaching Sociology* (1989), with Carol Riddell, and a collection co-edited with Pearlie McNeill, *Women's Voices, Refugee Lives: Stories from Bosnia* (1994).

Krista Cowman is Senior Lecturer in History in the School of Cultural Studies, Leeds Metropolitan University, UK. She has published articles on women's suffrage and women and socialism in the late nineteenth and early twentieth centuries. She is a member of the editorial board of *Women's History Review.* Her current research is on paid organizers in the Women's Social and Political Union.

Mary Eagleton is Reader in the School of Cultural Studies, Leeds Metropolitan University, UK. She has published in the areas of feminist literary theory and contemporary women's writing. She is the editor of *Feminist Literary Criticism* (1991) and *Feminist Literary Theory: A Reader* (1986, 1996) and the author of *Working with Feminist Criticism* (1996). She is at present writing a monograph on the representation of the woman author in contemporary fiction.

Rosemary Hennessy teaches in the English Department of the State University of New York at Albany, USA. She has written *Materialist Feminism and the Politics of Discourse* (1993), *Profit and Pleasure: Sexual Identities in Late Capitalism* (2000) and has co-edited *Materialist Feminism: A Reader in Class, Difference, and Women's Lives* (1997). She is currently at work on various projects that address the dynamics of organizing on Mexico's northern border.

Louise A. Jackson is Senior Lecturer in History in the School of Cultural Studies, Leeds Metropolitan University, UK. She is the author of *Child Sexual Abuse in Victorian England* (2000) and is completing a book on the social and cultural history of women police officers in Britain. She is the UK Deputy Editor of the journal, *Women's History Review*.

Linda McDowell is Professor of Geography at University College London, UK. Her main research interest is the connections between economic restructuring, new forms of work in the labour market and in the home and the transformation of gender relations in contemporary Britain. Her publications include *Capital Culture* (1997), *Gender, Identity and Place* (1999) and *Redundant Masculinities?* (2003). She is currently working on a study of the domestic and working lives of European migrant women in Britain in the 1950s.

Sara Mills is Research Professor at Sheffield Hallam University, UK. She has published in feminist linguistics and feminist post-colonial theory, including *Discourses of Difference: An Analysis of Women's Travel Writing and Colonialism* (1991), *Feminist Stylistics* (1995) and *Discourse* (1997). She is the editor of *Gendering the Reader* (1994), *Language and Gender* (1995) and *Feminist Practice* (2001). She is currently working on *Rethinking Gender and Politeness* and editing, with Raina Lewis, *Feminist Postcolonial Theory: A Reader*.

Griselda Pollock is Professor of Social and Critical Histories of Art and also Director of the AHRB Centre for Cultural Analysis, Theory and History at the University of Leeds, UK. She works on feminist theory, the visual arts, psychoanalysis and aesthetics and on culture and trauma. Her most recent writings include *Differencing the Canon: Feminist Desire and the Writing of Art's Histories* (1999) and *Looking Back to the Future: Essays on Art, Life and Death* (2000).

Chris Weedon is Professor of Critical and Cultural Theory at Cardiff University, UK. She has published widely on feminist theory, cultural politics and women's writing. Her books include *Rewriting English: Cultural Politics of Gender and Class* (co-authored with Janet Batsleer, Tony Davies and Rebecca O'Rourke, 1985), *Feminist Practice and Post-structuralist Theory* (1987, 1996), *Cultural Politics: Class, Gender, Race and the Postmodern World* (co-authored with Glenn Jordan, 1995) and *Feminism, Theory and the Politics of Difference* (1999). She is currently completing books on *German Women's Writing 1850 to the Present* and *Culture and Identity*.

Jenny Wolmark is Principal Lecturer in Critical and Cultural Theory at the University of Lincoln, UK. She has published widely in the area of feminist science fiction and is the author of *Aliens and Others: Science Fiction, Feminism and Postmodernism* (1993) and the editor of *Cyber-sexualities: A Reader on Feminist Theory, Cyborgs and Cyberspace* (1999). She is co-editor of the *Journal of Gender Studies*. She is currently working on the relationship between image and text in web-based and other electronic formats.

Acknowledgements

I am most grateful to the British Academy for awarding me a Small Research Grant which facilitated my research and to Linda Anderson and Cora Kaplan who supported my application. I am also happy to acknowledge the support of the School of Cultural Studies, Leeds Metropolitan University, particularly Simon Gunn and Gordon Johnston. Pat Cook at Leeds Metropolitan University and the staff at Blackwell aided with exemplary professionalism the production of the book. David Pierce was, as ever, generous with advice and encouragement. My major debt is to my sister contributors who responded to what must have seemed, at times, like an endless list of requests with unfailing humour and goodwill.

Introduction

Mary Eagleton

Paradoxes and Contradictions

Unsurprisingly, the millennium produced many feminist 'state of the discourse' addresses at conferences, in monographs, articles and special issues of journals. All trace a history, usually post-1968, and most recognize the force of two powerful emotions: a nostalgia for a past Golden Age of feminist collectivity and purpose, though such a period is invoked only to be immediately disputed, and a deep longing for a utopian future, though here too there are qualifications; the vision is rhetorical, a spur to action rather than a blueprint for any lived political reality. Weighing up the gains and losses, what has been done and what still needs to be done, is a complex process, all the more so because one is often trying to work between a political philosophy and practice, changes in the 'common culture' and the specific impact that feminism has had in the academy and on knowledge production. Juliet Mitchell (1999: 187) remarks in 'Feminism and Psychoanalysis at the Millennium':

> In the United States thirty-five years ago psychoanalysis was part of a natural discourse; today it is feminism which is part of a natural discourse. There is a kind of naturalized feminism at any bus stop that is actually not particularly political. Has it been ideologically absorbed into the academies and universities without being retained as a political movement?

1

Lynne Segal, in her impressive survey of thirty years of feminist activity, makes a similar point. She notes the impact of feminist discourse in areas such as equal opportunities work, self-help and therapeutic cultures and care practices but, equally, she perceives how '[t]he continuing dissemination of just such a "feminist" into "feminising" personal ethos can offer a feminism *without* an oppositional culture or politics' (1999: 227). Segal deliberately recasts Joan Scott's title, *Only Paradoxes to Offer* (1996) and suggests that what we are experiencing are 'not so much paradoxes as full-blown contradictions' (1999: 229). Significant changes in the common culture or the academy may not be met by similar advances in political and economic spheres or those advances, though real, may be offset by other retreats or areas of neglect. The estimation that is so difficult to make is whether the glass of feminism is half empty or half full.

The concern of Mitchell and Segal with the depoliticization of feminism and its institutionalization within the academy finds an echo in what Michèle Barrett has described as feminism's 'turn to culture' (1990, 1992). She sees a changing emphasis from 'things' to 'words', in discipline terms from the social sciences to the arts, humanities and philosophy. There is a twin move in which political and intellectual projects are described in cultural terms (she uses the example in her 1992 essay of the wide application of the term 'metanarrative') while, at the same time, cultural theory is itself politicized in what is to Barrett the inadequate sense that 'theoretical arguments made, and the vocabularies in which they are made, are read as if they were statements of political allegiance' (Barrett 1990: 23). Barrett is not dismissive of the cultural, or advocating a return to some 'hard' version of the social sciences and politics, but she is aware of the difficulty of working across disciplines and of the need to 'restore a sense of the political power of cultural meanings' (1990: 24).

The chapters that follow come from different disciplines, discourses and feminist positions but are just as conscious as the commentators above of both the need to support feminism's political project and the position of paradox/contradiction in which we so often find ourselves. Linda McDowell in chapter 1, for example, notes, as Barrett does, the 'cultural turn', in McDowell's case the interest of critical theory, including feminism, in spatial metaphors – the nomad or the borderland. But – and here comes the contradiction – a metaphorical space of movement, crossings, exploration, so important in the construction of different concepts of the self, of community, of ways of being, is set against the material reality that pleasurable mobility is only for the

2

affluent; the poor are immobile or subject to enforced movement and migration. Or, as a second example, the central focus of Rey Chow in chapter 5 is the fraught relation between feminism and psychoanalysis over sexuality. Feminism's Enlightenment project, concerned with a rational explication of women's social role, progress and change, seems at odds with 'the fugitive object of sexuality-cum-unconscious that defines psychoanalysis'. The driving force of Chow's analysis is, precisely, to unpick the tensions, ambiguities, contradictions in that relationship. Or, as a third example, Kum-Kum Bhavnani and Meg Coulson in chapter 4 conclude that the encounter between feminism and 'race' has to be understood as 'working with the paradoxes'. One aspect they consider is how to relate large political, economic or ideological structures to the local and the particular and, equally, to the agency of the individual woman.

In looking across the chapters in this book I want to draw out some of the paradoxes, problems and contradictions with which feminist theory continues to tussle, though anyone hoping that we will find neat answers had better stop reading now. The first is feminism's response to theory – the 'proper' theory for feminism and theory's relation to practice.

The State of Theory

At the end of chapter 1, Linda McDowell quotes from an earlier text of Rosi Braidotti where she questions the relation between 'the nomadic intellectual and the migrant women'. This phrase suggests not only the politics of mobility, which McDowell has discussed, but also the place of theory in feminism. The disquiet is that theory may serve only the needs of the privileged – white, educated, middle-class women – and become divorced from practice and day-to-day struggle. The problem of the relation between theory and practice is present in the 'theoretical/political structure' that Griselda Pollock maps (chapter 9) and challenged in Krista Cowman and Louise Jackson's invocation (chapter 2) of the Marxist notion of 'praxis' as both a coming together and a reshaping of the relationship between the two terms. No collection of essays on feminist theory would want to dismiss theory, especially as, Rosemary Hennessy reminds us in chapter 3, the struggle for social justice is in part a struggle *about* concepts and the university is a place that permits critical analysis. One way – by no means the only way – of rescuing the 'lost continent' of class, Hennessy argues, is through theory; feminism must play its part in that and not be complicit in the erasure of class as a concept. Moreover, it is wrong to see the status of feminist theory as secure. Within the privileged space of the university the expansion of feminist theory can be a form of incorporation; as I point out in chapter 8, it is depressing how readily the most challenging ideas are transformed into a sort of 'module fodder'. And all critical theories move up and down the pecking-order of recognition. Sara Ahmed's overview (chapter 12) of the range of feminist positions on this issue is a good introduction to the debate, as are Barbara Christian's influential essay 'The Race for Theory' (1989) and the special issue of *Signs* (1996) on 'Feminist Theory and Practice'.

But what kind of theory should feminism be employing? The anti-theory animus is often directed against what Gayatri Spivak calls 'capital *t* Theory', which she describes as 'the kind of ethereal feminist theory where the female sexed subject is constantly theorized in terms of psychoanalysis and counter-psychoanalysis simply in terms of absences in texts and so on' (1990: 120, 119). To many readers Spivak's comment may seem slightly odd. Though she disassociates herself from an 'ethereal' psychoanalytic theory, no one could be in any doubt that Spivak's own work is deeply engaged in theory and represents a for-midable challenge to the reader; for many, her work too constitutes a 'capital *t* Theory'. Indeed, as Braidotti points out elsewhere, what one understands by 'high' theory rather depends on where one is stand-ing (1997: 23–4). However, Spivak's caution is well made and the essays in this collection most influenced by psychoanalysis are con-scious of both the purpose of theory and the political and practical reasons for lucidity. Rey Chow (chapter 5) makes a careful assessment of the extent to which Freud can be seen as the friend or foe of femi-nism, while Chris Weedon (chapter 6) traces the impact of Freud, Lacan and post-Lacanian feminists, such as Julia Kristeva and Luce Irigaray, on theories of the subject and subjectivity. The fact that identity is not innate but the product of a process of development, is never successfully completed and is not totally within one's rational control was an important insight for feminism to take on board. Both Weedon (chapter 6) and Pollock (chapter 9) helpfully introduce some key concepts from Lacan: the mirror phase, misrecognition, the Imag-inary, the Symbolic. Pollock also explains terms from psychoanalysis essential to the understanding of visual culture: fetishism, castration, voyeurism, scopophilia, narcissism, hysteria. To avoid the ethereal, contributors to this collection ground these abstract terms. For instance,

Pollock shows how our attraction to visual artefacts like a painting, to narrative forms like a Hitchcock film or to idealized figures such as the film star or the fashion model relates to our own psychic formation and is always played out within a social order where power differences of race, class, gender and sexuality are ever-present.

Feminist theory's keen but critical interest in Freud and Lacan makes clear how any lingering view of it as a separatist space, peopled only by female theorists, no longer has credibility. In chapter 3 by Rosemary Hennessy the influence of Marx is central. Although she reviews a number of positions on class – socialist feminism, radical feminism, neo- and post-Marxist – it is a Marxist feminist analysis that she explores most fully, stressing the significance of the exploitative relation between capitalist and worker and the continued relevance of the concept of class in the post-1970s' transformed economies of the West. Chris Weedon (chapter 6) shows how Marx's concept of false consciousness and Althusser's theory of ideology have been important to a socialist feminist analysis of subjectivity in its search for a theory that recognizes both women's class position and the effects of patriarchy on women's subjectivity. Foucault's work has also been highly influential within feminism. For Sara Mills (chapter 7) and Weedon, his theory of the dispersion and acquisition of power can help us to understand how the relatively powerless may gain power, albeit temporarily. For Griselda Pollock (chapter 9), Foucault's concept of surveillance links to the visual as 'the eye of power'. Rey Chow (chapter 5) employs Foucault both to challenge the Freudian terms of castration and repression so that female sexuality can be redefined in terms of pleasure and social power and to question Freud's view of the social as an obdurate oppressive force rather than a locus in which to intervene and make change. Moreover, Foucault's concept of 'bio-power' can find urgent relevance in these days of 'designer babies' and 'wombs for sale'.

At the same time, contributors are often unhappy about theories that operate only at the macro-level. In recent decades, dominated by 'high' theory or 'capital *t* Theory', however one wishes to describe it, the necessary concern with the local and particular contexts that Bhavnani and Coulson (chapter 4) mention has, sometimes, been given pretty short shrift. They show how disastrous is that exclusion if one wants to understand the place of women in development studies. The relation between the macro and the micro, the abstract and the concretely specific, is present also in Krista Cowman and Louise Jackson's chapter. They consider large theoretical debates on the notion of time and post-structuralist critiques of historical 'truth', but they also emphasize the necessity of a micro-theory of data retrieval and archival work, which, significantly, can operate both inside and outside the academy, of constructing other histories and of examining the processes of institutional change. I make a similar point in chapter 8 with respect to literary history and the continuing relevance of a more sociological approach in, for example, the study of reading groups. In both disciplines, history and literature, detailed, small-scale work has effectively challenged received norms. These kinds of undertakings can give another twist to Barrett's 'cultural turn'.

Pluralities and Partialities

A second area of common interest throughout the chapters lies in the nature of feminist theory as, at once, seemingly plural and diverse while also partial and selective – another paradox. Particularly in the late 1980s and into the 1990s, when the books began to pour off the presses and feminist/women's/gender studies became more established in the universities, feminist theory seemed to burgeon, almost to increase exponentially. Not only can we now talk about many feminisms, as the chapters of Weedon, Hennessy and Braidotti show most clearly, but there are also numerous interrelations between feminism and other critical theories, as the frequent sorties into Marxism, psychoanalysis, post-structuralism and postmodernism illustrate. However, the most repeated assertion throughout this book is the impossibility of tackling the urgent issues of social change solely through the concept of gender. In that happy phrase from David Glover and Cora Kaplan, which I quote in chapter 8, femininity is 'a part-time occupation for full-time humans'. Hence the need to consider concurrently, race and class and sexuality and many other differences. Add to this an awareness that interpretation is itself always a multifaceted activity and we get a rough sense of the complexity of the undertaking. For example, McDowell's exploration in chapter 1 of the meanings of 'home' embraces identity, power relations (possibly leading to domestic violence), questions of labour, surveillance, the home as a 'repository of memories' or a marker of social status and its uncertain placing between public and private space.

However, at the same time – and this is another refrain throughout the book – the feminists who have most determined feminist theory have been a very select bunch, overwhelmingly white, middle-class,

Western women. Furthermore, as we have seen, certain theoretical perspectives gain currency over others and this relates to the power of the academy and certain groups within it. And, as I indicate in chapter 8, the institutions and social practices within which the academic feminist works constantly encourage her towards selection and, inevitably, partiality in the construction of the field of feminist studies. As Bhavnani and Coulson (chapter 4), adapting Ien Ang, stress, this truth has to be confronted: 'all feminists are partial feminists working with partial feminisms' and, therefore, 'there is a need for recognition and negotiation among feminisms and feminists'. Rosi Braidotti (chapter 10) is the only contributor to the book to give a positive inflection to partiality, but this is not because she endorses any elitist view of feminism and feminists. In explaining developments in feminist philosophy, she warns against what she terms a 'nationalistic system of indexation' which too rigidly compartmentalizes the subject. Braidotti talks of the partial not in terms of the limited or the biased, which are the meanings that exercise others, but as an aspect of 'nomadic' thinking, an adventurous feminist philosophy which resists categorization; this is the partial as opposed to the monolithic and the systematized.

Two concepts in particular, central to feminist thought in recent years, have unleashed a plurality of positions and responses. The first is difference. Michèle Barrett, in a 1987 article, sets up the argument in terms of the difference *between* women and men and the difference *within* each category. With respect to the difference *between*, it is obviously important to recognize continuing imbalances of power without essentializing the difference. As Sara Mills (chapter 7) demonstrates, gender stereotypes remain worryingly present in the culture; men and women are judged by others or may think of themselves specifically 'as men' or 'as women' and are often rewarded accordingly. But we need, Mills says, to get 'beyond binary thinking' and her chapter points to the inadequacy of an oppositional model of dominance versus subordination, men's language versus women's language. An examination of difference *within* the category 'women' can, as we have seen, highlight the inequalities of race, class, sexuality, though, even when these are recognized, it is easy for the differences to be commodified, as is evident in the figure of the token black woman or lesbian. Secondly, an emphasis on the difference *within* may erode a common identity as 'we women' which is important to feminism as a political movement. Iris Marion Young (1997) has suggested that feminists should think in terms of 'asymmetrical reciprocity'. This position recognizes that one cannot presume to know fully the other's standpoint or presume that the other's standpoint is identical to one's own. Rather, one needs to allow the space to acknowledge difference and to allow listening and learning to take place. For Rey Chow (chapter 5), looking at sexual difference, a crucial question for feminism is how Freud's method of differentiating sexuality becomes expressed in the social world in 'attitudes of reverence or contempt', another form of difference *between*. It is not enough, she suggests, to say that feminists are conflating description with evaluation; one also needs to ask why Freud himself fails to address the problem.

The second, and linked, concept is subjectivity. We can see a figure taking shape across the chapters – 'the woman', 'the feminist', 'the feminist theorist', 'the cyborg' – and also her specific cultural incarnations – 'the author' (Weedon and Eagleton), 'the reader' (Eagleton), 'the spectator' (Pollock). In varied cultural forms – the art of Jo Spence and Cindy Sherman (Pollock) or the writing of life stories, oral history, autobiography, personal testimony (Cowman and Jackson, Bhavnani and Coulson, Eagleton, Weedon) – female subjectivity is confronted, constructed, diversified, and the process of writing or visualizing the self is put into question. As Chris Weedon (chapter 6) effectively illustrates, the terms 'subject' and 'subjectivity' and the related terms 'experience' (an important concept for Cowman and Jackson also) and 'identity' have a complicated history. Early claims for women's status as full legal subjects were formulated around women's similarity to men – in other words, there is no difference *between*; we are all equal. However, post-nineteenth-century views of femininity have often confirmed a difference *between* and posited a subjectivity markedly different from that of men. Moreover, Weedon traces the problematic opposition of mind and body with respect to female subjectivity. Forms of feminism, such as liberal-humanist and some wings of socialist feminism, which have been largely indifferent to the body and have emphasized the rationality of the mind, have been countered by feminisms with a bodily interest, radical feminism and feminism influenced by psychoanalysis and post-structuralism. New understandings have been generated about the corporeality of the female subject, the materiality of the body and its relation to gender, race, class and age. Jenny Wolmark (chapter 11) introduces us to the body reformed under the impact of new technologies. Sara Ahmed (chapter 12) considers the making of the body, its surfaces and borders, through feelings. Truly, there has been, as Rosi Braidotti remarks, 'a return of the body'.

And What Next?

All the chapters in this book have a strong sense of unfinished business, of agendas which will carry feminism through the twenty-first century. However, the final two chapters are by their nature particularly forward-looking. Wolmark's discussion of cyberculture in chapter 11 is shot through with a rhetoric of the new, of transmutation, transcendence, the limitless, the celebratory. Almost all the material of the preceding chapters is here re-framed through the perspective of hectic technological change: concepts of reality, of time and space; subjectivity, difference and the body; the construction of social and political communities; the playing out of fantasy; the creation of new cultural forms and practices. Cyberculture takes us into fields of mind-expanding potential but also brings us back to familiar problems about, for example, the persistence of very traditional gender identities; the perpetuation of a mind (male) versus body (female) distinction; problems of unequal access to the new technologies; issues about how these new technologies are used.

The euphoric rhetoric is not Wolmark's own. She takes a cautious approach to the utopian strain in feminist thought with which I started this Introduction and which has been given free play in cyberculture. Nor, as I indicate, are contributors immobilized by a damp-eyed nostalgia. Diana Coole, writing in 1997, entitles her essay, 'Feminism without Nostalgia', and her insistence that we recognize the different world that we now inhabit in comparison with heady moments in the 1960s and 1970s, the particular demands and possibilities of the present, is one that all contributors would endorse. What, then, are the affects that can enable feminism to learn from the past and move with purpose towards the future? This is one of the important questions suggested by Sara Ahmed in chapter 12 as she returns to the relation between theory and practice, not to map out a series of programmes but, rather, to understand how emotions work 'as forms of mediation between knowledge/theory and practice/activism'. This involves a close reading of the emotions. Some emotions that inform feminism may also be implicated in the very power relations that feminism critiques. For example, as Ahmed discusses, feminists' senses of pain and anger are, for Wendy Brown, emotions that continue to tie feminists to a position of subordination from which they should be moving. But Ahmed also shows, through the work of Audre Lorde, how pain and anger can enable a moving to a different future. The concept of 'moving' is significant. Ahmed points out how salient are the meanings of 'moving' and 'being moved' both as an emotional affect and as a transformation that could be bodily, intellectual or political. The emotions that Ahmed leaves us with are not nostalgia or an unqualified utopian optimism. Rather, she looks backwards and inwards in a 'critical wonder' that asks fundamental questions about the world and is self-reflexive about feminism and women's studies and she looks forwards and outwards with hope for change. Though contributors to this volume come from a variety of feminist positions and in their chapters appraise a huge field of feminist interventions, all would, I think, agree with Ahmed's ardent conclusion: we are 'stuck' to feminism; we are 'stuck together' in feminism; in different ways and in different contexts, we work with wonder and hope for a new future.

References and Further Reading

Barrett, M. (1987) The concept of difference. *Feminist Review*, 26: 29–41.
— (1990) Feminism's 'turn to culture'. *Women: A Cultural Review*, 1 (1): 22–4.
— (1992) Words and things: materialism and method in contemporary feminist theory. In Michèle Barrett and Anne Phillips (eds), *Destabilizing Theory: Contemporary Feminist Debates*, pp. 201–19. Cambridge: Polity Press.
Braidotti, R. (1997) Comments on Felski's 'The Doxa of Difference': working through sexual difference. *Signs*, 23 (1): 23–40.
Christian, B. (1989) The race for theory. In Linda Kauffman (ed.), *Gender and Theory: Dialogues on Feminist Criticism*, pp. 225–37. Oxford: Blackwell.
Coole, D. (1997) Feminism without nostalgia. *Radical Philosophy*, 83: 17–24.
Mitchell, J. (1999) Feminism and psychoanalysis at the millennium. *Women: A Cultural Review*, 10 (2): 185–91.
Scott, J. (1996) *Only Paradoxes to Offer: French Feminists and the Rights of Man*. Cambridge, MA: Harvard University Press.
Segal, L. (1999) *Why Feminism? Gender, Psychology, Politics*. Cambridge: Polity Press.
Signs (1996) Feminist theory and practice. *Signs*, special issue, 21: 41.
Spivak, G. Chakravorty (1990) *The Post-colonial Critic: Interviews, Strategies, Dialogues*, ed. Sarah Harasym. New York: Routledge.
Young, I. M. (1997) *Intersecting Voices: Dilemmas of Gender, Political Philosophy and Policy*. Princeton, NJ: Princeton University Press.

1

Place and Space

Linda McDowell

The Significance of Place

The social theorist Manuel Castells (2000) has argued that growing numbers of people increasingly live in a world that he characterizes as a space of flows rather than a space of places. Compared to an older, more settled world, capital and labour are now increasingly restless, travelling across space in unforeseen ways and to a previously unsurpassed extent. Movement is facilitated by innovative technologies that reduce the friction of distance and link people, money and places in ever-expanding patterns of impermanent connections. Thus, the world is becoming globalized, increasingly dominated by a version of the capitalist economic system that Castells designates 'informationalism'. Informationalist capitalism, as Castells rather portentously notes, is defined by its 'capacity to work as a unit in real time on a planetary scale' (1996: 92). No wonder more excitable commentators have announced the (premature) 'end of geography' as globalization 'abolishes the significance of geographic distance' and 'makes all frontiers permeable' (Anderson 1997: 2). In this global system, identities based on place are transformed through real and virtual travel and migration into hybridized, nomadic versions of travelling subjects. And yet . . .

At the same time as certain disciplines are celebrating globalization, other commentators in several disciplines and diverse theoretical perspectives, feminist approaches among them, have claimed that location and locality still matter. An attachment to place, whether voluntary or chosen, retains its significance for life chances, ways of living, access to resources and cultural identities. Travel or mobility, at least as a choice, is still to large extent a privilege of the affluent minority. For most workers, the mobility of capital tends to mean either the devastation wreaked by deindustrialization or exploitative labour in an economy commanded and controlled from a distance by foreign capital that neither knows nor cares about the local conditions of existence. Perhaps, in this sense, Castells is correct to emphasize the flows not the places. However, individuals as workers and residents are fighting back (at both the local and the global scale) against footloose capital. As well as local political struggles based on making connections within the community, workers are using the same technological advances that multinational companies depend on to build connections between places to create alliances between employees of the same companies in different places. In this way they are building a new form of global/local politics. In other ways too, place seems to be becoming more not less important. In the final decades of the last millennium, growing numbers of nation-states began to splinter as claims to territory, based on ethnicity or religion or some constructed version of an imagined community, formed the basis of new identities and new nationalities. As the rise of ethno-nationalism is often linked to particular views about gender relations, it has become a significant issue for feminist scholars.

The significance of place and its relationship to gendered identities, however, is more than an empirical question for feminist scholarship. It is now well established that many of the assumptions of Western Enlightenment theory, which dominated the development of the social sciences in the nineteenth and early twentieth centuries, rely on a fundamental and essentialist binary distinction that maps onto gender divisions (Pateman and Grosz 1987; Pateman 1988). Whereas men were the idealized rational, civilized Enlightenment subject, full participants as workers and citizens in the public arena of the economy and politics, women were dependants, to be protected and kept close. They were to provide sustenance and nurture to their menfolk and children through the construction of a place of leisured and domestic calm. If men's role was in the public sphere then women's was to be in the private arena: an ideal complementarity between the sexes was established in which, according to the political theorist John Stuart Mill, neither was inferior, merely different. That this division was never complete, that it took a class and racialized form, that it varied across space and over time is indisputable but the ideology of separate spheres has cast a long shadow over Western industrial societies in innumerable ways. Social practices, state institutions, symbolic representations and cultural artefacts are all marked by ideas about gender distinctions, and the binary division between men and women, in which women are assumed to be naturally inferior, has perhaps been the most resistant to abolition.

The mapping of a place or location onto gender identities has been a key part of the establishment and maintenance of women's position and is reflected in both the materiality and the symbolic representation of women's lives. Interestingly, in feminist politics and scholarship, spatial metaphors have become a key way of thinking and writing about struggle and transformation. In the shift from a politics based on demands for equality and a theoretical rejection of modernist ideas, a more recent language suffused with notions of place, context and location has come to the forefront in feminist texts. Thus, for example, the art historian Griselda Pollock (1996) and Third World political theorist Chandra Talpade Mohanty (1991) have written about, respectively, feminist 'geographies' in the visual arts and 'cartographies' of political struggle. Adrienne Rich in her poetry and essays has long insisted on the significance of a 'politics of location' (1986). Her concern is paralleled by more recent notions in the writings of feminist scientists, including Donna Haraway (1991) and Sandra Harding (1991), about context dependant and 'situated knowledge' in which speaking from the margins provides an alternative, more grounded position from which to challenge conventional assumptions. The importance of mobility, of movements between one place and another, is reflected in both the literal and metaphorical use of concepts such as hybridity, of nomadic identities, of constructing and maintaining an identity in the borderlands (Anzaldúa 1987; Braidotti 1994; Kaplan 1996).

In her book about spatial concepts of human subjectivity, literary theorist Kathleen Kirby (1996) suggests that the ideas she discusses there perhaps fit more comfortably into geography as a disciplinary category than her own discipline. She notes, though, that 'to classical geographers, this study's fascination with representation, politics and the psyche might appear a little out of bounds' (1996: viii). But, in fact, even as she wrote, geography's boundaries were expanding to encompass all these issues and more. As a synthetic discipline concerned to say something about the significance of spatial variations, about place and location and difference across the boundaries of conventional distinctions, whether within the social sciences or across the social–natural science distinction, the geographical project remains a most ambitious undertaking. In this chapter I want to give a partial impression of its diversity and to look at the ways in which feminist theory and geographical approaches to the interrelationships between place or location and identity have converged. I also want to give a flavour of the ways in which feminist approaches to the gender division of space have evolved and, to do this, I have chosen to focus on a single concept: the home, in the sense of both the house and the homeland.

I want to illustrate some of the ways in which the home as a place became associated with women and the feminine, as well as some of the ways in which it has been rethought and retheorized in more recent analyses, challenging its static nature and its conservative associations. This shift in the meaning of the home is part of a wider challenge to the modern project. If time, travel and history tend to be associated with ideas of progress, change and masculinity, then space, place, location and geography have been associated with stasis and femininity (Massey 1992). However, more recent work by poststructuralist and postcolonial theorists, feminist scholars, geographers and anthropologists, among others, has challenged older certainties and associations, insisting on the significance of location, on space, borders and boundaries that both allow and refuse movement between places. If history was the discipline that personifies modernity, then, according to some, geography exemplifies postmodernity (Soja 1989). Ideas about the home and its association with female 'virtues' have, however, a continuing centrality in constructions and representations of place, community and nation, despite theoretical shifts in social thought and the significant material changes in people's associations with home and territory outlined at the beginning of this chapter.

Home/Place

Home, home-grown, homespun, home-made: the word 'home' is one of the most resonant words in the English language. As Bob Dylan insisted 'a house is not a home.' A home is more than a house; the term conveys simple pleasures, familial togetherness, privacy and freedom, a sense of belonging, of security, a place to escape from but also to return to, a secure memory, an ideal. These multiple connotations extend to a wider spatial scale than simply the dwelling itself. The notion of a homeland constructs what the critic Benedict Anderson (1991) has termed a 'deep horizontal comradeship' among strangers, an 'imagined community' based on shared myths and rituals, which creates the same sense of inclusion and exclusion as the home as a dwelling does at a smaller scale. Within are all those who belong there, the wall/boundaries exclude strangers from the place, from the geographical territory.

Home is about identity. As Gaston Bachelard (1969) indicates, it is our first cosmos, the location of memories, of identity itself; indeed, all space is imbued with ideas about home. But the notion of home – its meanings and associations – is never fixed and static but is instead fluid and multiple, changing over time as inhabitants leave, perhaps never to return, as their views alter and change over the lifestyle. It is a container for many activities, a repository of memories and a prime agent of socialization, providing a guide to the basic ways of living in a particular society and a map of the relations between strangers and household members as well as to familial and gender relations. The nostalgia lurking behind Bachelard's definition is absent from Valerie Walkerdine's reminiscences (1989). Walkerdine remembers the suburban home of her youth as a trap, an enticement that might still yet lure her back to the conformist suburbs of middle England. It is perhaps no accident that these different views are expressed by a man and a woman. Walkerdine's associations reflect the strong criticisms of the notion of home and domesticity developed in the early writings by what have become known as second-wave feminists (Wilson 1977; Barrett and McIntosh 1982; McKenzie and Rose 1983). For most women, the home is a site of social relations that are structured by power and inequality. It is the location of unpaid labour – still mainly the responsibility of women, despite the rapid rises in women's waged employment in the last decades of the twentieth century. For too many women, too, the home is a place dominated by fears of domestic violence and abuse, where women and children are the victims of male aggression. It is also less private than many commentators assume. Both public and private bodies and institutions have the right of access to the home, ranging from the public utilities companies to health visitors. The home is also, as Foucault (1980) argued so persuasively, the location of self-surveillance that ensures that even in the most private of acts the capillary structures of power in a modern state make certain that most behaviour conforms to societal norms.

15

In the language of socialist feminism, the home is the site of patriarchal relations, the appropriation of women's labour by men in order to enable the daily maintenance of the household members and the reproduction of their labour power on both a daily and a generational basis, since the home is also the location of a large proportion of the activities of early child-rearing (Walby 1990). This simple model of exploitative relations between an individual man and woman linked together by conjugal ties is, as feminist scholars of colour pertinently pointed out, a singular reading based on the specific position of middle-class, white women in industrial societies around about the middle decades of the twentieth century. Before, and increasingly since, those decades, a great deal of the domestic work and child care carried out in the home was actually undertaken for wages by working-class women and women of colour (Anderson 2000). These women who laboured in other women's homes, caring for other women's children and cleaning their homes, had to try to maintain a version of long-distance mothering and a sense of belonging at home from another place, often in another country (Pratt 1997).

The relevance of the patriarchal model of gender relations and singular models of the home as a sphere of exploitation is also increasingly challenged by shifts both in the nature of capitalist production and in household structures and relations. The argument in earlier feminist theories about patriarchy that the state colluded both with employers and with individual men to ensure women's role as domestic labourers seems, with hindsight, a surprisingly optimistic or benevolent interpretation of the world (McDowell 1991). Now multinational capital and the deregulated state seem scarcely interested in the daily reproduction of the working class *in situ*. Instead, in most of the industrialized countries of the 'West', an individualized model of personal responsibility for daily life has largely replaced state intervention and welfare policies. At the same time, individual men are increasingly reluctant to trade their independence for domestic care by a single woman, finding emotional solace in multiple relationships or commodified forms of support and hot dinners at fast-food outlets. In 2001, the average age of first marriage for British men had risen to 30 years. Larger numbers of women, too, are remaining single for longer, and having fewer children. These changes do not, however, negate the continuing significance of home. It remains central in its meaning as a repository of memories and its function as a location for a wide range of activities. Homes, in the sense of physical structures, are also concrete indicators of social position and status in both their external image and internal layout. Their position in a neighbourhood brings both costs and benefits and relative accessibility to other locations, goods, services and activities. The home is a site of multiple activities, including production, consumption and reproduction, a place of waged and unwaged work, of inequality and pain as well as pleasure and security. It is imbued with contradictory meanings and memories that change with time and is a key link in the relationship between material culture and sociality (Wilson 1977; McDowell 1983; Davidoff and Hall 1987). Such are the strength and complexity of these associations that the home as a symbolic representation and as the locus for material practices and social relationships has become a key focus of a great deal of theorizing in the varied disciplines of the humanities and the social sciences.

To capture something of this range in analyses of the home, I want to draw on the work of three feminist scholars: Minnie Bruce Pratt, bell hooks and Sharon Marcus, each of whom has taken a different approach to a feminist understanding of the meaning of home. While all three challenge conventional associations and assumptions about the meaning of home, the first two authors connect their personal experiences to broader political processes, whereas Marcus's work is a scholarly analysis of multiple texts in which she traces the significance of the apartment as a particular built form in fictional and other representations of nineteenth-century London and Paris.

Minnie Bruce Pratt in her essay 'Identity: Skin Blood Heart' (1984) reflects on the different places in which over the years she has felt 'at home', including her childhood home, the market town in which she lived in the early years of her marriage and her current location, living alone in a predominantly black area of Washington, DC. She recalls these places and reveals the social relations of power and oppression that construct them and that have to be negotiated in every daily encounter. She explores her location in networks of power of which she was largely unaware when growing up in a privileged Jewish middle-class family. She recounts memories of key places in her suburban childhood, places that suggest 'mutuality, companionship, creativity, sensuousness, easiness in the body, curiosity in what new things might be making in the world, hope from that curiosity, safety and love' (1984: 24). Pratt explains the limitations of her memories and understanding of this place, how her security depended on the fact that 'Laura Cates, Black and a servant, was responsible for me; that I had walks with my father because the woods were "ours" by

17

systematic economic exploitation, instigated, at that time, by his White Citizens' Council' (1984: 25).

Over time Pratt began to develop a different way of looking at the world that was 'more accurate, complex, multi-layered, multi-dimensioned, more truthful' (1984: 17) than the singular perspective of her early life. In her later life, she lived in a part of Washington, DC where, when she went to the local shops, she was almost always the only white person around. She provides a vivid picture of the neighbourhood, which she clearly loves:

> In the summer, folks sit out on their porches, or steps or sidewalks; when I walk by, if I lift my head and look toward them and speak, 'Hey', they may speak, say 'Hey' or 'How you doing?' or perhaps just nod. In the spring, I was afraid to smile when I spoke, because that might be too familiar, but by the end of summer I had walked back and forth so often, I was familiar, so sometimes we shared comments about the mean weather. (1984: 11)

Pratt feels comforted by these greetings as they make her feel at home, in a place she wants to be and to which she feels attached but where she also feels out of place. She knows from her understanding of difference and diversity, from the new multiple way of looking that she has grown into, that she brings with her to every chance meeting the 'history of race and sex and class' (1984: 12) in which she is not innocent. As she comments: 'It is an exhausting process, this moving from the experience of the "unknowing majority" (as Maya Angelou called it) into consciousness. It would be a lie to say this process is comforting' (1984: 12).

In these extracts from Pratt's essay, the ways in which the meanings of home are fluid and transitory are captured, showing too how personal experiences and developing political beliefs challenge conventional ways of thinking or long-held beliefs about home. bell hooks's (1991) well-known insistence that the home is a site of resistance for African-American women was written as a direct challenge to the conventional assumptions behind a great deal of feminist theorizing about the meaning of home and, like Pratt, hooks insists on a re-evaluation of feminist conceptions of the home. Both women also write from within their personal experiences, connecting the personal and the political, indeed showing how the personal is political. In her chapter about home in her collection of essays, *Yearning* (1991), bell hooks takes us straight into her neighbourhood and its comforting familiarity as she ventured out as a young girl in a segregated city into 'that terrifying whiteness – those white faces on the porches staring us down with hate' (1991: 41).

In the following passage she explains the significance of home for minority residents in cities that made them feel as if they had no rights in the public arena: 'Oh! That feeling of safety, of arrival, of home-coming when we finally reached the edges of her yard . . . such a con-trast, that feeling of arrival, of homecoming, this sweetness and the bitterness of that journey, that constant reminder of white power and control' (1991: 41). The activities of the home, hooks argued, have a key political dimension:

> Since sexism delegates to females the task of creating and maintaining a home environment, it has been primarily the responsibility of black women to construct domestic households as spaces of care and nur-turance in the face of the brutal harsh reality of racist oppression, of sexist domination. Historically, African-American people believed that the construction of a homeplace, however fragile and tenuous . . . had a radical political dimension . . . [The] homeplace was the one site where one could freely confront the issue of humanization, where one could resist. (1991: 42)

hooks points to the links that this idea of home as a site of resistance constructs between black women globally; between, for example, African-Americans and black women in South Africa whether working in the city as domestic servants for white women or trying to create a home in those districts that were inappropriately named 'homelands' under apartheid. Indeed, it has a wider resonance, perhaps, recogniz-ing the potential for resistance in women's home-based activities that have too often been dismissed as insignificant or irrelevant to wider political studies. In her moving memoir of life with the beat genera-tion, Carolyn Cassady (1990) has also argued that staying at home, raising their children and making a home for Neal Cassady and his friends, including Jack Kerouac, was as significant a gesture against the norms of 1950's society as her husband's more highly regarded mobility. Staying put may be an act of resistance.

hooks's essay also demonstrates the importance of connecting local circumstances to the global context. Thinking across spatial scales like this challenges what is taken for granted and so defamiliarizes con-ventional explanations of the local and the domestic. The significance of home in contemporary US cities is not unconnected to larger histories of movement between places and the circumstances under which they occurred. Thus, thinking spatially, about the relational construction of place through geographical connections between the places furthest away as well as nearby, reveals not only a more complex story about the significance of home in a particular place at a certain time but also allows connections and comparisons to be revealed.

The final challenge to conventional associations of home with femininity, privacy, conservatism and stasis is from the field of cultural studies and literary criticism and it is taken from Sharon Marcus's book *Apartment Stories* (1999). Drawing on a range of material from novels, architectural plans and descriptions, legal documents and contemporary and popular urban commentaries, Marcus challenges the widespread belief that the nineteenth century was the apotheosis of feminine domesticity when the separation of the public and private spheres was most evident. She argues that the urban apartment house – a common form in many nineteenth-century cities – embodies the intersection of the public and the private, city and home, or masculine and feminine spheres of influence:

> Unlike the isolated single family house and the barely liveable tenement, which opposed the city to the home, apartment buildings linked the city and its residences in real and imagined ways, and nineteenth century discourses about apartment buildings registered the connections and coincidences between urban and domestic spaces, values, and activities. For their inhabitants and observers, apartment buildings were miniature cities whose multiplication of individual dwellings both magnified domesticity and perturbed its customary boundaries. (1999: 2)

In Paris, one of the key actors in the construction of these stories and the regulation of activities was the female *portière*: a figure whom Marcus suggests is as important in nineteenth-century Parisian urban life as the male *flâneur* identified by Baudelaire. While Marcus's book is a challenge to the conventional wisdom about spatial separation in nineteenth-century cities in Western Europe and the US, it also provides a salutary warning of the dangers of ethnocentrism. The single-family, private dwelling is an historically and spatially specific form and, as Bahloul (1992) has shown in her study of a multi-dwelling building in colonial Algeria, the boundaries between the household and others, between public and private and even between the inside and outside of a dwelling are permeable and changeable. But even in the single-family dwellings that were built in such huge numbers in Victorian Britain, the domestic ideology of separate spheres depended on the waged labour of millions of working-class women for whom the middle-class home was a workplace.

Home/Land

A second significant set of associations between femininity and home, between gender and place, occurs at a larger spatial scale than that of the home and the city. It draws on a range of associations between the nation-state and idealized womanhood constructed through symbolic representations of the nation-state. Here gendered language, images and artefacts are used to create a particular image of nationalism and national identity. As political theorists have argued (Smith 1986, 1999; Anderson 1991) the nation-state is not only, nor indeed always, a territorial unity; it is also an imaginary community of distant strangers, united through the construction of communal myths, political rhetoric and cultural artefacts that define who is included and who is excluded from the nation-state. In an era in which the decline of communism and ethno-nationalist movements have resulted in the emergence or re-emergence of growing numbers of new nations, the co-constitution of gendered identities and national identities is of great importance, especially as it often relies on conservative images of women as homemakers. As the emergence of new states in the 1990s illustrates beyond doubt, the ways in which nationalism and nations are represented and imagined are fluid and contestable, being made and remade under different historical circumstances.

These connections between gender and nationhood have a long history and are particularly evident in the myths and material symbols used by different nation-states in struggles to establish their existence and/or independence from a colonial power. For example, in the development of national currencies – one of the key distinguishing features of an independent nation-state – allegories of the female form are frequently used as images to represent either the highest civil values of the new nation-state or its wealth and power. Thus, images of the female form representing truth or virtue, liberty or justice are typical, as well as images of women with children, fruit or corn to represent plentiful and fecund nature. In the first of these two sets of images of femininity, womanhood is presented as almost disembodied, above the mundane struggles of everyday life, and so representing the higher virtues of civilization. In the images in which femininity is associated with fecundity and the plentiful bounty of the natural world

21

place, the women pictured on the notes are shown in close contact with earthly values, in this case representing nature rather than 'society' or 'civilization'. Interestingly, on some of the notes issued by former colonies prior to independence in the twentieth century, these two representations of femininity are sometimes found in juxtaposition. On the notes of the former French colonies, for example, images of 'native' woman, unclothed or in exotic costumes, surrounded by tropical fruits or lush vegetation appear next to clothed, 'civilized', and often classical images of Western women.

Marina Warner (1985), in her analysis of representations of women as monuments and statues, found similar representations of the classical virtues as female: Justice above both the Old Bailey in London and the City Hall in New York City, for example; Liberty as a female colossus in New York; the female figure of Marianna, representing the French Republic. As Warner argues, these female figures and allegories were powerful not because they represented the material circumstances of women in these societies at the time, but rather the opposite. 'Often the recognition of a difference between the symbolic order inhabited by ideal, allegorical figures, and the actual order, of judges, statesmen, soldiers, philosophers, inventors, depends on the unlikelihood of women practising the concepts they represent' (Warner 1985: xx).

In the nineteenth century, when many of these images originated in industrial societies, the domestic ideology of women as angels of the hearth, above the sordid struggles of capitalist commerce and industry, facilitated these associations between femininity and the abstract virtues of a civilized society. I want to expand this illustration of the links between gender and national identity by looking in a little more detail at representations of Ireland, drawing in the main on the work of three geographers, Bronwen Walter (1995, 2001), Catherine Nash (1993) and Nuala Johnson (1995).

In representations of Irish identity, religion and opposition to colonial and imperial power play a significant and continuing role. As Walter has explored, in the myths, stories, poetry and events that celebrate both a shared and a separate past, masculine sacrifice in war and death is an integral part of the construction of national identity. Men's courage and resistance is documented through the statues and names on war memorials, whereas women seldom appear as named war heroines. Women overwhelmingly die as civilians. However, the rhetoric of nationalism, in whose name these men were sacrificed, is a profoundly gendered one in which women take their familiar and familial place as the guardians of the family, keeping home and hearth together in times of hardship. As Walter (1995: 37) notes, 'The trope of the family is widespread in the figuring of national narratives – homeland, motherland, fatherland, daughters and sons of the nation. This imagery serves to naturalise a social hierarchy within an apparent unity of interests so that its gendered formation is unquestioned.' Men are active, women are passive in nation-building myths in which the comradeship identified by Anderson (1991: 7) is one between men: a 'fraternity that makes it possible for so many millions of people, not so much to kill, as willingly to die for such limited imaginings'.

Women's location in the privacy of the home rather than in the public arena, whether as active participants in war or in politics more generally, was a central element of the construction of identity in Catholic Ireland. The Catholic church has long played a 'powerful leadership role in the national struggle and imposed a particular version of gendered differentiation. After the Famine the Virgin Mary was promoted as a role model for women' (Walter 2001: 18). A combination of self-sacrifice, submerged sexuality, family duty and motherhood defined 'proper' womanhood as well as associated it with passive duty, rather than active participation, in defence of the nation. However, it has also been argued that Ireland itself, as an imaginary construct, is feminine. Drawing on a wide range of scholarship about images of Ireland in official discourses, art, literature and music, Walter illustrates how Ireland was feminized in its colonial relation with Britain:

> Britain represented Ireland as Erin, a young, beautiful but weak woman who needed 'marriage' to her strong masculinised neighbour for control and protection. This feminine position of dependence was popularised in the second half of the nineteenth century by Matthew Arnold, who published theories about Irish 'Celticism'. Celts were constructed as a feminised 'race', characterised as artistic and charming, but impractical and unreliable. (2001: 18–19)

Catherine Nash (1993), in her analysis of images of Ireland in literature, painting and travel photography, argues that nationalist writers of the Irish Ireland movement reacted to this nineteenth-century construction of the Celtic as feminine by asserting masculinity as an essential characteristic of the 'Gael'. She notes that:

> while the idea of 'woman' remained the embodiment of the national spirit and the allegorical figure for the land of Ireland, this land now became the domain of the overtly masculine. The West [of Ireland] was redefined as Gaelic, masculine, wholesome, pragmatic and Catholic in contrast to the femininity and natural spirituality of the Celtic. (1993: 47)

23

Women continued to be represented as passive in idealizations of asexual motherhood. Nash suggests that the popularity of 'the cottage in the landscape' in genre painting 'came to carry the cultural weight of the idealisation of traditional rural, family life and its fixed morality and gender roles . . . a surrogate for the depiction of the rural Irish woman and the values of motherhood, tradition and stability' (1993: 47). Thus, the connections between femininity and home at different spatial scales are illustrated in a single image.

Although the symbolic representation of Ireland as female is particularly strong – the image of a protective or suffering 'Mother Ireland' was powerful as a response to British imperialism as well as among Irish diasporic communities – the actual representation of female figures in public spaces is seen as highly transgressive and destabilizing. The strong conservatism and Catholicism of Ireland was based on the fundamental belief, at least until the recent decades of modernization, that a woman's place is in the home and not in the streets, even as a steel or stone image. In her analysis of the monuments and statues of Ireland, Johnson (1995) found that representations of mythical and fictional women outnumbered 'real' women. She discusses the popular reactions to a statue of Anna Livia Plurabelle, a character from Joyce's *Finnegans Wake*, which was erected in Dublin to symbolize the city and its river. The statue has variously been nicknamed 'the floozie in the jacuzzi', 'the whore in the sewer' and 'the skivvy in the sink', undercutting its high art pretensions but also, Johnson suggests, reflecting a masculine discourse of dominance over women. Though the idealized figure of 'woman' is accepted in nationalist discourse, the 'woman's role in public space . . . is confined to that of prostitute or seductress strolling in streets normally occupied by men' (1995: 58).

Walter (2001) has argued that, with the election of Mary Robinson as the first woman President of Ireland in 1992, the use of feminized language and symbolism has changed in ways that emphasize active rather than passive versions of femininity. In her speeches, for example, Robinson tended to use the word 'cherish', suggesting a positive notion of female nurturing rather than the more traditional version of the self-sacrificing duty of 'caring' associated with a Catholic version of 'Mother Ireland'. Feminization was also signalled in the domestic symbols adopted by Robinson to represent the Irish diaspora. In her inaugural speech, she announced that annual reunions would be held at her presidential 'home' for representatives of diasporic communities, 'strongly echoing the importance of family and the high profile of the figure of the mother in Irish culture' (Walter 2001: 12). In the same speech, Robinson also said that she would light a candle in the window of her home as a permanent reminder to those who had stayed put in Ireland of the absent members of their 'imagined community'. Walter points out the gendered symbolism of the candle, a domestic object but also 'to men candles may signify a romantic view of the cosiness of the home as a haven, overseen by mothers and wives who "keep the home fires burning"'' (2001: 12).

Stateless and Placeless: Nomadic Subjects and Diasporic Identities

In this section I want to pursue some of the implications of migration and the development of diasporic communities such as the Irish in more detail, looking in particular at the implications for gendered identities. Historical associations between womanhood and nation, gender and nationality may by migration and mobility be challenged and destabilized rather than reconfirmed. Notions of home and away, here and there, location and dislocation, place and displacement are key terms in a number of contemporary theoretical discourses, as well as ideas about new ethnicities, hybridity and diasporic identities. At the beginning of the twenty-first century, displacement rather than attachment to a fixed and settled place or location has become a more 'normal' way of life for increasing numbers of people from the war-torn countries of central Africa to the temporary and permanent migrations for work in almost all the world's regions. Large-scale migration is not, of course, a recent phenomenon. The arguments of bell hooks about home as a site of resistance for black women reflect the savage dislocations of the slave trade, and the nineteenth-century cities re-examined by Marcus were partly built on migration, from rural areas to the city and between nations. In the nineteenth century almost 40 million people left Europe for the Americas and the great cities of the US became the homes of a cosmopolitan population that nevertheless recreated the cultural customs of 'home' in neighbourhoods that were designated as Little Italy and Germantown, depending on the origins of their inhabitants.

While the social theory of the modern era, reflected for example in the Chicago School of urban ecology that documented the ways of life in that city in the first half of the twentieth century (Park et al. 1925), focused on the consequences of mobility and the re-establishment of

25

home in the new world, in contemporary theorizing in both the humanities and the social sciences, travel and mobility itself have moved to centre stage (Kaplan 1996; Clifford 1997). Some feminist theorists (Wolff 1992) are sceptical about this focus, pointing out the gendered associations of travel as a privileged activity: travel to broaden the mind of the white bourgeois youth in the nineteenth century and as masculine rebellion in the post-war West (Phillips 1997). But there is also a growing feminist literature about the signifi-cance of women travellers in colonial and postcolonial times (Pratt 1992; Blunt and Rose 1994), as well as exciting new work about nomadic and diasporic identities, establishing the political potential-ities that lie in a location in the borderlands.

Migration – what the sociologist Stuart Hall (1990) has termed the movement of the Third World into the First World – has disrupted associations between territory and ethnicity. This migration has, Hall argues, altered the customs, cultures and identities not only of the 'travelling' peoples but also those of the 'natives', producing what he has termed a 'translation' of identity. In a parallel discussion, James Clifford (1997), an anthropologist, has noted the construction of 'translocal identities' in the world's metropolises. Translation is a somewhat optimistic concept, based on belief in the possibility of the development of a new tolerance in Britain. While the white British population may cast off its Little Englander/bulldog Britain attitudes and its racist behaviours, African-Caribbean and Asian populations may begin to reject claims to an essentialized identity and instead the diverse population will embrace their hybrid or translated identities. This clearly is a contested and politicized process working out in dif-ferent ways in different places and spaces.

The Politics of Location

At the beginning of this chapter, I suggested that there has been an exciting coincidence in the conceptual concerns of the social sciences and the humanities, especially among feminist theorists. In new work that straddles the boundaries of geography, literary and cultural studies, spatial metaphors and concepts play a key role. Caren Kaplan (1996: 144) has noted how maps become metaphors

> signalling a heightened awareness of the political and economic struc-
> tures that demarcate zones of inclusion and exclusion as well as the

interstitial spaces of indeterminacy. Topography and geography now intersect literary and cultural criticism in a growing interdisciplinary inquiry into emergent identity formations and social practices.

Identity and politics thus combine spatial practices, location and images of place in which people are differentially positioned by the large-scale processes of what geographer Derek Gregory (1994) has termed 'space-time colonization and compression'. A locational approach to understanding gendered identities demands an analysis of the ways in which the intersections of social processes of stratification and distinction and movements for social justice at different times and in different places result in different and changing gender identities and relations. Such a feminism must be informed by an understanding of what may seem like conventional geographical knowledge. It requires analyses of the ways in which local and global changes are mutually constituted, each informed by the other, and the ability to make connections between the multiple and heterogeneous feminist movements and struggles in specific places at particular times. Consequently, Mohanty (1991), among others, has argued that feminist politics is no longer necessarily based on a settled or territorially based identity but rather on the development of networks among an imagined community of women with interests in common. For Third World women migrants, these common interests are constructed by the ways in which capital positions them in marginal spaces, exploiting them as the new proletariat of the increasingly globalized economy outlined in the introduction to this chapter (Fuentes and Ehrenreich 1983; Rowbotham and Mitter 1994).

Despite its clear geographical connections, the concept of identity as an 'historically embedded site, a positionality, a location, a standpoint, a terrain, an intersection, a cross roads of multiply situated knowledge' (Friedman 1998: 19) is now a common one. In its conception and development, ideas from the humanities and the social sciences, from literary theory, from cultural and postcolonial studies, as well as global economics, have been influential. Friedman terms this coincidence of interests across disciplinary boundaries 'the new geographics'. This approach, she argues, 'articulates not the organic unfolding of identity but rather the mapping of terrains and boundaries, the dialectical terrains of inside/outside or centre/margin, the axial intersections of different positionalities, and the spaces of dynamic encounter – the "contact zone", the "middle ground", the borderlands, *la frontera*' (1998: 19).

27

While the optimism that informs notions of translation, trans-national feminism and a new geography or geographies of identity has been a significant spur to an exciting expansion of work on travel, displacement, migration, and diasporic identities, as well as informing the politics of identity, it is also important not to neglect the structural processes of inequality that characterize capitalist societies and that continue to divide the interests of people along class, gender and ethnic lines. The strength of different claims and the power of different voices remain unequal. Indeed, it has been argued that the structures of exploitation are currently starker than at almost any time throughout the twentieth century, leading some feminist theorists to suggest that post-structuralist perspectives might usefully be brought into contact with older work on material inequality (Phillips 1999; Segal 1999). While the notion of an emancipatory politics that is fluid, diverse and provisional may seem to some an overly optimistic aim and to others a realistic goal, it is also important to hold on to earlier feminist visions of a progressive transformation in the everyday lives of women.

A sobering counter to the emphasis on displacement and mobility in recent theoretical work as well as in empirical studies lies in realizing that most women in the world remain trapped or fixed in place. Their everyday lives and social relations are confined within often tight spatial boundaries, constructed through power relations and material inequalities. The opportunities but also the constraints of the locality continue to structure many women's, indeed most people's, lives, when the material costs of overcoming the friction of distance are beyond their means. However, the new technologies that compress distance and reduce friction for capitalist enterprises also open up increasing possibilities for interaction between imagined communities or communities of interest. While these communities may be spatially distant, there are greater prospects than ever before of building coalitions between them. As Rosi Braidotti (1994) reminds us, this new international politics of coalition raises key questions for feminist scholars in the 'centre', in the metropolises of the industrial West where migrant women constitute the bulk of what she terms 'domestic foreigners'. 'When', Braidotti asks,

> will we accept that internationalization begins at home? How close are we, the 'white' intellectual women, to the migrant women who have even fewer citizen rights than we have? How sensitive are we to the intellectual potential of the foreigners that we have right here, in our own backyard? . . . For internationalization to become a serious practice

we must work through this paradox of proximity, indifference, and cultural differences between the nomadic intellectual and the migrant women. (1994: 255)

Acknowledgement

The section entitled 'Home/Land' is a revised version of part of chapter 7 of my book *Gender, Identity and Place* (1999) published by Polity Press.

References and Further Reading

Anderson, Benedict (1991) *Imagined Communities*, rev. edn. London: Verso.

Anderson, Bridget (2000) *Doing the Dirty Work? The Global Politics of Domestic Labour*. London: Zed Books.

Anderson, M. (1997) *Frontiers: Territory and State Formation in the Modern World*. Cambridge: Polity Press.

Anzaldúa, G. (1987) *Borderlands/La Frontera: The New Mestiza*. San Francisco, CA: Aunt Lute Books.

Bachelard, G. (1969) *The Poetics of Space*, trans. M. Jolas. Boston, MA: Beacon Press.

Bahloul, J. (1992) *The Architecture of Memory: A Jewish–Muslim Household in Colonial Algeria, 1937–62*. Cambridge: Cambridge University Press.

Barrett, M. and McIntosh, M. (1982) *The Anti-social Family*. London: New Left Books (2nd edn 1991, London: Verso).

Blunt, A. and Rose, G. (eds) (1994) *Writing Women and Space: Colonial and Postcolonial Geographies*. New York: Guilford Press.

Braidotti, R. (1994) *Nomadic Subjects: Embodiment and Sexual Difference in Contemporary Feminist Theory*. New York: Columbia University Press.

Cassady, C. (1990) *Off the Road*. London: Black Spring.

Castells, M. (1996) *The Rise of the Network Society*. Oxford: Blackwell.

— (2000) Materials for an exploratory theory of a network society. *British Journal of Sociology*, 51: 5–24.

Clifford, J. (1997) *Routes: Travel and Translation in the Late Twentieth Century*. Cambridge, MA: Harvard University Press.

Davidoff, L. and Hall, C. (1987) *Family Fortunes: Men and Women of the English Middle Class*. London: Hutchinson.

Foucault, M. (1980) *Power/Knowledge: Selected Interviews and Other Writings, 1972–1977*, ed. and trans. C. Gordon. New York: Pantheon Books.

Friedman, S. S. (1998) *Mappings: Feminism and the Cultural Geographies of Encounter*. Princeton, NJ: Princeton University Press.

Fuentes, A. and Ehrenreich, B. (1983) *Women and the Global Factory*. Boston, MA: South End Press.

Gregory, D. (1994) *Geographical Imaginations*. Oxford: Blackwell.

Hall, S. (1990) Cultural identity and diaspora. In J. Rutherford (ed.), *Identity: Community, Culture, Difference*, pp. 222–37. London: Lawrence and Wishart.

Haraway, D. (1991) *Simians, Cyborgs and Women: The Reinvention of Nature*. London: Free Association Books.

Harding, S. (1991) *Whose Science? Whose Knowledge?* Milton Keynes: Open University Press.

hooks, b. (1991) Homeplace: a site of resistance. In *Yearning: Race, Gender, and Cultural Politics*, pp. 41–9. London: Turnaround Press.

Johnson, N. (1995) Cast in stone: monuments, geography and nationalism. *Environment and Planning D: Society and Space*, 13: 51–65.

Kaplan, C. (1996) *Questions of Travel: Postmodern Discourses of Displacement*. Durham, NC: Duke University Press.

Katz, C. (2001) On the grounds of globalization: a topography for feminist political engagement. *Signs*, 26: 1213–34.

Kirby, K. (1996) *Indifferent Boundaries: Spatial Concepts of Human Subjectivity*. New York: Guilford Press.

McDowell, L. (1983) Towards an understanding of the gender division of urban space. *Environment and Planning D: Society and Space*, 1: 15–30.

— (1991) Life without father and Ford: the new gender order of postfordism. *Transactions of the Institute of British Geographers*, 16: 400–19.

McKenzie, S. and Rose, D. (1983) Industrial change, the domestic economy and home life. In J. Anderson, S. Duncan and R. Hudson (eds), *Redundant Spaces and Industrial Decline in Cities and Regions*, pp. 155–99. London: Academic Press.

Marcus, S. (1999) *Apartment Stories*. Berkeley, CA: University of California Press.

Massey, D. (1992) Politics and space/time. *New Left Review*, 196: 65–84.

Mohanty, C. T. (1991) Cartographies of struggle. In C. T. Mohanty, A. Russo and L. Torres (eds), *Third World Women and the Politics of Feminism*, pp. 1–47. Bloomington, IN: Indiana University Press.

Nash, C. (1993) Remapping and renaming: new cartographies of identity, gender and landscape in Ireland. *Feminist Review*, 44: 39–57.

Park, R. E., Burgess, E. W. and McKenzie, R. D. (1925) *The City*. Chicago: Chicago University Press (reprinted 1967).

Pateman, C. (1988) *The Sexual Contract*. Cambridge: Polity Press.

— and Grosz, E. (eds) (1987) *Feminist Challenges: Social and Political Theory*. Boston, MA: Northeastern University Press.

Phillips, A. (1999) *Which Equalities Matter?* Cambridge: Polity Press.

Phillips, R. (1997) *Mapping Men and Empire: A Geography of Adventure*. London: Routledge.

Pollock, G. (ed.) (1996) *Generations and Geographies in the Visual Arts: Feminist Readings*. London: Routledge.

Pratt, G. (1997) Stereotypes and ambivalence: the construction of domestic workers in Vancouver. *Gender, Place and Culture*, 4: 159–78.

Pratt, M. B. (1984) Identity: skin blood heart. In E. Bulkin, M. B. Pratt and B. Smith (eds), *Yours in Struggle: Three Feminist Perspectives on Anti-Semitism and Racism*, pp. 9–64. Brooklyn, NY: Long Haul Press.

Pratt, M. L. (1992) *Imperial Eyes: Travel Writing and Transculturation*. London: Routledge.

Rich, A. (1986) *Blood, Bread, and Poetry: Selected Prose, 1979–1985*. New York: Norton.

Rowbotham, S. and Mitter, S. (eds) (1994) *Dignity and Daily Bread: New Forms of Economic Organising among Poor Women in the Third World*. London: Routledge.

Segal, L. (1999) *Why Feminism?* Cambridge: Polity Press.

Smith, A. D. (1986) *The Ethnic Origins of Nations*. Oxford: Blackwell.

— (1999) *Myths and Memories of the Nation*. Oxford: Oxford University Press.

Soja, E. (1989) *Postmodern Geographies*. London: Verso.

Walby, S. (1990) *Theorising Patriarchy*. Oxford: Blackwell.

Walkerdine, V. (1989) *Democracy in the Kitchen: Regulating Mothers and Socialising Daughters*. London: Virago.

Walter, B. (1995) Irishness, gender and place. *Environment and Planning D: Society and Space*, 13: 35–50.

— (2001) *Outsiders Inside: Whiteness, Place and Irish Women*. London: Routledge.

Warner, M. (1985) *Monuments and Maidens: The Allegory of the Female Form*. London: Picador.

Wilson, E. (1977) *Women and the Welfare State*. London: Tavistock.

Wolff, J. (1992) On the road again: metaphors of travel in cultural criticism. *Cultural Studies*, 7: 224–39.

2

Time

Krista Cowman and Louise A. Jackson

In April 1978 the American artist Judy Chicago exhibited *The Dinner Party* (figure 2.1) at the San Francisco Museum of Modern Art (Chadwick 1990: 346). The result of a collaborative four-year project involving over a hundred women, the work had been constructed as 'a symbolic history of women in Western Civilization' (Rosen et al. 1989: 122). A triangular table was laid with thirty-nine place settings, each representing an historic or legendary woman. Each place included a ceramic plate and an embroidered runner in a style appropriate to the era in which the woman had lived. The table stood on a tiled floor inscribed with a further 999 names. The work has been seen as controversial amongst feminists because of its central 'vaginal' imagery, which could be interpreted as essentialist, and because Chicago's name as artist overshadowed those of her collaborators. Yet for many, the piece remains extremely appealing because of the humour and scale of the idea: it unites, temporally and spatially, for the purpose of feasting and celebration, women who have been separated by centuries and continents. By bringing together past and present in one frozen moment, *The Dinner Party* uses art to challenge the strictures of time itself.

Chicago and her collaborators were also participating in a task that was central to the feminist project: the retrieval of women artists, writers, musicians and scientists who had been marginalized or forgotten by a male-dominated culture. In this chapter we will begin by examining the politics of 'retrieval' and of writing women's history. We shall then consider more broadly how feminists have used and worked with

Figure 2.1 Judy Chicago, *The Dinner Party*, 1979 © ARS, NY and DACS, London, 2002.

the concept of 'time' and, in so doing, how they have challenged existing assumptions. Finally, we shall consider how women's life stories can provide a central focus in theorizing and working with notions of time, perception, social position and identity. This chapter is concerned with both feminist 'theory' and the practicalities – methodological, institutional, material and social – of doing feminist research (inside and outside academia). The connections between theory and practice – and hence the notion of praxis – have always been emphasized within feminism because both converge on the political. Furthermore, it is through specific case studies or research projects that 'theory' (feminist and non-feminist) is challenged, qualified or shifted.

Hidden from History

In 1929 in *A Room of One's Own*, British writer, Virginia Woolf, asked what had happened to Shakespeare's sister and why it was that her life and history had been overshadowed by that of her brother:

> What one wants, I thought – and why does not some brilliant student
> at Newnham or Girton supply it? – is a mass of information; at what age
> did she marry; how many children had she as a rule; what was her home
> like; had she a room to herself . . . All these facts lie somewhere, pre-
> sumably, in parish registers and account books; the life of the average
> Elizabethan woman must be scattered about somewhere, could one
> collect it and make a book of it. (1993: 41)

Discussing her own involvement in feminism, Sheila Rowbotham
(1990: 29) has written: 'I can remember jumping up in one of the ple-
naries [at the first History Workshop in 1969] and announcing that
we were going to have a meeting about women, at which point all the
trade union men laughed.' These two quotations, separated by over
sixty years, share more than a common call for the writing of a different type of history in which women would figure as equal players
or, as Woolf says, 'a supplement to history' (1993: 41). Both were
written by feminists who had played their own part in the two significant movements of feminist activism since the nineteenth century,
commonly referred to as first- and second-wave feminism. Furthermore, they indicate that within first- and second-wave feminism, a
search for women's pasts – constructed by feminists and with a distinctive political agenda – was a crucial part of the broader feminist
project.

The success of Rowbotham's project can be quantified by casting an
eye over the programmes and prospectuses of most history depart-
ments in the Western world. It is now virtually impossible to under-
take a history degree without encountering material on women's
history (although in the great majority of institutions the subject still
remains discreetly contained within options). The most cursory glance
at the earliest texts to emerge from historians engaged with second-
wave feminism (or feminists who turned to history, a point which will
be returned to below) reveals books which, in the words of the preface
to *Hidden from History* came 'very directly from a political movement'
(Rowbotham 1974: ix). Their titles alone bore witness to their intention to restore to the historical picture something vital which was
missing. Women had been 'hidden from history'. Now they were
'becoming visible' (Bridenthal et al. 1987). Feminist historians were
'redressing the balance' (Davin 1987) between men and women in
history, 'retrieving women's history' (Kleinberg 1987) from its almost
invisible status. Second-wave feminists had long campaigned around
the fact that women formed a majority rather than a minority of the
global population. Now, that majority was able to find its past (Lerner

1979). And, as that past emerged, it began to pose fascinating challenges to the categorizations and chronology of the dominant historical canon. For example, 'Did Women Have a Renaissance?' the American historian Joan Kelly-Gadol enquired (1977), urging historians to think long and hard about the extent to which allegedly key historical moments were engaged with or perceived by their female contemporaries.

By the late 1980s, the amount of historical writing to emerge from the feminist movement had been so great that the authors toyed with the idea of *No Longer Invisible* for the revised edition of *Becoming Visible* (Bridenthal et al. 1987). It was rejected, largely because it was felt that a new set of objectives was now emerging which was broadening the project of feminist history still further. Beyond the initial retrieval stage, feminist historians were questioning the entire basis of the categorization of history. Work, labour and public life for women in the past were now joined by new topics: the family, private life, women's domestic worlds, the body. There were further calls to change the discipline entirely rather than simply to add to it, to create 'Herstory' rather than 'History' in an attempt 'to convey the idea that for too long history has been a male preserve, telling stories of men for men' (Black and Macraild 1997: 140). Feminist historians also realized that the project of history was not as simple as one of telling stories, of reconstructing a narrative for a particular audience in order to enlighten, or possibly simply to entertain. Events throughout the historical world in the 1980s and 1990s, which crystallized in the British context in the debate over the content of the new national curriculum (Clark et al. 1990), left historians in no doubt as to the importance of their subject. History's tales were not innocent narratives but held a wider political purpose, the potential to create or reinforce dominant paradigms, national identities and cultural norms.

The political movement of second-wave feminism made explicit connections between women's contemporary oppression and their invisibility in the historical record. An absence of historical precedent had long been used as an excuse for normalizing or perpetuating instances of historical discrimination, both legal and cultural. Women were paid less, it was argued in the 1970s, because they had always been paid less, because Western wages were predicated upon the existence of a male breadwinner with female wages representing 'pin money' for household extras and luxuries. Feminists turned to the archives to counter this, and emerged armed with examples of women who had successfully mounted challenges to 'oppressive norms' in the past, or women who had 'manipulated prevailing cultural norms to maximise what power they had' in extremely inauspicious circumstances (Bridenthal et al. 1987: xi). Sally Alexander spent nights campaigning with exploited cleaning staff in London, and days in the archives in the company of their ghostly foremothers, the sweated needlewomen of the nineteenth century (Alexander 1976). The battles women had fought in the past, their arguments and their campaigning tactics, their victories and their defeats were rediscovered and studied, not simply as an academic exercise, but with the explicit intent of using these examples and precedents from the past to inform and improve the lives of women in the present. How women had challenged inequality in the past remained a key issue, more vital to the project than the simple act of retrieval of 'great' women or the construction of new historical heroines, although a good many of these were thrown up along the way as work progressed.

As feminist historians turned to the history of their own movement, it emerged that even their current preoccupation with restoring a feminist past had an historical precedent. Studying early women graduates in the United Kingdom through the records of the British Federation of University Women caused Carol Dyhouse to remark on 'broken or lost traditions', the importance of 'recovering neglected areas of women's experience in the past' and of 'rediscovering or getting in touch with earlier traditions of feminist history and awareness' (1995: 467). Research into British education revealed that, just like second-wave feminists, women who pioneered entry into academia had themselves looked to the past to create role models, challenge the sexual divisions and discriminations of their own time, and query accepted norms via examples of historical feminism. At the London School of Economics, which was co-educational from its opening in 1895, Lilian Knowles was appointed to the first chair in Economic History. She quickly gathered a group of enthusiastic young scholars around her, many of whom had participated actively in the suffrage movement. Eileen Power, Alice Clark and Ivy Pinchbeck produced important studies of the earlier lives of women as an attempt to historicize their own feminist activism (Clark 1968; Power 1975; Pinchbeck 1981). In the United States, where a similar struggle for access to higher education had emerged, writing women's history was equally important to the first generation of female academics. Kathryn Kish Sklar examined the careers of a number of US academics and identified 'female support networks' as 'important sources of career support in their increasingly direct encounter with the historical profession' (1975: 182). In the cases of women such as Kate

Hurd-Mead, a medical practitioner who wrote a history of women in medicine, these networks could just as easily be forged in the Senior Common Room (Hurd-Mead 1933). Simultaneously, outside mainstream academia, many first-wave feminists began self-consciously to chart the history of their own movement, and their participation within it. The first histories of the British suffrage campaign were published by activists while the campaign was still in process (Pankhurst 1911; Fawcett 1912; Lytton 1914).

A common need to search for their past has led feminists in many countries into the archives in an attempt to understand their own history. In an ambitious survey spanning most of the world, Offen et al. (1991: xx) identified a common 'influence of the contemporary women's movement on kindling an interest in the history of women' in countries as diverse as Greece, Japan, Yugoslavia, India and France. However, whilst a wider feminist politics may have been the driving force behind the emergence of most women's histories, the geographical specificities of particular national feminisms directed these histories down different roads. Distinct preoccupations emerged within certain countries which reflected differences between national feminisms. In Britain, there were particularly close links between feminist and socialist history. These had direct implication for the subject matter of early British feminist history, and meant that for many years research on middle-class, liberal or conservative women was at best marginalized and more frequently not undertaken. In America, where the civil rights movement emerged alongside feminism, feminist historians were quick to identify race as an important category and to attempt to differentiate between the historical experiences of women from different racial groups. In Germany, many feminist historians engaged with the national preoccupations of their discipline and sought to research women's relationship to the Third Reich both as resisters and as participants (Koonz 1987; Bock 1991). Just as the women's movement had taken on different forms in different countries, the common quest for 'foremothers' emphasized that women had occupied a variety of places in the past.

The Challenge of the 'Enlightenment'

Thus 'History' as a discipline and an area of enquiry was vitally important to feminism. Yet many of the theoretical assumptions that underpinned notions of historical investigation – and indeed the concept of 'time' itself – were hugely problematic. In this section we examine how feminists, both influenced by and contributing to wider developments in cultural theory, have re-examined the connections between time, perception, subject position and identity.

The emergence of Western 'History' as a modern academic discipline, which seeks to investigate and explain the events of the past, is usually associated with the 'Enlightenment' project and its pursuit of rational, scientific enquiry. Moreover, it is possible to chart shifts in the dominant conceptualization of 'time' – past, present and future – in eighteenth- and nineteenth-century Western societies. First, the measurement of time itself was standardized as part of the process of rationalization but also in response to the growth of mechanization, which required a large number of 'docile' bodies to be in the same place at the same appointed hour (Thompson 1967; Foucault 1977). If pre-industrial societies measured time in terms of task or process (the time it takes for a bowl of rice to cook, or for a carpet to be woven), the development of large-scale factories led to the apparent uniformity and discipline of 'clock' time, which was linear. Clock time within and across countries was very gradually aligned with Greenwich Mean Time, making it possible to coordinate train timetables as travel and communication accelerated. Secondly, if natural phenomena – species of animal, vegetable and mineral – could be measured, classified, ordered and fitted into an agreed framework that explained their origins, so too could all previous human endeavour. On one hand, the reading and writing of histories and historical novels became a popular activity and, on the other, the 'protocols' of professional historical enquiry were put in place. The 'scientific' approach to history is usually associated with the German scholar Leopold von Ranke, whose central precept – in the words of English translators – was 'to show how things actually were' (Evans 1997: 18). 'History' as a discipline should not judge the past in relation to the values of the present but seek to understand it on its own terms. Careful objective and empirical observation, akin to the methodology of pure scientists, was required when it came to the evaluation of the past. Historians, too, depicted time as linear and teleological as they sought to trace 'cause' and 'effect'; in some accounts, which were labelled retrospectively as 'Whiggish', an historical process depicted in terms of progress or evolutionary development. Finally, the 'Enlightenment' project led to a new interest in the figure of the child, whose temporal growth to adulthood was to be measured, demarcated (in stages), medicalized and normalized (Steedman 1995). The human life-cycle itself, mental and physical, became the object of scientific enquiry. In both symbolic and material terms, the child was closely associated with the future health and happiness of the nation. Mothering and child-rearing practices were increasingly monitored; women's reproductive functions became a focus of medical intervention.

Feminism, too, can be seen as a product of 'Enlightenment' thought. Mary Wollstonecraft's *Vindication of the Rights of Woman* (1792) was a response to both Paine's *The Rights of Man* and Rousseau's *Émile* and their concern with the education of male rather than female children. In the context of revolutionary France, Olympe de Gouges challenged the notion of the male citizen. Similarly, in the United States, Abigail Adams attempted to persuade her husband, the future President John Adams, to include women in the new republic, writing in 1776: 'Do not put unlimited power into the hands of Husbands . . . Remember all Men would be tyrants if they could' (quoted in Kerber 1998: 12). Yet feminism has also taken issue with the precepts underlining the 'Enlightenment' notion of 'rational', 'scientific' enquiry.

Given that most histories pre-dating second-wave feminism tended to ignore or leave out women, it was apparent that 'History', far from being objective, is dependent on the subjective viewpoint of the historian. Black feminists highlighted the logocentrism and ethnocentrism of white women's history. For example, Lucille Mair Marthurin's 1975 study *The Rebel Woman in the British West Indies during Slavery* exposed white women's complicity in the exploitation of black women: 'the black woman produced, the brown woman served and the white woman consumed' (quoted in Bush 1990: xii). The rediscovery and republication of women's slave narratives, such as *The History of Mary Prince, A West Indian Slave, Related by Herself*, pointed to white women's brutality. Originally edited and published in 1831 by the secretary of the British Anti-Slavery Society, Mary Prince's account included graphic descriptions of treatment by her mistress:

> She taught me to do all sorts of household work; to wash and bake, pick cotton and wool, and wash floors and cook. And she taught me (how can I ever forget!) more things than these; she caused me to know the exact differences between the smart of the rope, the cart-whip, and the cow skin, when applied to my naked body by her own cruel hand . . . she was a fearful woman and a savage mistress to her slaves. (Ferguson 1987: 56)

Women do not have a common past. Furthermore, the processes of socialization and acculturation, which are informed in one way or another by past 'experiences' of exploitation and colonization, mean we all present our own readings of the past. A black Jamaican woman writing the history of her ancestors may do so with a very different emphasis from a liberal white Englishman or an Italian/American woman.

When 'traditional' historians argued that they had not included women because women had been absent from the sources on which they were working, feminist historians set about the task of retrieval, locating long-forgotten diaries, memoirs and artefacts produced by women. But it was also clear that the 'traditional' historians had a point. Women might have been written out of history because their contributions had not been valued in past societies (and, indeed, poor women and black women had been marginalized the most). Moreover, 'the past' can never be retrieved. Fragments or relics of the past survive in the form of artefacts and texts but these are an infinitely small percentage of all cultural production. These fragments are not 'the past' itself, neither are they self-evident 'truths'. Rather, they require interpretation. No one can ever fully know how things 'actually were'.

The Challenge of 'Experience'

If the past cannot be uncovered, the 'truth' never told, and if women all speak with different voices, can there ever be an authentic feminist 'history'? If a 'feminist' account of past time is simply one possibility amongst many others, no more or less 'truthful', then it loses its political cogency. Furthermore, what should a feminist study? Whilst second-wave feminism had placed women's 'experience' at the centre of enquiry in the 1970s, the interest in post-structuralism, which surfaced in literary, sociological and historical studies during the 1980s, served to critique this focus as essentialist. Experience could never be 'real' in any sense; rather, events are always interpreted and mediated through language, as they are remembered across time, making them discursive effects. American historians Linda Gordon and Joan W. Scott debated the uses (and abuses) of post-structuralist theory for feminist historians in the early 1990s (Gordon 1990; Scott 1990a). Their differences possibly stemmed from their research concerns at the time. Gordon had used the records of social work agencies in Boston, Massachusetts, to examine voluntary and state interventions in cases of family violence, aiming to highlight the agency of women and children whom she saw as 'heroes of their own lives' (also the title of the study). For Gordon, a focus on discourse analysis obscured physical 'experiences' of pain or violence – the extra-textual – and gave little space for human agency (Gordon 1990). For Scott, whose historical research centred on the gendering of the political sphere in eighteenth-century France, discourse analysis was vital to the feminist project in order 'to understand how, in all their complexity, collective and individual differences are constructed, how that is, hierarchies and inequalities are produced' (Scott 1990b: 859). Scott, whose ideas have been linked with what is often termed 'the new cultural history', developed her ideas in a further article entitled 'The Evidence of Experience' (1991) which, significantly, offered a return to 'experience' as a central focus of analysis. Rather than assuming that 'experience' is an a priori given, Scott argued that feminists should 'historicize experience and the identities it produces' (1991: 792): 'Historians must take as their project *not* the reproduction and transmission of knowledge said to be arrived at through experience, but the analysis of the production of knowledge itself' (1991: 792). Within this formulation, material or physical events are constituted as 'experience' through processes of naming, remembering, re-telling and assigning meaning. The relationship between the material and the discursive becomes the key line of enquiry.

The study of literary fiction raises further questions about the relationship between past and present. The retrieval of past women writers and the interest in 'authentic' and realist texts that arose from second-wave feminism were not merely about the identification of women's cultural heritage. It was also assumed that realist texts could bring author and reader together across time because of their shared position, and indeed 'experience', as 'women' (Mills 1989). However, the question of what, exactly, we can assume to be shared, has been problematized by the argument that there is no such thing as 'women'. Identities and 'experiences' are shaped by class, religion, sexual orientation and ethnicity. Furthermore, as the historicists amongst literary scholars argue, they are culturally and temporarily specific. Influenced by Michel Foucault's re-articulation of the idea that there is no absolute truth, that 'knowledge' and 'power' are intertwined, and that 'knowledge' is discursively constructed, the New Historicist approach to literary studies, most closely associated with the work of Stephen Greenblatt, Louis Montrose, and Jonathan Dollimore, emphasized the notion of 'inter-textuality' or 'cross-cultural montage' (Foucault 1970; Greenblatt 1980, 1988; Montrose 1981; Dollimore and

Sinfield 1985). If history like fiction is text, so too are science and theology. All texts, therefore, must be considered in relation to each other as effects of power relationships at the time in which they were produced.

New Historicism has evoked differing feminist responses. For feminists who were interested in continuities in terms of women's 'experience' and subjectivity and who wished to highlight a shared identity across time that might be biological and psychical as well as cultural, such an approach seemed politically dangerous; by denying that 'woman' existed outside of the text, patriarchy would simply continue to reproduce itself (Neely 1988). Other feminists whose approach had always been situated within a cultural materialist framework argued that New Historicism was based upon and indeed shared many of the ideas that had been developed by second-wave feminism. As Judith Newton has pointed out, feminist theory and scholarship was rendered invisible in the histories of New Historicism that were presented for student and academic audiences in the 1980s: 'Like housework, women's theoretical labor seemed part of life and therefore not like "real" – that is, male – theoretical labor at all' (1988: 95). Many key studies produced by feminist literary scholars working within a cultural materialist framework have shared New Historicist concerns with the 'cross-cultural montage' of scientific/medical discourse, newspaper reportage, social commentary, fictional and artistic representations, without specifically situating themselves in relation to New Historicism (Newton, 1988). This analysis of different forms of representation has been a particularly fruitful area in relation to attempts to understand the dynamics of gender, class and national identity in nineteenth-century Britain. In *Uneven Developments* (1988), Mary Poovey, trained as a literary critic, offered interpretations of medical texts, divorce law reform, the work of Florence Nightingale as well as literary texts to explore, as her sub-title indicates, 'the ideological work of gender'. Similarly, Judith Walkowitz, although emerging from a background in historical rather than literary study, examined, in *City of Dreadful Delight* (1992), a wide range of textual and visual representations of the city, including newspaper accounts of the 'Jack the Ripper' murders, to demonstrate how London was constructed as a terrain of sexual danger in the 1890s.

Whether positioned as New Historicism, 'cultural materialism' or 'the new cultural history', a range of literary/historical studies have shared an approach that is concerned with hermeneutics rather than grand theories of cause and effect. This approach has been accused of a cultural preoccupation with the relationship between representation and identity that has ignored the material circumstances of people's lives. It has also been accused of depoliticizing the study of gender, class and ethnicity. Feminism is above all a political and personal ideology as well as a theoretical position within the academy, which means that, for feminists, some explanations will always be more credible than others, certain principles and value judgements more valid. Feminists acknowledge a duty towards those women who inhabited the past: to ensure that their lives are evaluated with respect and hence 'truthfully'. To state so adamantly that there is no such thing as absolute truth is, of course, a contradiction in terms. We know that the past 'really existed' because we have all, ourselves, been there. We are all, effectively, time-travellers. The debates about post-structuralism and 'the cultural turn', certainly within history and sociology, have often been polarized and have often been based on the caricature of allegedly extreme positions. But they have enabled us to think in more depth about the ways in which experience and identity are constituted and played out over time. 'Experience' remains a valid focus of enquiry.

Within social science disciplines, agreed protocols still exist regarding 'proof' or 'evidence', grounded as it is in the analysis of artefacts. But what do we do when there is little in the way of formal evidence? Do we sever our link with the past? Do we simply forget because there are no material traces? For the American author Toni Morrison, whose novel *Beloved* examines the painful issue of infanticide within a slave community, the possibilities of the past can be recalled and deciphered emotionally and creatively as well as rationally. Although black slaves produced biographical narratives (as we have seen in the extract from *The History of Mary Prince*), these were used for publicity purposes by the anti-slavery moment, and it can be argued that they are carefully constructed to portray the black slave as a civilized, rational and obedient subject. Anger, pain and sorrow – the emotional – are sublimated to suit a white Western readership. For Morrison, the imaginative retrieval of the past through fiction and the process of coming to terms with it are important psychologically, philosophically and culturally: 'the exercise is . . . critical for any person who is black, or who belongs to any marginalized category, for, historically, we were seldom invited to participate in the discourse even when we were its topic' (1990: 302). Morrison talks of 'a kind of literary archaeology' – of places and images that remain – which enables her to get at what is 'truth' if not necessarily 'fact':

> You know they straightened out the Mississippi River in places, to make room for houses and livable acreage. Occasionally the river floods these places. 'Floods' is the word they use, but in fact it is not flooding; it is remembering. Remembering where it used to be. All water has a perfect memory and is forever trying to get back where it was. Writers are like that: remembering where we were, what valley we ran through, what the banks were like, the light that was there and the route back to our original place. It is emotional memory – what the nerves and the skin remember as well as how it appeared. And a rush of imagination is our 'flooding'. (1990: 305)

One could argue that Morrison's fiction deals with the inheritance of the present and the legacy of the past, rather than the past *per se*. It is through fiction and the imaginative process that collective memories are interpreted, worked through and finally laid at peace. It is, therefore, about coming to terms with the present. Morrison's approach, with its emphasis on emotions and imagination, offers a different framework for writing and thinking from that suggested by the rational scientific framework.

Life Stories

The concepts of 'experience' and 'memory' have, as we have seen, been subject to careful scrutiny but they remain central to feminist attempts to interpret women's lives, whether long or recently passed. In this section we will consider the role of personal memoirs and narratives in feminist research. Although Judy Chicago's *Dinner Party* was concerned with 'great women' or 'women achievers', feminist sociologists, linguists and anthropologists recognize the significance of collecting oral narratives and life stories from all groups of women including the 'ordinary' and the 'invisible' (Gluck and Patai 1991). For historians too, oral interviews have become increasingly important as a way of investigating the lives of those who have left little in the way of official documentation. Penny Summerfields's interviews with over forty women led her to re-evaluate earlier conclusions, based on printed sources, that women's work in Britain during the Second World War did little to alter the sexual division of labour in the workplace or at home (Summerfield 1998). The use of oral interviews raises particular methodological issues. The power dynamics between interviewer and interviewee, the question of whether a necessarily small and often self-selecting sample can be representative, and the relationship between actual events and the story that is then told about them are key areas for consideration. But these issues themselves can enrich rather than invalidate a project. Summerfield (1998: 286) concludes her study thus:

> I have learned from writing it why I was upset in 1977 by the two women at the adult education meeting, who told me that my story about the war was wrong. I did not have at my disposal at that time a way of understanding both our stories as 'right', theirs based (I would now argue) on a heroic representation of the woman war worker, mine informed by wartime representations of the marginal woman worker and by 1970s analyses of women's oppression. To paraphrase Luisa Passerini, no one's story is wrong, but we need more than the story itself to understand what it may mean.

Summerfield's sophisticated analysis shows how women's life stories, and their contextualization, can be a crucial source upon which to draw when evaluating the construction of feminine identities and subject positions.

The collection of life stories is not simply a priority for feminist academics. In Britain, feminist and socialist historians of the 1960s and 1970s recognized the importance of community-based 'people's history' that was independent of the 'ivory towers' of academia. Family history or 'genealogy' has become a booming interest area as women and men seek to trace ancestors and long-lost cousins and to flesh out the stories of kith and kin. The tracing of our own individual origins can shape, reinforce and challenge personal identities as, for example, 'white' identified citizens discover black ancestors and vice versa. Community history – whether of neighbourhoods or diasporas – emerges from and builds on a sense of collectivity and shared identity. Community groups, such as the Chapeltown Black Women's Writers Group (1992) and the Ethnic Communities Oral History Project (1989), have played an important role in charting and collecting the life stories of immigrant groups whose experiences have not been recorded in 'official' sources.

Where academics use oral history interviews to create written histories, there is an increasing awareness of the collaborative nature of this research. Kristina Minister, who has worked on oral history projects in Arizona, has described the ideal interview process as 'rich dialogue' rather than 'an impoverished list'. Oral historians, she believes, should be alert to 'emergent meanings and to opportunities to draw out narrators' experience, an experience that has not yet been examined linguistically' (1991: 36–7). A feminist approach to oral history interviewing opposes previous 'scientific' research models that position the interviewer as objective/'expert' observer and the interviewee as the object to be studied and that require a meticulously structured set of questions rather than a discursive format. Feminist research sees interviewing as a dialogic and reciprocal process, which must have a positive outcome for all parties concerned.

For feminist historians, sociologists and literary scholars working with women's autobiographical writing, whether unpublished diaries or published memoirs, the relationship between the 'I' who is writing and the 'I' who is reading is, similarly, an important area for discussion, whether decades or centuries separate the two activities. Where the text has been published and, as such, has entered the public domain, the intention is to produce a life story that claims authenticity and is probably written with a specific audience in mind. This may involve countering or contradicting other narratives regarding the author's actions, intentions and reputation. For the critical reader, however, the task of assessing the 'veracity' of the text is often an impossible one in terms of establishing external reference points that can be checked and cross-checked across the ravages of time. We are left, instead, with the task of analysing the identity that the author has assumed: 'The writer of auto/biography has, at the "moment" of writing, an active and coherent "self" that the text invokes, constructs and drives forwards' (Stanley 1992: 61). Autobiography always invokes the past as gone, and is a conscious attempt to rewrite and reassess it.

To return to the example of *The History of Mary Prince*: although this text featured the autobiography of a previously unknown woman whose reputation had not figured as an object of public concern, it did offer a direct challenge to earlier abolitionist representations of slave women. As Moira Ferguson has written: 'Mary Prince inaugurates a black female counter-offensive against a reductive conception of black women as flogged, half-naked victims of slavery's entourage' (1987: 29). Issues of veracity and personal reputation were, significantly, central features. Mary Prince's final owner, Mr Wood, who brought her from the Caribbean to England in 1827 where she finally escaped captivity, went on to make allegations regarding her 'baseness' and 'depravity' and to accuse her of libel (Ferguson 1987: 109). There are traces in other documentary sources that refer to a possible sexual relationship with a white captain, traces that are suggestive but can never be proved. Mary Prince's life story was taken down by a third party and used as a promotional vehicle for the anti-slavery campaign. Yet its apparent silence regarding her sexual experiences could be as much a result of self-censorship as of a desire to please a 'respectable' English audience. Taught to read by Moravians, whose congregation she went on to join, Mary Prince's identity in England was bound up with the creation of a new spiritual 'self' and a sense of shame regarding her previous sinfulness; whilst acknowledging this shame, she did not chose to name those sins in detail. The autobiography itself charts a geographical and spiritual journey from past to present as well as a process of physical emancipation.

Feminist interest in life stories and personal narratives has also been reflected in an awareness of the significance of women's life-cycles. Along with class, gender and 'race', the category of age becomes another important focus of analysis. It is difficult to understand women's narratives without considering cultural attitudes towards aging, rites of passage, sexuality, reproduction, and women's responses to these. For much of the historical past, it can be argued, the transformation from childhood to puberty to parenthood to menopause has been seen as more significant for women – often viewed as '*the* sex' – than for men. Any discussion of women's life-cycles involves a consideration of continuity as well as change across time and space. It also requires an evaluation of the ways in which bodies and bodily functions are imbued with cultural significance. Finally, it requires a consideration of how the culturally signified body is 'experienced' emotionally and psychologically. The study of women's life-cycles has led not only to a greater understanding of women's experiences *per se*; it has also led to research which challenges previous assumptions about other phenomena. Until comparatively recently, for example, historians evaluating the witch-hunts of the sixteenth and seventeenth centuries showed very little interest in the alleged 'confessions' of those accused as witches or in the witness testimonies of their neighbours, seeing them solely as fictional products (albeit collaborative ones) arising from a combination of folk-lore and demonology. Lyndal Roper (1994), however, has argued that these testimonies, although of course framed by cultural and religious belief, can be read as intensely personal narratives. In Augsburg in 1669 Anna Ebbeler, aged 67, was accused of poisoning a woman for whom she had worked as a lying-in maid and causing the death of her child; Ebbeler was subsequently executed. Roper was struck by the frequency with which accounts involving motherhood and childbirth, as well as conflict between women over these themes, appeared in witchcraft narratives. Influenced by the psychoanalytical theory of Melanie Klein, Roper has suggested that witchcraft narratives can be interpreted as psychic dramas. Within Roper's analysis, a mother's ambivalent reaction towards her own newly born child (hate and subsequently guilt) could have been projected onto her lying-in maid, resulting in a witchcraft accusation (Roper 1994).

The consideration of women's life-cycles has caused feminists to ask whether men and women experience, organize or 'count' time in the same way. Although for many the discipline of 'clock time' became increasingly significant from the eighteenth century onwards, for women involved in domestic labour and child care, the notion of task-oriented time may continue to dominate. In her analysis of the French feminist movement, Julia Kristeva has argued that liberal/socialist feminists of the late nineteenth and early twentieth centuries 'aspired to gain a place in linear time as the time and project of history' (1981: 18). The stress on egalitarianism and the rejection of biological essentialism achieved economic, political and professional equality; as it did so, it involved an acceptance of time as a linear trajectory and sought to reclaim a place for women as well as men within that. From 1968 onwards, however, a second wave of French feminists began to confront the notion of sexual equality, which had never been resolved within the socialist framework, and, as they did so, were involved in a direct encounter with questions of 'difference and specificity' (Kristeva 1981: 21). This led to a recognition of other temporalities than the linear and, in some feminist thought, to an association of female subjectivity with reproductive and lunar cycles. It is also possible to argue, in place of a purely essentialist position, that the association of women with cyclical time is a tradition that has been culturally and historically constituted, shaping understandings of 'the feminine' within the symbolic order. For Kristeva the question remains: 'What can be our place in the symbolic contract?' (1981: 23).

Finally, feminists who study women's experiences of life-cycle change have taken issue with 'scientific' assumptions about growth and development, in particular the way in which medical discourse has presented women's bodies as 'maturing' over time to the point of child-birth and then 'deteriorating' as menopause sets in (Martin 1987). Rather, old age and the passing of time can be celebrated and associated with knowledge and deepened experience, as it has been in feminist sci-fi and utopian fiction. If the 'Enlightenment' project led to a focus on women's bodies as objects of the scientific gaze, feminism has responded by stressing the importance of subjectivity and of creating our own meanings.

Conclusion

Underpinning the use of time in historical thought and writing there has often been a discernible 'Whiggish' tendency to use time as a unit of measuring abstract notions of human progress. However, within the feminist historical project, explorations back in time have offered modern-day activists the means to normalize their own activism and public life by demonstrating the existence of clear historical precedents. The retrieval of women into the historical record is a vital means of legitimizing many current feminist claims and concerns. Feminist thought has also challenged assumptions about knowledge, temporal development and the passing of time that were set in place with the emphasis on rational 'scientific' enquiry during the course of the nineteenth century. It has called for a re-evaluation of historical periodization, since stretches of time that have been judged as significant or progressive from a male perspective may take on a different complexion if one looks at the position of women. Hence the so-called 'cultural flowering' of the Renaissance and the re-emergence of Humanist thought must be set against the persecution of women as witches. Feminism has also argued against scientific interpretations of the human life-cycle, of the human body and its temporal transformation, seeing science itself as culturally mediated rather than externally and objectively positioned. Finally, feminist thought continues to argue for the centrality of 'experience' as a focus of research. Women's identities and subject positions can be understood more fully if we explore the intersection of the physical, the material, the cultural and the social: those processes of remembering and re-membering, telling and re-telling, and their relationship to the passing of time.

References and Further Reading

Alexander, S. (1976) Women's work in London: a study of the years 1820–50. In J. Mitchell and A. Oakley (eds), *The Rights and Wrongs of Women*, pp. 59–111. London: Penguin.

Black, J. and Macraild, D. (1997) *Studying History*. Basingstoke: Macmillan.

Bock, G. (1991) Antinatalism, maternity and paternity in national socialism. In G. Bock and P. Thane (eds), *Maternity and Gender Politics: Women and the*

Rise of the European Welfare States, 1880s–1950s, pp. 233–55. London: Routledge.

Bridenthal, R., Koonz, C. and Stuard, S. (eds) (1987) *Becoming Visible: Women in European History*, rev. edn. Boston: Houghton Mifflin (first published 1977).

Bush, B. (1990) *Slave Women in Caribbean Society 1650–1838*. Bloomington, IN: Indiana University Press.

Chadwick, W. (1990) *Women, Art and Society*. London: Thames and Hudson.

Chapeltown Black Women's Writers Group (1992) *When Our Ship Comes in: Black Women Talk*. Castleford: Yorkshire Art Circus.

Clark, A. (1968) *Working Life of Women in the Seventeenth Century*. London: Frank Cass (first published 1919).

Clark, J. C. D., Collicott, S. L., Davin, A., Marks, S., Nelson, J. and Samuel, R. (1990) History, the nation and the schools. *History Workshop Journal*, 29: 92–134.

Davin, A. (1987) Redressing the balance or transforming the art? The British experience. In S. J. Kleinberg (ed.), *Retrieving Women's History: Changing Perceptions of the Role of Women in Politics and Society*, pp. 60–78. London: Berg.

Dollimore, J. and Sinfield, A. (eds) (1985) *Political Shakespeare: New Essays in Cultural Materialism*. Ithaca, NY: Cornell University Press.

Dyhouse, C. (1995) The British Federation of University Women and the status of women in universities. *Women's History Review*, 4: 465–85.

Ethnic Communities Oral History Project (1989) *The Motherland Calls: African Caribbean Experiences*. London: Ethnic Communities Oral History Project.

Evans, R. (1997) *In Defence of History*. London: Granta.

Fawcett, M. (1912) *Women's Suffrage: A Short History of a Great Movement*. London: T. C. and E. C. Jack.

Ferguson, M. (ed.) (1987) *The History of Mary Prince, A West Indian Slave, Related by Herself*. Michigan: University of Michigan Press (first published 1831).

Foucault, M. (1970) *The Order of Things: An Archaeology of the Human Sciences*. London: Tavistock (first published 1966).

— (1977) *Discipline and Punish: The Birth of the Prison*, trans. A. Sheridan. Harmondsworth: Peregrine (first published 1975).

Gluck, S. B. and Patai, D. (eds) (1991) *Women's Words: The Feminist Practice of Oral History*. London: Routledge.

Gordon, L. (1990) Book review: *Gender and the Politics of History* by J. W. Scott. *Signs*, 15: 853–60.

Greenblatt, S. (1980) *Renaissance Self-fashioning: From More to Shakespeare*. Chicago: University of Chicago Press.

— (1988) *Shakespearean Negotiations: The Circulation of Social Energy in Renaissance England*. Berkeley, CA: University of California Press.

Hurd-Mead, K. Campbell (1933) *Medical Women of America: A Short History of the Pioneer Medical Women of America and a Few of their Colleagues in England*. New York: Froben Press.

Kelly-Gadol, J. (1977) Did women have a renaissance? In R. Bridenthal and C. Koonz (eds), *Becoming Visible*, pp. 137–64. Boston: Houghton Mifflin.

Kerber, L. K. (1998) *No Constitutional Right to be Ladies: Women and the Obligations of Citizenship*. New York: Hill and Wang.

Kleinberg, S. J. (1987) *Retrieving Women's History: Changing Perceptions of the Role of Women in Politics and Society*. London: Berg.

Koonz, C. (1987) *Mothers in the Fatherland: Women, the Family and Nazi Politics*. London: Cape.

Kristeva, J. (1981) Women's time, trans. A. Jardine and H. Blake. *Signs*, 7: 13–35.

Lerner, G. (1979) *The Majority Finds its Past*. Oxford: Oxford University Press.

Lytton, C. (1914) *Prisons and Prisoners*. London: Heineman.

Mair Marthurin, L. (1975) *The Rebel Woman in the British West Indies during Slavery*. Kingston: African-Caribbean Publications.

Martin, E. (1987) *The Woman in the Body: A Cultural Analysis of Reproduction*. Milton Keynes: Open University Press.

Mills, S. (1989) Authentic realism. In S. Mills (ed.), *Feminist Readings*, pp. 51–82. London: Harvester Wheatsheaf.

Minister, K. (1991) A feminist frame for the oral history interview. In S. B. Gluck, S. B. Patai and D. Patai (eds), *Women's Words: The Feminist Practice of Oral History*, pp. 27–42. London: Routledge.

Montrose, L. (1981) 'The place of a brother' in *As You Like It*: social process and comic form. *Shakespeare Quarterly*, 32: 28–54.

Morrison, T. (1990) The site of memory. In Russell Ferguson et al. (eds), *Out There: Marginalization and Contemporary Cultures*, pp. 299–305. Cambridge, MA: MIT Press.

Neely, C. T. (1988) Constructing the subject: feminist practice and the new Renaissance discourses. *English Literary Renaissance*, 18: 5–18.

Newton, J. (1988) History as usual? Feminism and the 'new historicism'. *Cultural Critique*, 9: 87–121.

Offen, K., Pierson, R. and Rendall, J. (eds) (1991) *Writing Women's History: International Perspectives*. London: Macmillan.

Pankhurst, E. S. (1911) *The Suffragette*. London: Gay and Hancock.

Pinchbeck, I. (1981) *Women Workers and the Industrial Revolution*. London: Virago (first published 1930).

Poovey, M. (1988) *Uneven Developments: The Ideological Work of Gender in Mid-Victorian England*. Chicago: University of Chicago Press.

Power, E. (1975) *Medieval Women*. Cambridge: Cambridge University Press.

Roper, L. (1994) Witchcraft and fantasy in early modern Germany. In L. Roper (ed.), *Oedipus and the Devil*, pp. 226–48. New York: Routledge.

Rosen, R., Brawer, C., Landau, E., et al. (1989) *Making their Mark: Women Artists Move into the Mainstream, 1970–85*. New York: Abbeville.

Rowbotham, S. (1974) *Hidden from History: Three Hundred Years of Women's Oppression and the Fight Against It*. London: Routledge.

— (1990) Sheila Rowbotham. In M. Wandor (ed.), *Once a Feminist: Stories of a Generation. Interviews by Micheline Wandor*, pp. 28–42. London: Virago.

Scott, J. W. (1990a) Book review: *Heroes of their Own Lives* by Linda Gordon. *Signs*, 15: 848–53.

— (1990b) Response to Gordon. *Signs*, 15: 859–60.

— (1991) The evidence of experience. *Critical Enquiry*, 17: 773–97.

Sklar, K. Kish (1975) American female historians in context 1770–1930. *Feminist Studies*, 3 (1–2): 171–98.

Stanley, L. (1992) *The Auto/Biographical I*. Manchester: Manchester University Press.

Steedman, C. (1995) *Strange Dislocations: Childhood and the Idea of Human Interiority 1780–1930*. London: Virago.

Summerfield, P. (1998) *Reconstructing Women's Wartime Lives*. Manchester: Manchester University Press.

Thompson, E. P. (1967) Time, work-discipline and industrial capitalism. *Past and Present*, 38: 56–97.

Walkowitz, J. (1992) *City of Dreadful Delight: Narratives of Sexual Danger in Late-Victorian London*. London: Virago.

Wollstonecraft, M. (1985) *Vindication of the Rights of Woman*. Harmondsworth: Penguin (first published 1792).

Woolf, V. (1993) *A Room of One's Own* (1929). In M. Barrett (ed.), *A Room of One's Own and Three Guineas*. Harmondsworth: Penguin.

3

Class

Rosemary Hennessy

The Importance of Concepts

The most compelling question for feminism is this: what are the concepts that are necessary now in the struggle for social justice? This may seem like an odd claim, perhaps even an outrageous one. But pause to consider it for a minute. Often the enterprise of feminist theory has been dismissed as the work of 'elite academics' – abstract, obscure or, even worse, irrelevant to the pressing concerns of women and men. While it may be that some – even most – feminist theory is not even read by many of the world's women, this is not to say that the work of thinking about what and how we know does not matter. Quite the contrary. Although they are rarely made visible, theories inform the ways of making sense on which organizing, education and all forms of action and 'activism' invariably depend. Theories – or explanations of how and what we know and live – rely on concepts that are embedded in them. These concepts are like the scaffolding for building social movement or, to use another metaphor, they are the directionals for charting any course of action. Often invisible as guides, concepts undergird our ways of making sense, from the profound and visionary perspective to the most mundane and obvious. When we ask 'what are the concepts feminism needs now?' we are indeed asking a 'philosophical' question that is also and necessarily a practical one as it is a question that speaks to a very basic and inevitable component of feminist practice.

Feminists in the over-developed world have struggled to make spaces where people can take time out to consider the concepts that inform and enable their practice. Universities have now become the institutions that most allow these spaces; their provision of the resources and institutional structures for the work of feminist theory is the result of years of feminist struggle. Universities are not, of course, the only places where feminist reflection and writing are done. Many non-governmental and non-university organizations foster this work as do alternative media. But these institutions struggle harder for funding and are institutionally much smaller and often less established than the academy. While the time and structures for intellectual work may be most readily provided by universities, it is important to remember that theories and concepts circulate throughout other institutions: in the media, in social movements, in common sense.

When we ask 'what concepts does feminism need?' or 'where will we find the concepts that are necessary to explain the historical conditions we are trying to change?' these questions imply some consensus on common aims for feminist work. In other words, answering these questions will inevitably, if at times only implicitly, speak to what feminism strives to accomplish, its visions and goals. In considering the concept of class, for example, we might want to take into account how it speaks to the general objectives of feminism. We might want to ask: 'Can this particular concept or this particular formulation of it explain aspects of social life and human relations in a way that advances the struggle for social justice and for the equitable meeting of human needs that feminists are committed to?'

Class: The 'Lost Continent' in Feminist Theory

Keeping these questions in mind, let us proceed to consider 'class' as a concept. In order to assess its usefulness for feminist work, we might first look at some of the ways in which class has been understood and used by feminists. For feminists in the over-developed world especially (that is, in the US, Canada, the EU), class is both an invisible and a contentious concept. When it appears as the overlooked member of the 'race, class and gender' trinity or when it appears as an 'obvious' indicator of a person's social status, class is often under-conceptualized. What I mean by this is that many times when the term 'class' is discussed as an empirical reality, it is not really explained as a critical concept that might advance the aims of feminist movement.

Why is 'class' this sort of 'lost continent' in feminist theory? One answer lies in the historical conditions that shape the dominant ways of knowing under capitalism. In the past three decades a new phase of capitalism has developed. Some of its notable features are evident in the ways in which the regulation of capital accumulation and the organization of production and consumption have been modified. We see this in the erosion of the welfare state's regulation of capital greed, in the expansion of the 'free market', the intensified search for cheap labour, the emergence of transnational corporate agencies and a global civil society devoted to entrepreneurship and consumption. Under this phase of capitalism, consumption in the over-developed world has become the main source of wealth, of citizens' political power and, for some, the primary arena for social change. There has also been a fragmentation of traditional relations of labour both in terms of working conditions and attitudes.

These changes in capitalism have been called 'postmodern' or 'advanced capitalism', and the policies guiding them are referred to as neoliberalism. Neoliberal policies help protect the unregulated accumulation of capital through national and international treaties – such as the North Atlantic Free Trade Agreement (NAFTA) or the Free Trade Area of the Americas (FTAA) – or through transnational organizations like the World Trade Organization, the International Monetary Fund and the World Bank which are not accountable to the democratic processes of any nation. Neoliberalism holds that economic crises are the result of excessive government intervention and regulation and they can best be remedied by returning state-supported economic ventures to the private sector (for example, by privatizing public education and health care, social services, prisons), re-establishing the family as a cushion to absorb the social effects of hard times and re-personalizing economic dependency, savings, work.

Neoliberalism is not just a set of economic policies, however; it also entails ways of knowing that promote a range of values and beliefs, among them competition, individualism and the notion that 'there is no alternative' to capitalism. Neoliberal forms of consciousness will tend to keep the structures of capitalism from view; for example, in offering ways of knowing the world that sever the cultures of capital and consumption from relations of labour. In academic circles, postmodern knowledges of various sorts have bolstered neoliberalism by aggressively discouraging analysis that reveals links between new cultural forms and changing relations of labour. To the extent that these values claim to be irrefutable, they dismiss the possibility of other ways of meeting human needs and the critical concepts for advancing these alternatives. Class is one.

More and more it has become commonplace to assert that class as a concept no longer carries any political weight, to accept as a given that differences of race, sexuality, gender, national and ethnic identity or religious diversity have replaced class realities as sites for political analysis and struggle or to claim that the 'failure of socialism' is empirical evidence of the limitations of class analysis. But no matter how much human diversity may seem to be the most pertinent point of social struggle, discrimination and injustice – and changes in the workforce or in more 'multicultural' representations of national identities might be cited to make that point – these changes still depend on persistent class relationships basic to capitalist production. Patterns of employment, accumulation and consumption may be changing, becoming decentralized and globally distributed differently, but the class structures that allow the accumulation of capital to take place remain. Socialism's failures have been real but they have to be measured against the staggering human cost incurred by capitalism's advance.

We now live in a situation where four-fifths of the world's people suffer under capitalism's exploitative social relations, where the gap between those who own and control the world's wealth and those who labour and own little or nothing is widening, and where women still perform most of the world's necessary yet undervalued labour. The erasure of the concept of class cannot be considered apart from this profile. Issuing primarily from the knowledge industry of the advanced capitalist sectors, the 'disappearance of class' as a concept for explaining our social world is not innocent. If feminism is not to be fully incorporated into capitalism's 'free market' and individualist corporate-driven consumer logics, feminists will need to seize upon concepts that are useful in the battle against them. Class is one.

Approaches to Class

Fortunately, we already have a rich archive of class analysis to draw upon, some of it central to feminist struggle for over a century. The most powerful theory of class or class analysis has been developed from the work of Karl Marx, specifically from Marx's critique of capitalism. As a critique of patriarchy, feminism coalesced into a social movement around the same time that Marx was developing his critique of capital.

In fact, it is fair to say that both feminism and the socialist and communist struggle Marx was part of are contemporaneous products of the crisis of democracy spawned by the modern industrial revolution. Feminists have been engaged with the philosophy of history, or historical materialism, and the critique of capital that Marx and other Marxists developed since the nineteenth century. At times, feminism's relationship to Marxism has been one of fraught, critical solidarity, intervening in and working over the concepts of historical materialism, challenging its limits, and extending the reach of its explanations.

The signatures that this feminist work has claimed are various. They include socialist feminism, Marxist feminism, red feminism, materialist feminism. The lines of distinction among them are not always clear or consistent and the terms are open to debate because they are sites of political and ideological, even class, struggle. Tracing a genealogy of any one of these terms or using any one of these names to identify your work invariably entails making an argument for what the name means, in the process explaining the concepts it relies on and claiming a (political) standpoint. While labels are important, then, in themselves they explain little. This is especially so in an historical time when Marxism as well as feminism are more than ever embattled.

In the 1970s in the over-developed world, a new wave of socialist feminist writing began to circulate, emerging initially out of grassroots organizing and without any national organization or party affiliation. Important in this writing were debates over what came to be called dual systems theory (Hansen and Philipson 1990). Many socialist feminists in the 1970s argued that there are two interlocking and mutually dependent systems of oppression – patriarchy and capitalism – and they called for analysis that would address both Marxism's class analysis and feminism's analysis of patriarchal oppression. The argument ran that Marxism's class analysis insufficiently addressed women's oppression under capitalism and that there are dimensions of women's lives that concepts rooted in class analysis could not explain: for example, practises like rape or domestic violence, the renewal of daily life that takes place in relations of care, the objectification of women's bodies, the power dynamics of gender and sexuality. Dual systems approaches argued that the two social systems of capitalism and patriarchy are neither identical nor autonomous.

Critics of this approach contended that in fact it did not move much beyond the assertion that the interface between the two systems of patriarchy and capitalism was the root of women's oppression (Hansen and Philipson 1990: 19). Another problem with the dual systems approach lay in the assumption that the family is a sphere of social activity separate from the capitalist production that takes place in the market and factory. Some critics suggested that domestic labour is not separate but a necessary though invisible component of capitalist production. Women's labour of caring for children, elders, husbands, the labour of preparing food and other basic necessities is not wage work but it is socially necessary for capitalist production in the sense that it enables those who are working for wages to return to work the next day. In this respect, domestic labour reproduces the labour power the worker exchanges for a wage and is in this sense an essential source of the profits the capitalist reaps. From this vantage point, the argument went, any explanation of women's place in capitalist class relations needs to begin not with the presumption that there are two systems of oppression but rather with the ways in which capitalism uses the patriarchal structures that preceded it and developed alongside it.

Socialist feminism in the advanced capitalist countries developed in tandem with and was considerably influenced by radical feminist theory and practice, an approach that saw women's oppression by men as the overarching reality in women's history. In contrast to the radical feminist emphasis on patriarchal oppression, socialist feminists stress the importance of class inequality and they understand the concept of class quite differently when they use it. Socialist feminists acknowledged their debt to Marxist explanations of class and at times even gave priority to Marxist explanations of social relations. But in actuality many socialist feminist attempts (in the 1970s) to address the relation of class analysis to gender inequality often amounted to adding class on to a radical feminist approach: class was seen as an adjunct to gender inequality or the fundamental power relation was taken to be that between men and women (Naiman 1996: 13). The notion of women as the oppressed group and men as the oppressors is problematic at least in part because not all women share a common oppression. While feminist debates throughout the 1980s addressed this problem in terms of increased attention to women's diversity, the challenge of identifying how this diversity plays out in capitalist relations, as well as what it is that brings women together and what constitutes the common ground of their fight for social justice, remained.

While the debates that dominated socialist feminism thirty years ago have receded from feminist discussions, the problematic dimension of their legacy is evident in the analysis of power and social structures that has become the mainstream of women's studies. To the extent that socialist feminists ultimately appropriated Marxism as a theory of oppression, they contributed to the translation of class analysis into the 'oppression theory' that became popular among the 'new Left'. Oppression theorists criticize what they see as the economic determinism of traditional Marxism and its view of the working class as the most revolutionary force in history (Naiman 1996: 13), but in the process they also forfeit the crucial concept of exploitation that lies at the heart of Marxist class analysis. (Exploitation, as I will explain below, is fundamental to the concept of class for Marxism and refers to a very specific power relation in which the capitalist gets his profits from the unpaid labour of workers.) Instead, theories of multiple oppression stress the interrelation of 'classism, racism, sexism' in history and society. The concept of 'classism' which features in this approach understands class relations as an oppressive social practice parallel to sex and race oppression. Class in this sense is a cultural system or set of status distinctions, often explained in terms of the goods one consumes that mark one's social standing, or it may refer to the distribution of resources that function as the markers of 'privilege'. For some (radical) feminists, 'classism' as a social system is a byproduct of the patriarchal oppression of women by men.

These radical feminist versions of oppression theory have been overtaken in feminist theory more recently by neo- and post-Marxist understandings of class. They are related in the sense that, like the 'racism, sexism, classism' approach, they too claim that everything in society is interconnected but their explanation of the social system can seem to have a more materialist starting-point. Neo- and post-Marxist approaches to class tend to pursue one of two theoretical trajectories that might loosely be characterized as empiricist and postmodern (Torrant 2001). It is important to note that these two ways of explaining class in feminist theory are similar to conceptions of class that circulate more broadly. In other words, these notions of class are not unique to feminism.

Empiricist approaches to class treat it as one component of social stratification or status. As we will see, this is quite different, indeed a break, from Marxist (or historical materialist) explanations of class as an exploitative social relationship. The empiricist approach to class was most famously developed by Max Weber, but these ideas have now entered the common culture and many versions of this concept of class no longer acknowledge their debt to Weber. This version of class sees society as constituted by an economic order, a legal order and a cultural order – all of which interact and none of which is determining.

Here class refers to any group of people found in a market situation and an individual's class position is ultimately decided by the kind of opportunity offered in the market. The problem is that this analysis takes market relations to be obvious. It does not 'lift the veil' of commodity exchange that takes place in the market to make visible the social relations out of which commodities, goods and services are produced. Beginning with the vantage point of the market does not allow us to see and explain the relations of labour that bring goods into the market. This is especially troublesome for a feminist analysis that may want to account for the invisible labour of women in the domestic sphere but also for any analysis that wants to disclose the relations of labour that lie behind 'free market exchange'.

Following the erasure of relations of labour in this neo-Weberian approach to class, property (which for Marxists is a social relation) is presumed to be a matter of individual possessions. Here the economic order is merely the way in which economic goods and services are distributed and used. When economic relations are reduced to market relations, the concept of exploitation disappears along with the exploitative relations of labour on which the Marxist concept of class is based. The problem with the empiricist (or Weberian) analysis of class is that here class refers to any group of individuals who share a common market situation defined in terms of the goods or properties they possess. The more common-sense notion of class as white or blue or pink 'collars' or as lifestyles is derived from this approach. While class appears here as a group identification or a particular social status, it is essentially an individual difference in the sense that the distribution of wealth and resources is understood in terms of assets allocated among individuals.

Another approach to class developed more recently lies in a body of work that might be loosely termed postmodern or post-Marxist and which includes contributions from many feminists pursuing a 'cultural materialist' analysis. This work has in common the premise that culture is not linked in any determinate way with social relations that are not cultural. It may also claim, at times implicitly, that society is exclusively cultural, that there are no social relations that are non-cultural or non-discursive, that is, not language practices. Some postmodern analysis asserts that social relations are first and finally textual, that there are no objective foundations (like class relations) outside language; furthermore, for these postmodernists, language and meaning are inherently unstable, the effect of the radical 'play' of relations among the signs and signifiers that comprise language. From this perspective, all social antagonisms, like the language or discourses in which they are rooted, are fluid, even reversible; power does not operate through top-down hierarchies or structures but rather through diffuse forces. Many cultural materialists have distanced themselves from the more idealist versions of this position that reduce social life to texts. Instead, they claim that social relations have to be understood as historical practices. But for cultural materialists the making of meaning still has a clear priority and for some it indeed constitutes the social entirely. Consequently, class relations have no reality outside their discursive formulation.

Marxist Feminist Class Analysis

If we return to my original question – 'what are the concepts feminists need in order to understand and change the situation of the majority of the world's women?' – we can evaluate the concept of class offered in these theories in relation to the aims of feminist practice. We can also ask 'what would it mean to reclaim the lost continent of class concepts from historical materialism and elaborate a Marxist and feminist analysis of class?' Marxist feminists contend that a full understanding of gender inequality requires a close examination of the objective characteristics of social systems and of the functioning of power within them. They see historical materialism as providing the most powerful explanation of the social relations in which gender is situated and the most incisive critique of capital. Historical materialism's first premise is that history and society require the presence of real living individuals. The fundamental material reality of human life is the requirement that humans produce the means to meet their survival needs. Capitalism is one way this production has been organized and like other modes of production it encompasses a whole way of life.

Under capitalism, the means to meet human needs are collectively provided by all human labourers who exchange their labour power for a wage and yet these means of production (the raw materials, technologies for producing) are owned and controlled by only a few. Capitalism is inextricably grounded in this contradictory social relationship that is geared to the accumulation of profit by the owning group. The accumulation of profit is the motor of capitalism, driving the capitalist to expand production and continually to search for new sources of raw material, new markets for goods, and cheaper labour for production and servicing. In his analysis of capital, Marx enables us to see that the accumulation of profit under capitalism is fundamentally rooted in relations of labour. In fact, he argues that capital is not money or wealth or any other obvious and common-sense thing; rather, capital is a social relation. This social relation takes place during the course of the working day when the worker sells his or her labour power to the capitalist in exchange for a wage. In the course of the working day it is the unpaid labour of workers that provides the value added to the commodities they produce and that is the source of profit for the capitalist. It is this social relationship that allows capitalism to be capitalism and not another way of producing. And it is this social relation that is fundamental to the Marxist concept of class.

Let me review this concept briefly here. During the working day the worker exchanges her labour power for a wage. Let us say that this worker is a woman named Carmen who works at a factory in Mexico making gift bags and that she makes 350 pesos or approximately 35 US dollars (£20) a week as her wage for 48 hours of work. This wage has to cover the costs of the basic necessities for Carmen's subsistence – that is, for food, clothing, rent – in order for her to be able to return to work each day. She makes approximately 7,000 bags in a day and works a five-day week during which she produces about 35,000 bags for her $35 weekly wage. One bag sells in a US store like Hallmark or Nieman Marcus for approximately $3.00 (£2). So in one week Carmen has produced bags whose value in the retail market is approximately $3 × 35,000 or $105,000 (£70,000). On his side, the capitalist has invested in the raw materials – paper and glue for the bags – as well as the rent and overheads for the building, any tools and machines needed in the bags' assembly and transport and, of course, the wages paid to the workers. The value added to the bags is the price the bags command on the market minus the overheads and the wages paid to the workers.

How long does Carmen have to labour to produce the value that is returned to her as wages or the cost of her own subsistence, that is, her weekly wage? About two minutes. The rest of the working day her unpaid labour adds value to the raw materials she assembles, but this value is not given back to her in her wages; instead it goes to the capitalist. It is in this sense 'surplus' or unpaid labour. Even when the costs of overheads and the wear on the machinery, as well as the costs levied by the retailer, are subtracted from the price of the bags, the remaining value added to these bags as a result of Carmen's labour is vast. It is this surplus or unpaid labour that is the sole source of profit for the capitalist. Without this profit-making organization of production you do not have capitalism. It is in this sense that this social relationship between labour and capital is fundamental to capitalism.

It is, moreover, a relationship of exploitation. Exploitation is a concept that describes a very specific power relation in which the benefits that accrue to one party (in this case the capitalist) arise only from the detriment (in this case the unpaid labour) of the other party, the worker. This is a quite different power relation from oppression or domination which may entail power over another without the benefit of one party arising from the detriment of another. As a concept in historical materialism, class refers to this distinct exploitative relationship and these specific positions in capitalist relations of production: the owner of the means of production or the capitalist and the worker who sells her or his labour power for a wage. Under capitalism, class relations are lived by collective actors and the two key oppositional collective actors are the bourgeois owners and the workers. In actual situations, this distinction is compounded by the reserve army of labourers and the professional middle class.

In the over-developed capitalist areas there is also a difference between a primary sector of the working class, where workers are relatively secure, and a secondary sector, where workers are poorly paid, lack benefits and are more liable to be laid off. The concrete collectivities through which people act do not always obey the formal outline of class relations I have sketched here but often take the shape of temporary coalitions that are dominated by segments of a single class. Bourgeois-dominated coalitions form 'ruling blocs' that rely on the media as well as the machinery of the state and the processes through which they operate. One of the greatest fears of the ruling bloc is that subaltern populations might develop alliances with people in other positions in the class structure. In the face of this threat, the ruling bloc has had to devise strategies to keep alliances from forming among those who are being exploited. The strategies span institutions and include state repression and violence as well as assigning loyalties along lines of racial, ethnic, national, sexual and gender difference.

Many workers in over-developed countries do not consider that their lives have much in common with Carmen's, for the most part because they have access to more money from higher wages and they enjoy a level of comfort from the consumer goods that define their lives: a nice house (which may be rented or mortgaged), a car (which the bank may own), credit cards for charging other necessities. While most workers in the US and Europe may work and live under different conditions from workers in the world's *maquilas* and sweatshops, we share a similar relation to capital. Like Carmen in the example above, most workers in the advanced capitalist sectors are compelled to labour many hours more than the working time necessary for their own reproduction and the surplus labour and the value it adds to the commodities they produce and the services they provide are appropriated by the big capitalists.

Since the 1970s the structure of the labour force in over-developed countries has been profoundly reshaped through technological innovation, shifts in the spaces and times of production, the rise of a service economy and the decline of organized labour. Seeing these changes, many people in over-developed countries say that 'the proletariat' has disappeared. But this conclusion comes from confusing class relations with consumer habits, 'lifestyle' and status. Wage- and salary-earners – that is, those who are working class because they are labourers not owners – now account for about 80 per cent of the working population in most Western countries and almost 90 per cent of the labour force in the US (Singer 1999: 178). The shift in the workforce in the over-developed world from a labour force concentrated in industry to one primarily concentrated in services has not meant the end of the working class; it has just given the working class a new profile. In many cases this 'new working class' is even less secure than the industrial 'proletariat' of a half-century ago since the service industry has ushered in many part-time and low-paying jobs. The woman at the cash register is paid less than the guys on the assembly lines and her conditions of work are just as alienating (Singer 1999: 180).

While the changes in work have been profound, they have not been fundamental. Many service workers live precariously, shuttling between a job where they often have little control to a home life stressed by the effort to make ends meet in the face of rising debts, uncertain educational opportunities for children, and limited health care for ageing parents. What unites most wage-earners is not the consumer niche we inhabit – where we shop (Harrods or K-Mart), the car we drive (BMW or used Chevy pick-up) or the style of the clothes we wear – but our role as the critical majority in production. As Daniel Singer (1999: 182) so aptly put it:

> In the decisive historical question of whether the working class is still the main agency of radical transformation, the problem is not one of size. Numerically, it is far from dwindling. The problem – not new, but more acute than in the past – is how to unify this class, how to give it a common purpose, despite its apparent divisions and real diversity.

If feminism is to grow as a force for transformative change in the world, we need to articulate much more firmly and clearly the class position that binds most of us, reminding one another that capital's mechanisms of eviction and control operate not only in the brutality and alienated relationships of production in the workplaces of our sisters in the Third World sectors, but also in the forms of consumer consciousness that invite us to misrecognize our shared, though different, position as workers.

Most Marxists agree with Friedrich Engels that gender inequality predated capitalism and that the new ruling class benefited from it. Marxist feminists have differed as to whether women can be understood as a class, but those who believe they can have not understood this class position in terms of women's status, rather in terms of their place in relations of labour (Delphy 1984; Ferguson 1989). Other Marxist feminists claim that the power men hold over women under capitalism is better understood as 'status'. Such a concept allows us to differentiate the power men actually do hold over women and the contradictoriness of that power, since the reality is that most men hold very little societal power in their everyday lives. Certainly it is true that for centuries most people holding structured positions of power have been men, and men as a group are enabled to occupy these positions more than women. But the fact that 'it has been a man's world' does not mean that men in positions of power are acting for the benefit of all males. In fact, the only power most men have, and that has been legally sanctioned, is their power over women (Naiman 1996: 23). Similarly, the fact that most men in power have been white males gives the appearance that it is gender or race that grants one power (Naiman 1996: 24). While gender inequality benefits capitalism, it is not essential to it and the loosening of patriarchal arrangements in the advanced sectors seems to bear witness to this.

One of Marxist feminism's main contributions to class analysis lies in what have come to be known as the domestic labour debates. This work was an effort to address the ways in which labour done outside the market-place of wage economy under capitalism, and most often relegated to women, can be explained in terms of the socially necessary benefits it provides to capital and its place in the capitalist class system. Following this logic, some socialist and Marxist feminists inaugurated a campaign for wages for housework. Their argument went that, while the household labourer may not be 'productive' in the sense that she does not directly produce surplus value, none the less when she acts upon wage-purchased goods her labour becomes part of the concealed labour embodied in labour power Thus, as we have seen, the housewife's labour introduces women into capitalism's class relations as necessary actors in the reproduction of labour power.

While capital both erodes and relies on the 'private' arena of the family, paying women wages for housework will not remedy the exploitation of women. Once women are paid a wage for their invisible labour they will not necessarily achieve a higher social status, as the history of paid domestics teaches us. Because the need to reproduce labour power is not part of the calculus of socially necessary labour covered by wages, this labour is either underpaid or not paid, invariably not valued, and often invisible as labour by being understood as a woman's natural role. Moreover, it is not necessarily women's labour and in some households in the developed world it is now being done more frequently by men. None the less, it is important to remember that to date across the globe most of women's labour remains invisible and the amount of labour that goes into this 'care economy' or 'love economy' has not been reduced by the introduction of new technology into the home (Wichterich 1998: 98). Only a third of the work performed by women is paid; two-thirds is unpaid and left out of the economic statistics (Wichterich 1998: 97). In the case of men the proportion is almost exactly the reverse.

An historical materialist feminist approach to class draws upon the Marxist recognition that capitalism has always been a global system and strives to address the international sexual division of labour that has maintained it. Among the important contributions of this work is the development of analyses that allow us to understand the ways in which the category 'woman' is differentiated across this global system, how bourgeois womanhood, for example, and the relations of consumption bourgeois women were recruited into as 'housewives', were historically linked to and made possible by women producers in other sectors of the relations of production (Mies 1986). While some of the early treatments of the international sexual division of labour underlying capital's class system oversimplify the complex and uneven ways in which production and consumption are interfaced and the colonization of the 'Third World' with consumer markets, they none the less lay the groundwork for developing a feminist class analysis that begins with the requirement to think class relations within the frame of an international sexual division of labour that has always been basic to capitalism as a world system (Mies 1986; Mitter 1986).

Much of the preceding discussion implies that a key feature of capitalism's gendered division of labour is the ways of knowing that help to reinforce capitalist relations of production through the beliefs, values and norms with which we make sense of the world. The drift into postmodernism has heightened debate in academic feminism over how to explain the relationship of knowledge and the knowledge of difference (gender, sexuality, race, nationality) in particular to class relations under capitalism. Marxist feminists want to hold on to the concept of ideology for explaining the production of knowledge because it allows us to conceptualize the fact that knowledge is produced under certain conditions and that those conditions have a causal effect, though not necessarily a simple one, on the forms that culture and knowledge take.

Put broadly, ideology is a concept that allows us to address the relationship of culture to capitalist class relations. Culture includes all of the meaning-making systems, practices, and discourses in a society: the prevailing truths, contesting knowledges, residual and emergent intelligibilities, codified beliefs as well as inchoate structures of feeling. Those ways of knowing that legitimize the human relations that capital relies on constitute 'ideology'. For the Marxist feminist, ideological struggle over knowledge is ultimately a struggle for mastery over the forces of production and the state. From this perspective, gender and race are two especially pertinent ways of knowing difference under capitalism. They are sites of ideological struggle and also serve in their dominant formulations to legitimize and explain away the contradictory class relations on which capitalism's relations of production rely. In this sense, as concepts, they are of a different order from class.

Feminism, Transformative Politics and Class

One often hidden facet of class politics lies in knowledge work. One of the challenges for feminist theory in the new millennium is to find ways to confront and overcome feminism's successful professionalization and incorporation into knowledge work, especially in the university, while in the process not losing sight of the role of critical reflection in the larger context of feminist struggle. Now that a good portion of First World feminism has been absorbed into the professions, self-reflective critique of the class dimensions and implications of that process for feminist politics is sorely needed. Some feminists have begun to suspect that the trend in academic feminism towards imagining political struggle solely in terms of a discursive terrain is not only making the class position of academics invisible to themselves but also limiting our ability to understand and combat the dominant, if now invisible, economic interests of neoliberalism (Stabile 1994: 54).

If the academy, as we saw earlier, has provided a fertile place for the development of feminist theory, its traditions and disciplinary regimes have also functioned to impede developing exchange between the production of feminist theory there and the feminist thinking that takes place in other social sites. Given the university's fostering of sustained feminist critical thought, it is the responsibility of academic feminist theory to continue to develop knowledges that reflect upon the class politics of the academy, while at the same time finding ways to develop links to forms of feminist critical enquiry that do not conform to academic standards and that circulate in other spaces. The challenge for feminism lies not in finding ways to break out of institutional constraints and become more 'inclusive', but rather in developing concepts that can allow us better to understand the real material conditions that both link and so variously affect our lives. In the end, these concepts are intimately bound to the horizons for change we imagine, the kind of world we dare to dream about and set out to achieve.

The obstacles women face in the struggle for social justice today are immense, and certainly no single path or concept can effectively confront them all. The effectiveness of the feminist movement will in large part be shaped by the degree to which critical thinking rooted in common goals across international alliances can be forged. As the offspring of liberal democracy and industrial development, feminism in the over-developed world has historically turned to the state to demand rights for women. Socialist and Marxist feminists have taken a critical view of this strategy because they have seen change enacted through the state as at best effecting reforms that can benefit only some women while leaving the basic class structures of inequality on which the state is based intact. In other words, they see representative democratic states under capitalism as premised on property relations (not representing 'the people' but rather property or corporate interests). Consequently, rights within the corporate state tend to be distributed according to these property (class) relations. Some Marxist feminists see the struggle for rights as short-term goals that do improve the lives of women but insist on keeping the long-term goal of social transformation in view as the framework for these struggles. Class relations shape the process and temper the achievements feminists have gained. While sexual violence or reproductive rights may not seem immediately to be class issues, few forms of violence against women are untouched by class relations. Even the freedom to organize has a class dimension as it has not been available to all women equally (Threlfall 1996: 293). For example, while poor and rural women benefit from the rights attained by professionals, their access to these rights is often restricted because of their class position.

Demands for civil rights from the state cannot lose sight of the class structures of global capital in which they are situated. In the past two decades, as neoliberalism has become the defining socioeconomic regime, the consequences for women and for feminism have been grim. While it is impossible to generalize, there are certain telling broad strokes in the global picture. At the dawn of the new millennium 70 per cent of the world's poor are women (Wichterich 1998: 124). Of 190 countries in the world, nearly all have reduced the role of the state and moved to a greater reliance on private ownership and market forces to spur growth. Of Third World and post-communist countries that have adopted structural adjustment programmes to stimulate economic efficiency and reduce the role of the state, there is evidence to show that the accumulated effects have fallen hardest upon women who confront changes from a distinct position of structural disadvantage (Molyneux 1996: 236). On one hand, feminism has been increasingly incorporated as a result of alliances struck with political parties, institutions and trade unions. On the other hand, and based on a wide range of socioeconomic indicators, the situation of most women has shown little or no improvement (Molyneux 1996: 233).

Home-working, which is primarily women's work, has become a requisite ancillary sector for clothing and electronics production. In the service economy, the victors in the reorganization of production have been a chiefly male core of permanent employees around whom small suppliers, casual workers and freelancers on casual contracts revolve like satellites. The computer age has not brought equality for women nor the elimination of routine drudge work. In fact, many women have become keyboard drones as telework has moved to the cheap labour pools of Bangalore, India or the Caribbean. Traffic in women's bodies remains a major facet of global trade and is controlled by transnational syndicates that make profits by the billions.

The state's changing role under neoliberalism has meant a rollback in many of the rights feminists had achieved in the realm of family, work and welfare, and a general backlash against feminism itself has occurred (Molyneux 1996: 233). In assessing the consequences of neoliberalism and their effects on women's lives, feminists need concepts that make visible the forces that underlie the widening gap between rich and poor, the persistent gendered division of labour, and the brutal consequences for most of the world's women. We need concepts that allow us to understand the social relationships behind wages, profit and the common-sense knowledges through which we make sense. Class is one of those concepts.

Attending to class, not as a marker of cultural status but as a set of social relations that undergird capitalism, has immense implications for women's transformative politics internationally. For one thing, it means clarifying the international dimension of this struggle. Terms like 'global' and 'transnational' are often used to denote a feminism whose border crossing is basically a cultural practice (compatible with the border crossing of hybrid identities, consumer and lifestyle practices). But international feminist struggle is based on the reality that capital relies on relations of labour that may be quite rigid even as they traverse and cross national interests. It grounds its solidarity in the shared goal of striving for alternative ways to produce in order to meet human needs equitably and justly. Women's movements already exist in and outside the over-developed world that are based not on transgressive cultural practices and identities or the desire to get more power within capitalism but in the struggle to meet human needs more adequately and fairly (Rowbotham 1992). Johanna Brenner has asked the provocative question: 'where lies feminism's transformative promise?' Her answer suggests that feminism cannot be renewed on the basis of its old middle-class constituencies but depends on rebuilding working-class self-organization. By this she means a collectively structured process of resistance to and demands on corporate capital (Brenner 2000: 211). Rather than a cross-classed movement for democratic rights, this women's movement would be based on organizations allied to and part of other struggles and located organizationally within working-class movements (Brenner 2000: 205).

Feminism as a movement in the over-developed world was able to make gains in the 1960s and 1970s without really taking on capitalist class power. To change the situation of working-class women from the vantage point of societies in the North will require concepts that keep this history from being repeated. It will demand a vision of a radically reorganized society and revolutionary strategies that include short-term as well as long-term goals for a significant reorganization of production and for international solidarity. Certainly there are structural limitations that pose barriers to women's self-organization, and international feminist organizing will have to find creative ways to overcome them (Brenner 2000: 208). Some of this work is already taking place (Threlfall 1996; Wichterich 1998). As a concept for social transformation, class is a necessary and immensely empowering weapon for feminism in this movement. It opens a network of related concepts for critically understanding the social relations of our time, for learning from the past, and for identifying the often invisible structures of power that undergird our lived experience. It invites us to keep our eyes on the challenge of meeting human needs that collectively binds us to one another rather than our obvious individual or group identities. Above all, it allows us to join with others from our position as capital's principal actors to imagine and insist that a more just alternative is possible.

References and Further Reading

Althusser, L. (1971) On ideology and ideological state apparatuses. In *Lenin and Philosophy*, trans. Ben Brewster, pp. 127–86. New York: Monthly Review Press.

Barrett, M. (1980) *Women's Oppression Today: Problems in Marxist Feminist Analysis*. London: Verso.

Brenner, J. (2000) *Women and the Politics of Class*. New York: Monthly Review Press.

Davis, A. Y. (1983) *Women, Race, and Class*. New York: Vintage.

Delphy, C. (1984) *Close to Home: A Materialist Analysis of Women's Oppression*. London: Hutchinson.

Eisenstein, Z. (ed.) (1979) *Capitalist Patriarchy and the Case for Socialist Feminism*. New York: Monthly Review Press.

Engels, F. (1942) *The Origin of the Family, Private Property and the State in the Light of the Researches of Lewis H. Morgan*. New York: International.

Ferguson, A. (1989) *Blood at the Root: Motherhood, Sexuality, and Male Dominance*. London: Pandora.

Field, N. (1995) *Over the Rainbow: Money, Class, and Homophobia*. London: Pluto.

Fraad, H., with Resnick, S. and Wolff, R. (1994) *Bringing it all Back Home: Class, Gender, and Power in the Modern Household*. London: Pluto Press.

German, L. (1989) *Sex, Class, and Socialism*. London: Bookmarks.

Giddens, A. (1973) *The Class Structure of the Advanced Societies*. New York: Barnes and Noble.

Hansen, K. V. and Philipson, I. (eds) (1990) *Women, Class and the Feminist Imagination: A Socialist Feminist Reader*. Philadelphia, PA: Temple University Press.

Haug, F. (1987) *Female Sexualization: A Collective Work of Memory*. London: Verso.

Hennessy, R. (2000) *Profit and Pleasure: Sexual Identities in Late Capitalism*. New York: Routledge.

— and Ingraham, C. (1997) *Materialist Feminism: A Reader in Class, Difference, and Women's Lives*. New York: Routledge.

Holmstrom, N. (2002) *The Socialist Feminist Project: A Reader*. New York: Monthly Review Press.

Marx, K. (1959) *Capital*, Vol. 1. Moscow: Progress.

— and Engels, F. (1988) *The Communist Manifesto*. New York: Norton.

Mies, M. (1986) *Patriarchy and Accumulation on a World Scale*. London: Zed Books.

Mitter, S. (1986) *Common Fate, Common Bond: Women in the Global Economy*. London: Pluto.

Molyneux, M. (1996) Women's rights and the international context in the post-communist states. In M. Threlfall (ed.), *Mapping the Women's Movement*, pp. 232–59. London: Verso.

Naiman, J. (1996) Left feminism and the return to class. *Monthly Review*, 42 (2): 12–28.

Rowbotham, S. (1992) *Women in Movement: Feminist Social Action (Revolutionary Thought/Radical Movements)*. New York: Routledge.

Sargent, L. (ed.) (1981) *Women and Revolution: A Discussion of the Unhappy Marriage of Marxism and Feminism*. Boston, MA: South End Press.

Singer, D. (1999) *Whose Millennium? Theirs or Ours?* New York: Monthly Review Press.

Stabile, C. A. (1994) Feminism without guarantees: the misalliances and missed alliances of postmodernist social theory. *Rethinking Marxism*, 7 (1): 48–61.

Threlfall, M. (ed.) (1996) *Mapping the Women's Movement*. London: Verso.

Torrant, J. (2001) Class ideology, family: toward a materialist critique of the (post)modern family. Unpublished paper, State University of New York at Albany.

Weber, Max (1978) *Selections in Translation*, ed. N. G. Runciman. New York: Cambridge University Press.

Wichterich, C. (1998) *The Globalized Woman*. London: Zed Books.

Wright, E. O. (1985) *Classes*. London: Verso.

4

'Race'

Kum-Kum Bhavnani and Meg Coulson

Feminism and the 'Race' Encounter

Feminist work has collided with work on 'race'/ethnicity and racism, a collision that is now fairly well documented (Moraga and Anzaldúa 1981; Amos and Parmar 1984; duCille 1994; Mirza 1997; Bhavnani 2001). However, despite this recent history, and many acknowledgements of the importance that racialized understandings play within feminist discourses, there seems to be some uncertainty about how best to proceed with the development and integration of such understandings. In this chapter we will review some of the main issues that have informed the discussions to date and also suggest ways in which the discussions of 'race' and feminism can go forward. In this process we will reflect on some of the shifts and developments in our own approaches and thinking. The encounter between 'race' and gender has a longer history than is often acknowledged. For example, the colonial history of Britain meant that this encounter framed discussions in India (Ware 1992). In addition, discussions concerning indigenous peoples have frequently been imbued with both the gendered and the racialized assumptions of the conqueror's worldview (Jensen 1977). In other words, those who took power, such as the British in India or the colonial pilgrims in the US, proceeded as if their system of gendered inequalities was the only way in which social groups ought to organize themselves and, thus, promoted those ways of living, being and thinking as *the* universal measures of human civilization and achievement.

Many readers of this chapter will know of Sojourner Truth who, speaking at a women's rights convention in Ohio in 1852, insisted on black women's interest in their rights and powerfully demonstrated how womanhood is cut through by differences of 'race' and the different political priorities and struggles of black women compared to white (Giddings 1984). In her speech 'A'int I a Woman?' she deconstructed prevailing ideas of womanhood by showing that those ideas were particular to white, middle- and upper-class women and that encounters between black and white women occurred within relationships of unequal power – gendered and racialized power – as well as class inequalities. Truth's speech appears to have had little impact *at that time* for as a black woman she was considered peripheral by the leaders of the suffrage and women's movements of the nineteenth-century US.

A similar encounter between 'race' and gender, but with rather different consequences, occurred when second-wave feminism, emerging from the late 1960s in Western societies, quickly borrowed the notion of self-determination, adapted from anti-colonial struggles, and political ideas from the American civil rights and black power movements. (In passing, we wish to note that the ironies and contradictions of the borrowing we refer to here were given little attention at the time.) What emerged, however, from this borrowing was the slogan 'sisterhood is powerful' which captured the aspirations of second-wave feminism to a politics of universal sisterhood. This desire for universal sisterhood obscured the white, middle-class reference point at the centre of Western feminism in all its political shades (from liberal to socialist to radical feminist) which all draw, more or less critically, on Enlightenment thinking. It was only when women of colour challenged, amongst other things, hierarchies of power within feminism and the ways in which feminism, for all its universal claims, has maintained racist exclusions, theories and practices that this mixture of optimism and complacency in the women's liberation movement was disturbed.

The idea of woman as an ahistorical, unlocated, undifferentiated category and *the* subject of *a* feminist project could not be sustained. The logic of feminist critiques of masculinist thought, when applied within feminism, meant that white women could no more claim to be or to represent women in general than white men could represent humanity as a whole. No woman was simply a woman. 'Different' women raised their voices; they insisted on the particularity of their experiences and aspirations from positions which combined woman

with 'race', class, coloniality, sexuality, dis/ability, age and other differences in a great variety of ways. Postmodern thinking and post-
structuralist critiques of Enlightenment narratives, of essentialist
subjectivities and of absolute meanings connected with these critical processes within feminism. Recognizing differences amongst
women – in practice, in struggles, in theorizing – showed feminism as
something less solid, more complex and diverse than had appeared to
be the case.

In this chapter, we ask what has become of this challenge
from women of colour within the feminisms of the early years of this
present millennium. In doing so, we are asking a question which is
unlikely to have an exact answer. So much – and so little – has
changed. We will consider some of the twists and turns, clashes and
dead-ends in this process and we will use particular examples to illustrate recent work.

Woman/Women, Feminism/Feminisms

In the mid-1980s, when we were both working in the same institution in the UK, we discussed our way through the challenges of
the encounter of 'race' and gender to write an article on 'race'
and feminism, 'Transforming Socialist Feminism: The Challenge of
Racism' (Bhavnani and Coulson 1986). We worked together,
recognizing our differences across 'race', sexuality, age, and the complexities of our different histories. We wrote within one of the main
political/theoretical frameworks of feminism of that time and place,
socialist feminism. In so doing, we wanted to express a political alliance
across difference, an alliance particular to our participation in the
arguments about 'race' which were challenging socialist feminism. Our intention was to contribute to a process that might crack
open racist and exclusionary feminist assumptions and so begin to
transform socialist feminism into something that could become, in
Barbara Smith's words, 'the theory and the practice that struggles to
free *all* women: women of color, working-class women, poor women,
disabled women, lesbians, old women – as well as white economically
privileged, heterosexual women' (Smith 1982: 49; cited in Bhavnani
and Coulson 1986: 81). While we would stand by most of our
argument and the examples discussed in the article, the aspiration
to make an overarching feminism inclusive of all differences
has remained elusive. This is less because 'race' has had no impact on

75

feminist thinking and practices in the period since then and more because feminism has changed; ways of 'doing' feminism and of being feminist have become even more fragmented and diverse now than in the mid-1980s.

The main political perspectives around which early second-wave feminist ideas became organized – liberal feminism, socialist feminism, radical feminism – although not irrelevant, have been bypassed or overtaken by the impacts of post-structuralist and postmodern thinking and affected by the rise of cultural studies. Politically, the world has changed: the collapse of state socialist regimes across eastern and central Europe and the demise of their organizational and ideological centre, the USSR, have both strengthened global capitalism and its market ideologies and eroded the credibility of even the most reflexive of socialisms as a means to critique and challenge capitalism and its sustaining ideas. While inequalities between states have increased, inequalities and differences between and within classes and peoples have also increased, including inequalities amongst women. Economic, political and military global pressures (which some think of as the new world dis/order) have increased migration and the pressure for migration between states, especially between poorer and richer states and between war-torn states and those close to them, with the result that populations within nation-states have tended to become more diversified by 'race' and ethnicity and also by religion.

The Western political movements for change that erupted in the 1960s and 1970s have also, themselves, undergone many changes. For example, during the 1980s and 1990s feminism made inroads into academia which became one of the sites of struggles for equal opportunities policies in terms of 'race' and gender. With the establishment of women's studies in the academy, universities and colleges became major locations for feminist theorizing and a significant point of access to feminist ideas. As we have discussed elsewhere (Coulson and Bhavnani 1989), these shifts had contradictory effects, including a growing distance between feminist theory-making and political activism. Beyond the academy this distance rendered inaccessible much of the theoretical debate within feminist thought. At the same time, ambiguities and uncertainties remained (and still remain) about the place of feminism in mainstream academic frames of reference. For instance, although feminist scholarship is legitimated within sociology through the use of key texts such as Patricia Hill Collins's *Black Feminist Thought: Knowledge, Consciousness and the Politics of Empowerment*

(1990), it is also the case that the discipline has barely added 'raced women' into its model of humanity. Too often, 'raced women' still appear as a special interest or are tacked on to a general consideration of 'race' or gender, and the inclusion of women of colour is not grasped as an opportunity to work through the political and intellectual transformations which that inclusion requires/demands.

The turn to postmodernism is also an important one to note here. While not wanting to repeat the discussions and arguments about postmodernism, we would stress that this turn had creative consequences particularly in the destabilization of singular identities. Yet it has also had consequences in moving the focus away from racism and towards insights in psychology, literature and sexuality (Tong 1998). In so saying, we are not arguing that such insights are not intrinsic to 'race'; rather, that the writings on the literary, psychological and sexual implications of feminist thought implicitly, if not explicitly, excluded 'race' from their remit. Hortense Spillers's *Comparative American Identities: Race, Sex, and Nationality in the Modern Text* (1991) is a notable exception to this trend. However, the trap of academia generally is that theory-spinning can become so interesting, so fascinating in itself that it can become a conversation amongst the few. The arguments around 'I'm a feminist but . . .' are important for all feminists; however, we suggest, equally important is the argument 'I'm a postmodernist but . . .'. There are problems in going too far with the 'post' deconstructions and critiques, for such a journey can be politically and practically debilitating, but we are left asking: how far is too far and how does one know when one has travelled too far or not far enough?

In documenting the above history, we suggest that feminism has always been multiple; that is, there were and are many forms of feminism holding sway at any one time, and in the 1980s and 1990s a key way of categorizing feminism(s) was based on whether the feminism(s) could be seen as located within or outside academic institutions. The challenges to feminism have also invariably been plural in scope. A theoretical and political consequence of the varied challenges to prevailing feminisms has involved acknowledging different feminisms and their limitations, which Ien Ang has called 'partial feminisms' (Ang 1995: 73). This is a position that comprehends not only a postmodern approach to feminism but is also one that suggests that political solidarity requires recognition and negotiation among feminisms and feminists, recognizing that all feminists are partial feminists working with partial feminisms.

'Race' Confronting Feminism

The challenge to white women in this recent history has been to recognize that they/we are raced in addition to being gendered and to
work out how to understand and disentangle the privileges attached
to whiteness and their implication in racism. Some feminists have
attended to this (Frankenberg 1993; Ware and Back 2002) and there
has also been discussion of the problems that can develop in focusing
upon whiteness, for such a focus can reinstate whiteness at the centre
of enquiry, re-marginalizing women of colour and Third World women
in the process. (We use Third World to refer to the countries of Africa,
Asia excluding Japan, Latin America and the Middle East.) Women of
colour and Third World women have always raised questions of
our/their inclusion and there is a substantial literature to demonstrate
this (Moraga and Anzaldúa 1981; Grewal et al. 1988; Moreton-
Robinson 2000). In other words, work by women of colour and Third
World women, as well as work on whiteness, has shown that 'race'
continuously confronts feminism by forcing attention to colonialism,
identity and difference. This confrontation not only grounds feminist
theorizing but also generates a reshaping of all forms of feminist work,
while also reshaping related ideas.

For example, issues of identity and difference have shifted their
focus of interest and intervention as a result of feminist interventions.
As a concept, identity has been variously deployed across many disciplines. In everyday usage, it may be placed on either side of the contradiction between 'absolute sameness' and 'individuality, personality'
(*Oxford English Dictionary*). This conundrum of connection and
separateness is partially unlocked by suggesting that identity may be
thought of as a site where 'structure and agency collide' (Bhavnani
and Phoenix 1994: 6). The (sometimes disparaging) reference to the
political movements around 'race', gender and sexuality as 'identity
politics' has been an impetus for galvanizing many constituencies into
rethinking their work and it is also the case that feminist scholarship
(amongst others) has urged analysts of identity themselves to rethink
the political and theoretical implications of their focus. Thus, the discussion as to what constitutes 'identity politics' and, indeed, whether
'identity politics' is a politics that encourages fundamental change has
been hotly debated. It is argued by some that the reliance on personal
identity leads to an individualist notion of change, with the consequence that larger forms of change, such as changing political and

economic institutions, recede into the background. In contrast, others have argued that to consider identity as an important way for rethinking politics is political in itself, a revolutionary political approach, for it is only comparatively recently that such an approach has gained legitimacy for many groups. The shift within identity politics has been to consider the ways in which identities, themselves embedded in axes of inequality, interconnect with each other. That is, the charge of racism directed at feminism has led not only to a reflection on the interconnections of axes of inequality with gender but also to a reworking of what constitutes identity, with the result that interconnections amongst seemingly distinct identities become more transparent. The shifting nature of identities (which may be clearly seen in age, a dimension always present in identity but also constantly in flux) is now taken for granted and has become more evident partly due to feminist thinking.

Identity can also open up discussions of subjectivity, evident in the work of Fanon (1967), Kollontai (1971) and Ogundipe-Leslie (1994). While such a direction demands a close understanding of psychoanalytic insights, and thus, some would argue (though not us), that it leads away from analysing how organized political change might occur, it is also the case that identity leads into discussions of agency and subjectivity. The latter is marked by the tension between social and/or psychic determination and the struggle for agency. Agency is an issue that has for too long been side-stepped in many discussions of subordination and change, although this, too, is in flux. This greater attention to agency is due, in part, to the impact of cultural studies on academic thinking as well as to feminist work that has discussed, for example, the 'constrained agency' of young women (Bhavnani et al. 1999: 575). In short, concepts of identity, made more complicated by the charge of racism, have shaped feminist thought which, in turn, has helped to reshape the concept itself.

Difference and Writing Stories

An anti-humanist insistence on always deconstructing subjectivity ignores political context and the importance of resistance. (Aziz 1997: 76)

There are many discussions of difference. It has been considered as differences of gender (Bock and James 1992), as differences in power, in inequality and in terms of experiencing the world. This final one can lead to the suggestion that many differences are incommensurable. In addition, difference has been analysed as differences of social relation, subjectivity and identity (Brah 1996). The argument for maintaining difference at the centre of feminist thinking is a strong one in that it is productive of more complex debates about possible directions for feminist work, such as how to think about 'race' in relation to different locations and time periods, how to move across difference without denying its existence, and how to create change in unequal human circumstances by harnessing difference. But, as Mary Maynard has noted, it also has its dangers where, for example, it reaches the point of implying that the expression of solidarity would be impossible (Afshar and Maynard 1994).

It is interesting to step aside for a moment from discussion of developments in theory and concepts to consider another facet of change relating to and influenced by feminism, the writing of stories. While discourse, narrative and story have become widely used concepts in social theory as a focus of deconstruction and interrogation, there has also been an extensive proliferation of published stories about women's lives, not to mention representations in film, radio and other media. The growth in women's story-telling – auto/biography, life-writing, fictional work – has been facilitated by the establishment of black, Third World, feminist, lesbian and queer courses in colleges and universities, publishing presses and bookshops. Transformations in the technologies of communication have helped sustain this momentum even as many of these specialist presses and bookshops have closed or been reabsorbed into the mainstream. Compared to the early 1970s, there is now a great body of work, much of it self-representational, which speaks out of the lives of women of many different backgrounds, identities and locations such that, if we choose to read across it, we can find an extensive literature on women and difference.

Much of this work is not academic, some of it is not 'literary' in any traditional sense, and it may or may not be considered political. It has, however, created another dimension of knowledge of the complexities of identities and subjectivities in the lives and imaginations of diverse women in diverse locations and has demonstrated how 'race', ethnicity, sexuality, dis/ability and age, for example, work within any woman's life. We cannot, here, tease out the wider implications of these developments, interesting as these might be. At present, we simply wish to make two points. First, story-telling should be taken seriously and recognized for the often generous access it can give to women's representations of themselves, their lives and circumstances. Secondly, there is a political edge to story-telling which may come from writing/telling and/or from reading/seeing. Stories have become a significant means of destabilizing boundaries of difference, of speaking into silences and of opening up possibilities for making connections. For example, Molly Talcott draws on the life stories of Colombian women who work as flower producers, and the women who take care of the workers' children (*madres communitarias*) not merely to show the diversity of women's employment but to demonstrate simultaneously how neoliberal forms of globalization rest acutely on the instability of the boundary between production and reproduction in women's lives. At the same time, these forms of globalization remain silent about the ways in which worldwide poverty is increasingly feminized (Talcott 2002).

Consider as a further example how the telling of life histories by indigenous Australians, in particular those from the stolen generations taken as children from their families, language and culture, has been a crucial part of a political process of bringing into public view what has for long been hidden from and denied in white Australia. Listening to and recording some of these stories became part of the work of the official National Inquiry into the Separation of Aboriginal and Torres Strait Islander Children from their Families (Human Rights and Equal Opportunities Commission 1997). The film version of one such story, *The Rabbit Proof Fence*, directed by Phillip Noyce and based on Doris Pilkington-Garimara's (2002) telling of the amazing childhood escape from captivity of her mother and aunt, has shown to large audiences in Australia and elsewhere. In addition, fiction as a particular form of story-telling has sometimes been able to jump ahead of much feminist theorizing and politics, raising more complex and disturbing issues as, for example, in Toni Morrison's unequivocal racialization of whiteness in the opening sentence of *Paradise* (1998): 'They shoot the white girl first.' Finally, Mary Eagleton, in her reading of Alice Walker's story 'Advancing Luna – and Ida B. Wells' alongside J. M. Coetzee's *Disgrace*, suggests that in both these works 'there is a play between history and fiction and the fiction is an attempt to say what history wants to silence' (2001: 195); in this case, the political dilemmas of black on white, male on female rape.

Thus, feminism, 'race', identity, difference, stories are interconnected. However, even as we draw on them to emphasize the agency of women that is an integral element of all feminist thinking, we also wish to ensure that structure, by which we mean political, economic and ideological frameworks, is not relegated to second place, to a place where it is acknowledged parenthetically and thus side-stepped. In other words, we argue that it is not possible to deduce an outcome from the structures at play and this is not only because people make decisions about possibilities in their lives, however constrained such decisions may be, but also because there are always more historically particular factors involved in any situation than are immediately apparent. These factors we rename as 'the local' and 'the particular'. In the rest of the chapter we provide two instances to illustrate our argument about 'race' and feminism, about the local and the particular alongside the structural.

Colonialism, Third World and Development Studies

'Race', colonization and development are connections that are made by many whose work is based in Third World regions and some of these analysts also include women/gender. Much has been written about colonialism and its relation to development projects in the Third World which, in turn, has meant that feminist thought based in the First World is slowly shifting to include considerations of Third World feminisms. For the purposes of this chapter, we will not discuss the wealth of literature that engages with Third World feminisms/gender, post-coloniality and development, though readers interested in this area could consult the following: Mani (1998), Nnaemeka (1998), Burton (1999), Barriteau (2001) and Ling (2002). Our focus is on development studies and the place of women.

It is widely conceded that development has failed the Third World (see Bhavnani et al. 2003 for a longer discussion of these issues). This failure has become sharper with the end of the Cold War and the subsequent rise of globalization. In such discussions, what are often noted as examples of this failure are the increasing feminization of poverty, the continued degradation of the environment and that the contexts for peace and security to survive are, in many parts of the world, non-existent. While a number of arguments exist to explain this failure, it is widely accepted that a misplaced emphasis, for over two decades, on modernization strategies, a lack of attention to women's contributions and a disregard for culture have contributed to this failure. Development may be thought of as purposeful projects to achieve social change (Kabeer 1994), as a means of poverty reduction as suggested by the World Bank, or, more explicitly, as a means of ensuring redistribution in a society (Franke and Chasin 1994). Vandana Shiva, however, argues that when development is understood as only economic development, such as increasing the gross national product of a nation, then it becomes 'maldevelopment' (Mies and Shiva 1993). Notwithstanding the diversity of views of what development is, and what it could be, it is the case that women's presence in development has a rich history.

The history of women in relation to development is often documented as shifting from 'women in development' (WID) in which it was argued that development projects needed to add women in, although such addition left definitions of development untouched; to 'women and development' (WAD) which suggested that women and development must be seen synonymously, each drawn upon to recast the other; and to 'gender and development' (GAD) in which it is argued that gender captures most closely the unequal power relations of women and men in development. All of these approaches have been critiqued not only for homogenizing Third World women but also for neglecting a larger analysis of the interconnections amongst women's subordination and capitalism, patriarchy and 'race'/ethnicity. 'Women, culture, development' (WCD) is a new paradigm that critiques the tendency in much development discourse to see women as in need of rescue from their culture, and for implying that Third World women are cast as people without agency (Chua et al. 2000; Bhavnani et al. 2003). A WCD approach explicitly centres the relationship between production and reproduction and ensures that women's agency is visible. It views culture as lived experience, which means that women are not seen only as gendered people, but also, for example, as part of ethnicized groups. Furthermore, in bringing culture into the foreground, a WCD lens guarantees that, in addition to gender and ethnicity, religion, age, sexualities and class are not omitted from analysis or practice. Thus, an engagement with difference is an integral component of the WCD approach and, hence, it demands that the local and the particular are analysed simultaneously with the structural. 'Women' is used in preference to 'gender' for it is argued that the latter, through its focus on structural power inequalities due to gender, can lose sight of the agency and resistance that women bring to their situations. Thus, WCD draws enthusiastically from feminist/women's studies, cultural studies and critical development studies, while simultaneously critiquing them for the different ways in which each area is inadequate in its attention to 'race', Third World and women/gender issues.

We discuss WCD for it seems to us that to guide prevailing, hegemonic feminist work into new directions it is not only necessary to engage the arguments advanced by women of colour in the First World, but also to engage writings by women based in the Third World which speak to issues of concern for Third World women. For example, the work done by Tostan to eliminate female genital cutting/mutilation in Senegal (Melching 2001) reflects on how to work towards the elimination of female genital mutilation/cutting without reproducing the insensitivities (at best) of 'Western' feminisms. Tostan (which means 'breaking out of the egg' in Wolof) is a non-governmental organization in Senegal that has worked with rural peoples for some time in a basic education programme. In 1996, some of the women who had been in Tostan came together to establish the 'Malicounda Commitment', a series of pledges that female genital mutilation/ cutting should be stopped (Mackie 1998). As a result, Tostan spearheaded a widespread grassroots opposition to female genital mutilation/cutting and the practice was declared illegal by the Senegalese government in January 1999 (*New York Times*, 18 January 1999). This is but one example of a strategy developed by women in the Third World which raises questions about the ways in which First World feminists, of colour or not, might create coalitions with women in the Third World.

Gender and development raise issues not only in the context of the Third World but also in the context of the wealthier regions such as North America, the countries of Western Europe, Australia and New Zealand through the issue of migration. While it is the case that all of these places have passed legislation against racial discrimination, the operation of their immigration policies means that racism, or 'xenoracism' (Fekete 2001), is legitimated through legislation on migration. It has long been argued, something we commented upon in our 1986 essay, that migration is, almost by definition, a phenomenon that gives rise to racism through the operation of mentalities of 'insider/outsider', 'citizen/non-citizen', 'the integrity of the (Western) nation-state' and similar. More recently, the racialization of migration has been discussed in the context of asylum-seekers; that is, the 22 million people seeking to flee untenable circumstances and who are in need of international protection. These people also appear to be at the new cutting edge of migration controls. As Ambalavaner Sivanandan comments, 'They demonised the blacks to justify slavery. They demonised the "coloureds" to justify colonialism. Today they demonise asylum seekers to justify globalism' (quoted in Fekete 2001: 23). Organizations such as the International Organization of Migration (IOM) have been set up to discuss how best to 'manage migration' in the context of globalization. Liz Fekete (2001) argues that the coordination of First World policies through inter-government and supranational bodies such as the IOM feeds into the vilification of refugees and asylum-seekers in popular media and politics.

The hostility to refugees, who are all too often seen as disrupting 'normal' life in the countries to which they flee, soon degenerates into racism and xenophobia. However, it is rare to see critics of xenophobic and racist policies towards asylum-seekers comment on the silence about women migrants and asylum-seekers. Many women who migrate find themselves seeking employment as domestic workers. For example, women who migrate from the Philippines and Mexico and find employment as domestic workers in countries such as Saudi Arabia and the United States are a group of migrants who have even fewer rights than other migrants in the countries to which they migrate. Migrant women, particularly when they are employed as domestic workers, often lose their human rights while their wages ensure that global poverty becomes increasingly feminized. Thus, the racialized discourses (at times unacknowledged) that organize all discussions of colonialism and of development are the same discourses that underlie discussions of globalization. The problem, however, is that women and gender are not integrated into such discourses and, thus, the interconnections between 'race' and gender, interconnections which delineate the realities of women's lives, are lost.

Feminism and 'Race': Australia 2000

The challenge of 'race' and racism to feminism in Australia was sharply invoked in the publication in 2000 of *Talkin' Up to the White Woman: Indigenous Women and Feminism by* Aileen Moreton-Robinson. In it she insists that white, middle-class Australian feminists need to move over, to listen to indigenous women, to look at their/our own racialization and at practices within the position/identity of white privilege and to unpick that power. She demands that they see why indigenous women cannot simply be 'added in' to feminism and thus forces them to rethink their/our own identities/subjectivities and the projects, limits and possibilities of feminism. This is a text in the tradition of the Combahee River Collective's 'A Black Feminist Statement' (1981) and Hazel Carby's 'White Woman Listen! Black Feminism and the

Boundaries of Sisterhood' (1982) and the many other writings from the mid-1970s onwards in which women of colour have confronted the racism in second-wave feminism and taken issue with white feminists.

Two decades later, Aileen Moreton-Robinson builds on this body of work to develop her highly focused and specifically located argument. At one level, perhaps, the relatively late arrival of this particular kind of engagement between 'race' and feminism in Australian theorizing can partly be explained by the closer involvement of Australian academic feminism with 'French feminism' than with aspects of relevant feminist debates in the US or the UK. Moreton-Robinson writes to represent an indigenous standpoint within Australian feminism, analysing the silences in white feminism in Australia and the legacy of colonialism and the dispossession of the indigenous peoples. She recognizes that the published stories of indigenous women in which they are 'Tellin' it Straight' (the title of the first chapter of her book) now constitute a substantial body of work and are an important source for self-presentation by indigenous women.

Moreton-Robinson also analyses the political activism of indigenous women and their 'take' on whiteness in feminism in a chapter headed 'Tiddas Speakin' Strong'. Between these chapters are four more which discuss: white feminism's (un)awareness of whiteness and theorizations of difference; the representation of indigenous women in the work of white women anthropologists; how indigenous women have been represented in white feminist writing; and white feminist self-presentations as recorded in interviews with the author. This methodology enables indigenous and non-indigenous bodies of knowledge to meet and disturb one another. 'Whiteness [is made] visible in power relations between white feminists and Indigenous women through examining their self-presentation and representation in various discourses' (Moreton-Robinson 2000: xxi). The argument is addressed to the subject position of 'the' white, middle-class woman, usually defined as a dominant subject position and, in particular, to white feminists in academia who carry the responsibility of having become the main producers of feminist theory. Her method very effectively demonstrates the incommensurability between different groups of women in Australia at this point in time in which whiteness for one group is 'overwhelmingly and, disproportionately predominant' (2000: 185), while for the other group it can be so taken for granted as to be almost invisible, rarely named or interrogated. The problem, as Marcia Langton has pointed out, quoting Richard Dyer, is that: 'as long as race is something only applied to non-white peoples, as long as white people are not racially seen and named, they/we function as a human norm. Other people are raced, we are just people.' Langton continues: 'there is no more powerful position than that of being "just" human' (2001: 7).

Australia's particular historical legacy of colonization continues to inform relations between 'races', ethnicities, classes and genders. Ien Ang refers to the unresolved 'original sin foundational to Australian white settler subjectivity' (1995: 71). This 'foundational sin' involved British invasion, the establishment of penal colonies, white settlement of the land based on the dispossession of indigenous lands, lives and cultures and the denial of indigenous realities expressed in the legal fiction of *terra nullius* (empty land). Ang considers how this original 'foundational sin' continues to impact within Australian feminism which, she suggests, tends to behave like a nation still under the ownership of white women who may choose to invite some 'other' women to join on the 'nation's' terms. More specifically, this gate-keeping is under the effective control of white Anglo women. Ang is concerned with the ways in which this original colonial dynamic operates within feminism to the marginalization and exclusion of women outside the indigenous/white invader–settler relation and she reflects on her position as a woman of Chinese descent within Australian feminism. Apart from self-representation by women of other 'race' and ethnic identities and their own claims for visibility, migrant women have tended to be homogenized into such categories as NESB (non-English-speaking background). 'There is so little feminist engagement with the challenge of constructing a "multicultural Australia"' (Ang 1995: 71). We suggest that this lack of engagement reflects the weight of unfinished business around Australia's 'foundational sin' which remains an obstacle to imagining a more coherent development of Australia as a multiracial, multicultural society capable of developing the potential of its diversity.

Another example of this failure to engage is evident in a 2002 postcard campaign for a fair and humanitarian Australia. It features a tall ship and proclaims that 'we are all boat people', an important statement of solidarity with asylum-seekers and refugees who are so vilified by the Australian government. Unintentional as this may be, indigenous Australians are out of this picture; they are not part of the 'we', for, of course, they did not arrive by boat. Thus, to a large extent, theoretical and policy discourses on 'race' (indigenous/white), on 'multiculturalism' (other racialized, ethnic, non-English-speaking groups) and gender have tended to develop along parallel rather than interconnected and intertwined tracks.

As Ang also notes, Australian whiteness has its own particularities. Even Anglo/Celtic Australian whiteness 'is relatively marginal to world-hegemonic whiteness . . . produc[ing] a sense of non-metropolitan, postcolonial whiteness', and she quotes Meaghan Morris on 'white settler subjectivity' which 'oscillates uneasily between identities as coloniser and colonised' (Ang 1995: 69). Geography conspires in this marginality as Australia is a 'northern' (as in relatively affluent and advanced) country sitting more or less uneasily in the southern hemisphere. Recognizing this uneasy oscillation can only be part of a full interrogation of Australian whiteness which cannot evade the realities of power and the challenges involved in working to dislodge them. A recent issue of *Australian Feminist Studies* (2000), entitled 'On Whiteness', promises to take such a task seriously but there is much hard work to be done to unseat the privileges of whiteness in Australian feminism and to take on the specificities of female racism and white racism in general. Gillian Cowlishaw (1999) has also done relevant work in this area. Discussion of this specific example from recent work in Australia illustrates the uneven and particular development of encounters between 'race' and feminism in different locations (Australia) and contexts (feminism in Australia at the beginning of the new millennium) despite the global accessibility of feminist work for those with access to the appropriate networks and means of communication. Alongside these particularities of location and context there are continuities – of identities, of difference and of histories of being colonized.

In Conclusion: Working with the Paradoxes

At many levels, including the personal, cultural, political and global, feminism(s) continue to be challenged by racism. In this chapter we have pointed to ways in which 'race' continuously confronts feminism(s) through the legacies and practices of colonialism and their implications for identity and difference. The result is that feminism is constantly reshaping itself (Bhavnani 2001). The kind of universalism and certainty with which Western second-wave feminism began has been profoundly disturbed. The intervention of 'race' into feminism and the challenges and critiques launched by women of colour have been a most important part of these disturbances. The processes unleashed by the entry of difference in general, and 'race' in particular, into feminism have developed momentum and direction with complex political implications. We have worked our way round some of the resulting paradoxes, asking what might be new ways of joining up the dots, tracing the interconnections between feminism(s) and 'race'. For all the achievements to which (mainstream/hegemonic) feminism(s) can lay some claim, there is still a white, middle-class reference point within what passes for feminism within and without academia in the West. The basic tasks of race-ing gender and gendering racism still require attention as we have indicated in our brief discussions of development studies and Australian feminisms. Such struggles take place at theoretical, administrative and political levels and continue even as feminisms multiply and 'new' variants of racism are produced.

We celebrate the shift from 'woman' to 'women' which recognizes differences amongst women and the deployment of 'gender' and 'genders' which keeps power inequalities between women and men in the picture. But, like many others, we note the problems of difference when it is detached from identification and leans towards a dynamic of fragmentation of all identities until everyone is left with the loneliness of separate, uniquely multifaceted and fluid identities/subjectivities with little to suggest the possibility of reaching across the chasm that surrounds each human being. 'I'm a postmodernist but . . .' might be one way of indicating a reluctance to follow a path of deconstruction to a point at which the journey becomes politically and practically debilitating. We look for ways of working self-critically with and across difference to open up possibilities of making connections, imagining new futures and acting with solidarity. Similarly, it has been important to acknowledge that 'I'm a feminist but . . .' can now express not a reluctance to identify with feminism as a political project but rather a recognition that all feminisms are partial and particular. No one feminism can speak for all women, and it is not even desirable that this should be so, although others might disagree.

In describing and analysing the confrontations, more questions emerge; for example, how have political practices shaped these confrontations and how have they been shaped by them? Such questions bring us back to issues of structure and agency modified by local and particular contexts, played out through identity and difference. Although everything appears more complex and even opaque as we develop a practice of interrogation, some generalizations remain: stark poverty, racism and exclusion, war and violence, growing material inequalities and life chances. Our history as socialist feminists leads us to insist that it is possible for new forms of feminism to rise out of earlier forms, not totally discontinuously but also not simply as an evolution. In recognizing that the encounters of 'race' and feminism involve disturbing confrontations and political paradoxes, we see our chapter as 'work in progress' on these issues.

References and Further Reading

Afshar, H. and Maynard, M. (eds) (1994) *The Dynamics of 'Race' and Gender: Some Feminist Interventions*. London: Taylor and Francis.

Amos, V. and Parmar, P. (1984) Challenging imperial feminism. *Feminist Review*, 17: 3–19.

Ang, I. (1995) Other women and postnational feminism. In B. Caine and R. Pringle (eds), *Transitions: New Australian Feminisms*, pp. 57–73. London: Allen and Unwin.

Australian Feminist Studies (2000) On whiteness. *Australian Feminist Studies*, special issue, 15: 33.

Aziz, R. (1997) Feminism and the challenge of racism: difference or diversity. In H. S. Mirza (ed.), *Black British Feminism*, pp. 70–77. London: Routledge.

Barriteau, E. (2001) *The Political Economy of Gender in the Twentieth Century Caribbean*. New York: Palgrave.

Bhavnani, K-K. (ed.) (2001) *Feminism and 'Race'*. Oxford: Oxford University Press.

— and Coulson, M. (1986) Transforming socialist feminism: the challenge of racism. *Feminist Review*, 23: 81–93.

— and Phoenix, A. (eds) (1994) Editorial introduction: shifting identities, shifting racisms. *Feminism and Psychology*, special issue, 4 (1): 5–18.

—, Foran, J. and Kurian, P. (eds) (2003) *Feminist Futures: Re-imagining Women, Culture and Development*. New York: Zed Books.

—, Kent, K. and Twine, F. Winddance (eds) (1999) *Feminisms and Youth Cultures*. *Signs*, special issue, 23: 1.

Bock, G. and James, S. (eds) (1992) *Beyond Equality and Difference: Citizenship, Feminist Politics, and Female Subjectivity*. London: Routledge.

Brah, A. (1996) Difference, diversity, differentiation. In A. Brah (ed.), *Cartographies of Diaspora*, pp. 95–127. London: Routledge.

— (1999) The scent of memory: strangers, our own, and others. *Feminist Review*, 61: 4–26.

Burton, A. (ed.) (1999) *Gender, Sexuality and Colonial Modernities*. London: Routledge.

Carby, H. (1982) White woman listen! Black feminism and the boundaries of sisterhood. In Centre for Contemporary Cultural Studies (ed.), *The Empire Strikes Back: Race and Racism in 70s Britain*, pp. 212–35. London: Hutchinson.

Chua, P., Bhavnani, K-K. and Foran, J. (2000) Women, culture, development: a new paradigm for development studies? *Ethnic and Racial Studies*, 23 (5): 820–41.

Collins, P. Hill (1990) *Black Feminist Thought: Knowledge, Consciousness and the Politics of Empowerment*. Boston, MA: Unwin and Hyman.

Combahee River Collective (1981) A black feminist statement. In C. Moraga and G. Anzaldúa (eds), *This Bridge Called my Back: Writings by Radical Women of Color*, pp. 210–18. Watertown, MA: Persephone Press.

Coulson, M. and Bhavnani, K-K. (1989) Making a difference: questioning women's studies. In E. Burman (ed.), *Feminists and Psychological Practice*, pp. 62–72. London: Sage.

Cowlishaw, G. (1999) *Rednecks, Eggheads, and Blackfellas*. London: Allen and Unwin.

DuCille, A. (1994) The occult of true black womanhood: critical demeanor and black feminist studies. *Signs*, 19 (3): 591–629.

Eagleton, M. (2001) Ethical reading: the problem of Alice Walker's 'Advancing Luna – and Ida B. Wells' and J. M. Coetzee's *Disgrace*. *Feminist Theory*, 2 (2): 189–203.

Fanon, F. (1967) *Black Skin, White Masks*. New York: Grove Press.

Fekete, L. (2001) The emergence of xeno-racism. *Race and Class*, 43 (2): 23–40.

Franke, R. W. and Chasin, B. (1994) *Kerala: Radical Reform as Development in an Indian State*. Oakland, CA: Institute for Food and Development Policy.

Frankenberg, R. (1993) *White Women, Race Matters: The Social Construction of Whiteness*. London: Routledge.

Giddings, P. (1984) *When and Where I Enter: The Impact of Black Women on Race and Sex in America*. New York: William Morrow.

Grewal, S., Kay, J., Landor, L., Lewis, G. and Parmar, P. (eds) (1988) *Charting the Journey: Writings by Black and Third World Women*. London: Sheba Feminist.

Human Rights and Equal Opportunities Commission (1997) *Bringing Them Home: Report of the National Inquiry into the Separation of Aboriginal and Torres Strait Islander Children from their Families*. Sydney: Commonwealth of Australia.

Jensen, J. (1977) Native American women and agriculture. In E. C. DuBois and V. L. Ruiz (eds), *Unequal Sisters: A Multicultural Reader in US Women's History*, pp. 51–65. New York: Routledge, 1990.

Kabeer, N. (1994) *Reversed Realities: Gender Hierarchies in Development Thought*. London: Verso.

Kollontai, A. (1971) *The Autobiography of a Sexually Emancipated Communist Woman*. New York: Herder and Herder.

Langton, M. (2001) The nations of Australia. Alfred Deakin Lecture, 20 May. Australian Broadcasting Corporation (http://www.abc.net.au/rn/deakin/docs/langton.doc).

Ling, L. H. M. (2002) *Postcolonial International Relations: Conquest and Desire between Asia and the West*. New York: Palgrave.

Mackie, G. (1998) A way to end female genital cutting (http://www.fgmnetwork.org/articles/mackie1998.html).

Mani, L. (1998) *Contentious Traditions: The Debate on Sati in Colonial India*. Berkeley, CA: University of California Press.

Melching, M. (2001) What's in a name? (Re)contextualising female genital mutilation. In S. Perry and C. Schenk (eds), *Eye to Eye: Women Practicing Development across Cultures*, pp. 155–70. New York: Zed Books.

Mies, M. and Shiva, V. (1993) *Ecofeminism*. New Delhi: Kali for Women.

Mirza, H. S. (1997) *Black British Feminism: A Reader*. London: Routledge.

Moraga, C. and Anzaldúa, G. (eds) (1981) *This Bridge Called my Back: Writings by Radical Women of Color*. Watertown, MA: Persephone Press.

Moreton-Robinson, A. (2000) *Talkin' Up to the White Woman: Indigenous Women and Feminism*. Queensland: University of Queensland Press.

Morrison, T. (1998) *Paradise*. New York: Alfred A. Knopf.

Nnaemeka, O. (ed.) (1998) *Sisterhood, Feminism and Power: From Africa to the Diaspora*. Trenton, NJ: Africa World Press.

Ogundipe-Leslie, M. (1994) *Re-creating Ourselves: African Women and Critical Transformations*. Trenton, NJ: Africa World Press.

Pilkington-Garimara, D. (2002) *Follow the Rabbit Proof Fence*. Queensland: University of Queensland Press.

Smith, B. (1982) Racism in women's studies. In G. T. Hull, P. B. Scott and B. Smith (eds), *All the Women are White, All the Blacks are Men, but Some of Us are Brave: Black Women's Studies*. Old Westbury, NY: The Feminist Press.

Spillers, H. J. (ed.) (1991) *Comparative American Identities: Race, Sex, and Nationality in the Modern Text*. New York: Routledge.

Talcott, M. (2002) Cultivating flowers, cultivating change: globalization, women workers and the Colombian flower industry. Unpublished MA thesis, University of California at Santa Barbara, California.

Tong, R. (1998) *Feminist Thought: A Comprehensive Introduction*. Boulder, CO: Westview Press.

Ware, V. (1992) *Beyond the Pale: White Women, Racism, and History*. London: Verso.

— and Back, L. (2002) *Out of Whiteness: Color, Politics and Culture*. Chicago: University of Chicago Press.

5
Sexuality

Rey Chow

Psychoanalysis and Feminism: Incompatible Agendas?

Any discussion of sexuality in modern times would need to acknowledge the unparalleled contributions made by Sigmund Freud, even though the nature of those contributions remains controversial. Freud's *Three Essays on the Theory of Sexuality* is considered by many critics to be his most important statement on the subject and, together with *The Interpretation of Dreams*, constitutes the centrepiece of Freud's writings on human existence. In the *Three Essays*, Freud makes the well-known argument that human sexuality is traceable to infancy and childhood and that it is manifest in the numerous forms of what are considered sexual aberrations. 'A disposition to perversions is an original and universal disposition of the human sexual instinct', he writes (Freud 1975: 97), and this instinct is fundamentally different from that of animals in that it is not, in and of itself, oriented towards the biological end of procreation. As Steven Marcus (1975) comments, in his 'Introduction' to *Three Essays on the Theory of Sexuality*, the ground-breaking point advanced by Freud is that 'the sexual instinct is plastic and labile, that it can be displaced, that it is not entirely dependent upon its object – or the object world – and that it may indeed be at first independent and without an object' (1975: xxviii). In this plastic and labile condition, sexuality is inextricably bound up with the unconscious, which is the object and foundation of psychoanalysis: 'What is specific to psychoanalysis is the articulation of sexuality with the unconscious; in other words, for psychoanalysis, human sexuality is the sexuality of the subject of the unconscious, to which it is the key, as Freud's early works on hysteria made clear' (Brousse 1992: 406).

Being 'the weak spot' in the process of human cultural development (Freud 1975: 15) and thus never fully compliant with the constraints of civilization, sexuality none the less must come into contact with the latter. Although Freud is, in the *Three Essays*, primarily interested in taxonomizing the variations of the sexual instinct, in his other works he frequently draws attention to the stunting effects human society has on sexuality and explores the hazardous paths that human beings must go through in order to attain social acceptance and mental sanity. The social, in so far as it is presented as an intractable arrangement in which sexuality gets punished, restrained, diverted and sublimated, appears in Freud's work as a source of oppression. Mandatory, with its own forms of rewards, the socialization of sexuality is always about conflict rather than harmony. As Marcus (1975: xli) puts it:

> Freud is . . . one of the last great legatees of the Romantic tradition in European thought. His theories are grounded in the idea of conflict, and this conflict exists in the realm of the normal as much as it does in the pathological. Even his conceptions of integration are touched by it. He sees integration as falling within the larger contexts of conflict and of incompatible needs, contradictory aims, and implacably opposed demands. Such integration as he finds is never complete, rarely adequate, and more often than not unstable. He never envisages the human or the social world as composing now or in the future to some harmonious order.

Freud's work can thus be understood as a two-pronged project. His bold, speculative theorization of human sexuality as a phenomenon with specificities that cannot be entirely divorced from, yet cannot be reduced to, biology is balanced by a steady, voluminous series of narratives depicting the multifaceted efforts, 'normal' and 'perverse', made by men and women to grapple with their sexuality under the collective pressures of their society. Jean Laplanche summarizes Freud's insights into human sexuality, in a remarkable phrase, as ' "instincts lost" and "instincts regained" ':

> The whole theme of *The Three Essays on the Theory of Sexuality* (Freud, 1905) could be summarized as 'instincts lost' and 'instincts regained'. The whole point is to show that human beings have lost their instincts,

especially their sexual instinct and, more specifically still, their instinct to reproduce. The thesis of the first two sections of the *Three Essays* at least is that human instincts have no fixed or definite object, and no goal, and that they follow no one, stereotypical path . . . The 'instincts regained' aspect of the *Three Essays* can be seen in its account of the trans-formations of puberty [*die Umgestaltungen der Pubetät*]. This theme might be termed 'instincts mimicked' or 'instincts replaced' . . . Although it is apparently natural, the genesis of a wish to have a baby is, in Freud's description, far from simple. A woman has to struggle through a veri-table labyrinth before she learns to *wish* for something that any living creative instinctively *wants*. (1989: 29–30; emphasis in original)

As Laplanche's passage indicates, for Freud the socialization of sexu-ality is a painful story about cultural adaptation. Especially for women, this is a story of how they must *mimic* a 'sexuality' that is, strictly speaking, not their own, until they have become the 'normal' version of womanhood. Not surprisingly, then, it is precisely on the question of female sexuality that the encounter between feminism and Freudian psychoanalysis tends to be the most contentious and explosive.

In so far as he shows how women, like men, must in the course of maturation abandon their own mobile, perverse sexuality in order to become acceptable and respectable, Freud can be seen as an ally to feminism. The logic of his analysis implies that since the repressive demands put on women are more arduous than those put on men, they ought to deserve greater sympathy. The manner in which Freud constructs the story of female sexuality, however, is highly disturb-ing to read, not least because of the excessively positive value he attaches to certain anatomical characteristics against which women are judged to be deficient. While readers will need to turn to Freud's works to follow his arguments in their expository intricacies (see Freud 1924, 1925, 1927, 1931, 1938), let me briefly recapture the highlights of his narrative of female mutism.

As Freud tells it, the story of how human beings arrive at their prop-erly socialized sexual identities comprises several stages. In the case of the male, the key is the Oedipal stage, during which the little boy, still bound to his autoeroticism, sexually desires his mother and, out of jealousy, wishes to kill his father. The intensity of this Oedipus complex is eventually dampened by another emotion, the fear of castration. As he is threatened with the possibility of losing his own penis, the little boy learns to identify with the authority of the father and gives up his autoeroticism, including his desire for his mother, which is gradually transferred to other women. This act of surrendering an immensely pleasurable part of himself to the dictates of authority gains him access to the adult world, even though as a transaction between sexuality and society it is often incomplete and tends to result in various neuroses or 'aberrations' that accompany male adulthood (such as fetishism). In the case of women, Freud argues a different scenario: the Oedipus complex is here preceded and assisted by the castration complex. Whereas the fear of castration for the little boy is a punishment and a consequence (he tends to imagine that everyone has a penis like him and ignores the female anatomical difference, until he is threatened with castration and begins, belatedly, to internalize the possibility of not having one), for the little girl castration is a prerequisite, the meaning of which is immediately understood by her. When confronted with the sight of the male organ, Freud writes, the little girl 'behaves differently. She makes her judgement and her decision in a flash. She has seen it and knows that she is without it and wants to have it' (Freud 1925: 187–8). In her awareness of her own condition of castratedness, the little girl develops 'penis envy'. This leads her to loosen her relation with her mother (since the latter is held responsible for her lack of a penis) and to transfer her affections to her father and later to other men. The path she must take to correct her deficiency involves marriage and childbirth. If she is lucky, her desire for the missing penis will be appeased, finally, by the birth of a son.

To readers of the twenty-first century, this classic account of anatomy-as-destiny, of men's and women's distinct manners of arriving at their socially approved sexual identities, which I have retold in a deliberately simplified manner in order to foreground the stakes involved, can only come across as ludicrous. The problems it presents are glaring and have been pointed out frequently by feminist and other critics: the privileging of the nuclear family, of heterosexual coupling, and of male sexuality (or the male trajectory of attaining 'normal' sexuality); the privileging of the penis as a symbol of positive cultural value; the disparaging of women based on their anatomical difference and the narrating of female sexuality (or the female trajectory of attaining 'normal' sexuality) in terms of a compensatory attempt to make up for an original lack. A radical critique of the patriarchal philosophical premises of Freud's theory has been offered, for instance, in Irigaray's important work *This Sex Which is Not One* (1985), which proposes the imaginative and utopian alternative of a sexual paradigm based on a positive evaluation of female corporeal specificities. It is, however, equally important to remember the speculative spirit in

which Freud offers these stories. As Jeffrey Weeks puts it, 'There is
. . . an alternative way of seeing the importance of anatomy: as symbolically important, representative of sexual differences which
acquires [*sic*] meaning only in culture' (1986: 62–3). Freud's point is
that sexuality and the identities it imposes on men and women are
always contingent and never fully achieved even as such identities are
crucial to social survival. As Rosalind Coward (1983: 266) writes:

> The Freudian account shows that the very process by which the sense
> of individual identity is acquired is the process by which social position
> is achieved . . . Crucial in this is the acquisition of position of sexed sub-
> jectivity, not given by an intrinsic sexual disposition, but constructed
> through our entry into a culture polarized around anatomical difference.
> (1983: 266)

At the same time that it shows how individuality is acquired
through the process of socialization, psychoanalysis also 'shows how
individuality is precarious, contradictory, only maintaining coherence
by holding fiercely to a socially defined and fixed role' (Coward 1983:
267). To the extent that Freud's premise is, as noted above, that of a
permanent conflict between sexuality and society, it may be argued
that his disparaging remarks on female sexuality and its futile struggles are simply testimonies to that fundamental conflict, whereby
women bear the brunt of civilization and its discontents in a far more
compelling manner than men. That Freud's work, despite his sympathy for women's plight, repeatedly confirms the stereotypical view of
them as the weaker sex thus stands as symptomatic of the tenacity of
that same conflict and of the heavy ideological price it exacts. Responding to the enigmatic status of women in Freud's thinking, Kofman
(1985), for instance, has offered a perceptive deconstruction of Freud's
texts against their own grain.

Feminism, on the other hand, has from the outset defined itself by
an explicit political project, one in which the causes of women's social
oppression and subordination can be carefully probed and hence,
ideally, eradicated. As different editors of fairly recent feminist theory
anthologies attest: 'The first idea that is likely to occur in the course
of any historical thinking about feminism is that feminism is a *social*
force' (Humm 1992: 1; emphasis in original); '[the] belief in the social
origins of women's oppression was and is common to all shades of
feminist opinion', though 'there have always been different forms of
analysis arising from the shared assumption' (Jackson and Scott 1996:
7). The contested nature of the debates about sexuality – defined

variously by way of masculinist ideology, economic exploitation, compulsory heterosexism, white hegemony, and representational politics – can be seen in the significant number of feminists who participate in them from multiple disciplinary perspectives. From the generation of activist writers (see Greer 1971; Millett 1977; Firestone 1979; Friedan 1983), who often looked back to historical predecessors such as Mary Wollstonecraft, Virginia Woolf, Simone de Beauvoir, to later theorists of sexuality and gender relations (see Chodorow 1978; Gallop 1982; hooks 1984, 1991; Rubin 1984; de Lauretis 1987; Scott 1988; Moore 1988; Spelman 1988; Butler 1990; Collins 1990 and their numerous fellow-thinkers), feminism's interest in female sexuality has been consciously interventionist rather than simply expository (see Humm 1992: 56–9 for brief summaries of feminist achievements in different disciplines up to the early 1990s). If Freud's work on sexuality stands as an attempt to explore, with hesitation and uncertainty, a realm of phenomena that can never be neatly clarified and stabilized, feminism's agenda has the rather different, perhaps opposite, goal of clarifying, naming, explaining, and thus changing women's social positions. (See the introductions to each section in Humm 1992 for useful discussion of the historical stages undergone by feminism in Britain and the United States.)

In this regard, there is perhaps a fundamental incompatibility between the rationalist, progress-oriented aim of feminist undertakings and the fugitive object of sexuality-cum-unconscious that defines psychoanalysis. For many feminist thinkers, the encounter with Freudian psychoanalysis and its understanding of female sexuality simply produces the consensus that the latter is part and parcel of the age-old phallocentric tradition that belittles and impedes women with an anachronistic form of sexual essentialism. Juliet Mitchell (2001: 16) describes this clash of agendas this way:

> Psychoanalysis is not and has never claimed to be a political discourse. Feminism is nothing if it is not this. As a political practice in search of a political theory, it can use concepts and arguments from elsewhere to analyse its own object – the position of women – in the relevant contexts, but it cannot convert these concepts and arguments into political ones in and of themselves . . . Psychoanalysis . . . does not contextualize. Any political practice must, by definition, contextualize – how else can political mobilization be contemplated, let alone achieved?

According to Mitchell, feminists' attempt to select the (apolitical) object of psychoanalysis as feminism's own political object 'was, and is, a mistake' (2001: 16). Mitchell's conclusion is provocative because it is such a resolute one. Rather than accepting it *tout court*, I would like to use the rest of this chapter to propose another, perhaps less final, way of examining the encounter between psychoanalysis and feminism over sexuality, so as to tease out more of the intensities and ambiguities involved before each of us goes on to form her own judgement.

The Problem of Differentiation

Because Freud asserts that there is only one sexuality, his description of female sexuality may be seen as a way of accounting for modes of differentiation within the trajectory of the same phenomenon. In this light, conceptual attributes such as lack and castration, which are assigned to femininity, would arguably be just that – concepts, with a special function to play in the schema Freud is constructing. This would be the function of negation and antithesis, without which no phenomenon can be grasped or analysed. For feminists, however, such conceptual attributions are never entirely separable from the social denigration of women. They tend, therefore, to read Freud's narratives literally by equating his references to 'lack' and 'castration' with actual assaults. This is what Mitchell means when she writes:

> [B]ecause the Freud–Lacan account explained how sexual difference was established as denigration on the side of the feminine, that explanation substituted for an explanation of oppression. The lack that is psychologically ascribed to women became treated as an actual lack . . . The psychological mode of oppression was taken as the cause of oppression. What might have been a politically useful search for a commonality of different contexts became instead . . . the target of an overarching criticism. (2001: 14)

For Mitchell, the problem therefore lies in feminism's conflation of the psychoanalytic elucidation of female sexuality as devalued with the historical causes for such devaluation. Is feminist theory completely wrong in making such a conflation though?

This fundamental conflict points to much larger problems of methodology, especially the kind of methodology used in representing marginalized cultural groups, their sexual practices, and their life activities. As Freud's sympathetic readers repeatedly remind us, sexuality as he understands it has nothing essential about it. 'The Freudian hypothesis, if taken seriously, must leave no room for theories which take sexuality as a given. It must displace any argument in which sexual identity of [*sic*] sexual behaviour is thought to arise out of a sexual predisposition' (Coward 1983: 277–8). Similarly, Brousse (1992: 408) argues: 'As Freud had already suggested when he placed the oedipus complex at the centre of his theory, human sexuality can only be understood as the result of a process of sexuation; it does not spring either from anatomy or from social role.' Even the most devastating depictions of women's sexuality are, accordingly, simply part of the process of recognizing or marking, the provisional, precarious character of attributed sexual differences, rather than a condoning of them. How then might one begin to deal with the socially persistent enforcements of such 'provisional, precarious' attributed sexual differences *of the erroneous kind*? The problem at hand, it seems, is not exactly that sexuality should or should not be treated as a given but that the social, in which sexuality finds its points of anchoring, is, for better or for worse, always a given. There is a way in which not just the individual but also society itself is engaged in what Laplanche so perceptively refers to as mimicry: society has learned to think of and treat women in a derogatory way – 'as if' they were really deficient, inferior and so on. This social performance is just as critical as the individual's own mimicry of so-called normal womanhood. And it is this other mimicry, materializing at the collective rather than individual level, which lies at the core of feminist enquiry. Rather than focusing on the variations of the sexual instinct, and rather than pitting the individual (and her sexuality) against the social as such, feminist theory's enquiry begins with the social as a kind of already-acquired presupposition about sexuality – as the catastrophe that has already claimed women – and asks 'how did this happen?'

At the heart of these cross-purposed debates is the problematic of differentiation. For Freud, the investigation of sexuality proceeds as a series of structural oppositions that keep fragmenting *from within*: sexuality becomes specified as human sexuality (that is, differentiated from animal sexuality in general); human sexuality is divided into the positive and the negative versions of masculinity and femininity; masculinity and femininity are then further broken down into modes of perversions, usually on the basis of a binary relation – for example, voyeurism and exhibitionism, sadism and masochism, mourning and melancholy, neurosis and psychosis, and so forth. In each case, a particular activity, identity or symptom is split up *internally* to become yet another finer set of differentiations, so much so that one would have to realize, with Lacan and Lévi-Strauss, that 'the universals described by Freud are the universals of differentiation, constitutive of culture' (Coward 1983: 273). For feminist theory, of course, the question is rather: at what junctures and in what manners do such mechanisms of differentiation turn into *more* than just differentiation – into attitudes of reverence and contempt? In other words, what is the differentiation that enables differentiation to operate and how is this meta-differentiation to be delineated? Its capacity for nuancing the mechanisms of differentiation from within notwithstanding, Freud's work seems consistently unable or unwilling to handle precisely this question of the *evaluative* transformation undergone by differentiation at certain points – specifically, of how differentiation turns negatively into hierarchical distinction and discrimination. From the perspective of those who happen to occupy the socially denigrated positions of sexual differentiation, it is clear why some other explanation is needed.

Disrupting the Repressive Hypothesis

Ironically, however, from the conflation of Freud's differentiation mechanism with the historical causes for women's oppression and subordination, some versions of feminist theory continue to derive a certain momentum. In so far as a prevalent story of victimization continues to be told about women, Freud's theory of sexual repression, together with its concepts of lack and castration, has, despite his intentions and despite feminists' criticism of his work, given rise to a powerful paradigm of rewriting history. At the level of a discursive intervention, lack and castration not only function as descriptive differentiations of sexuality from within but also enable an entire logic of thinking about identity – as captivity and liberation – to emerge. While for Freud sexuality itself is the oppressed other, the rebel permanently taking flight from the bonds of civilization, for feminism 'woman' occupies the similar position of an embodied force seeking emancipation from the chains of male domination. This paradoxical collaboration between the referent of sexual repression and its implicit demand for liberation, on the one hand, and the significatory power of discourse, on the other, is given a name by Michel Foucault – the repressive hypothesis, a term Foucault uses to refer to the widespread, post-Freudian attitude towards human sexuality as always repressed.

Unlike Freud, Foucault's aim is not to ask why or how we are repressed but how we come to believe that we are:

> The question I would like to pose is not, Why are we repressed? But rather, Why do we say, with so much passion and so much resentment against our most recent past, against our present, and against ourselves, that we are repressed? By what spiral did we come to affirm that sex is negated? What led us to show, ostentatiously, that sex is something we hide, to say it is something we silence? (1980: 8–9)

For Foucault, sexuality can no longer be thought of as 'a stubborn drive, by nature alien and of necessity disobedient to a power which exhausts itself trying to subdue it and often fails to control it entirely'. Rather, it needs to be theorized as 'an especially dense transfer point for relations of power' – one, moreover, that is 'endowed with the greatest instrumentality' (Foucault 1980: 103). If it succeeds in posing a challenge to the paradigm of lack and castration that is lodged firmly in the narrative of sexual repression, Foucault's critique of Freudian psychoanalysis at the same time acknowledges that it is an extraordinarily effective mode of discourse. Indeed, Foucault's own notion of discursive power is in part based on his understanding of how *talk* about sexual repression (as instigated by Freudian psychoanalysis) has activated an unprecedented proliferation of practices and discourses, leading thus to more obsessions with the topic, *ad infinitum*.

Unlike Jacques Lacan, who takes Freud's discussion of sexuality in the direction of language and semiotics in order to explore the psychoanalytic subtleties of subjection-through-sexual-difference, Foucault takes that discussion instead in its historical manifestations. The perversions and abnormalities Freud discusses as variants of a polymorphous sexuality, Foucault rewrites as Western society's way, since the eighteenth century, of controlling populations through the implementation of specific mechanisms of knowledge and power. In particular, he discusses four types of institutional practices that together form 'strategic unities' in enforcing 'normal' sexuality: hystericization of women's bodies, pedagogization of children's sex, socialization of procreative behaviour, and psychiatrization of perverse pleasure (1980: 104–5).

Foucault's interest in the social regimentations and penalizations of sexual behaviours suggests that while his work proceeds fully in accordance with Freud's argument that the sexual instinct is non-essentialist in character, he has chosen to side-step that argument in order to focus, instead, on the complex rationalizations of human sexuality in modern times through steady institutional surveillance. Rather than a matter of 'instincts and their vicissitudes' which require ever more efforts of categorization, sexuality in Foucault's work is a vast, heterogeneous apparatus that includes legal, moral, scientific, architectural, philosophical and administrative discourses, all of which are linked to the production of knowledge with ever-shifting boundaries and effects of inclusion and exclusion.

For some feminist critics also, it has become increasingly apparent that the Freudian paradigm of lack, castration and repression, despite its great influence, might not be the most precise way of rewriting women's history and that femininity must be recognized not only in terms of deprivation but also in terms of social power. Among the academic works produced in the past two decades are those that do not concentrate exclusively on protesting against women's victimization but more on exploring the differences that constitute women's uniqueness as culture workers. In their studies of British and American literature, for instance, Jane Tompkins (1985) argues for the power embedded in the sentimentalism often associated with women's writings, and Nancy Armstrong (1987) reads the canonical novel by way of the power enjoyed by middle-class domestic women. In the discipline of film, Linda Williams (1989) demonstrates how the objectification of female bodies in pornographic film does not by necessity reduce women to passivity and helplessness. In the field of American studies, Robyn Wiegman (1995) argues for the inextricability of gender from racial power.

Shifting the emphasis away from the manners in which women were excluded (or repressed), these and other feminist critics approach their topics by showing the access women have to certain forms of social privilege, the active roles they have taken to empower themselves and the contributions they have made to the systematic discursive productions of female sexuality itself. These critics help clarify the important point that sexual differentiation is not necessarily synonymous with or the negative outcome of sexual oppression; that it may be treated as the social given, however treacherous, around which women authors, women characters, women performers, women theorists, and women audiences may and do negotiate their share of social agency. Accordingly, feminist theory's relationship to female sexuality has also been undergoing a significant shift: from anger at captivity and the desire to break free, to pleasure, plurality and a recognition of women's and feminism's participation in global power networks.

Rey Chow

Female Sexuality and Bio-power

Toward the end of volume I of *The History of Sexuality*, Foucault moves into a crucial discussion of what he calls 'bio-power'. His analyses of the various institutional practices, devised and implemented in European society since the Enlightenment for handling human sexuality, lead finally to the point that such practices are part of a bio-politics, the calculated management of life through the administration of bodies and the systematic perpetuation of the rationale for continued human reproduction. If the discussions about sexuality are reconsidered from the vantage point of this latter part of Foucault's book, sexuality would perhaps need to be seen as just a step – albeit an indispensable one – in Foucault's attempt to come to terms with something much larger and more elusive – what he would call 'the entry of life into history' (1980: 141). To cite his thought-provoking point at some length:

> [W]hat occurred in the eighteenth century in some Western countries, an event bound up with the development of capitalism, was a different phenomenon having perhaps a wider impact than the new morality; this was nothing less than the entry of life into history, that is, the entry of phenomena peculiar to the life of the human species into the order of knowledge and power, into the sphere of political techniques . . . Western man was gradually learning what it meant to be a living species in a living world, to have a body, conditions of existence, probabilities of life, an individual and collective welfare, forces that could be modified, and a space in which they could be distributed in an optimal manner . . . If one can apply the term *bio-history* to the pressures through which the movements of life and the processes of history interfere with one another, one would have to speak of *bio-power* to designate what brought life and its mechanisms into the realm of explicit calculations and made knowledge-power an agent of transformation of human life. (1980: 141–3; emphasis in original)

The ascendancy of life over death, naturally, has profound consequences. On the one hand, as Foucault's own work indicates, the disciplining of the individual human body, including its anatomy, its energies, its habits and its orientations, has taken on economic, scientific and political proportions. On the other hand, it has become necessary to regulate and administer humans as a species, as a global population, by manipulating and regulating the effects of all of their activities. What is generated in the process of material improvements is therefore not only more biological life but also *the imperative to live*. This constitutes an ideological mandate that henceforth grants justification to even the most aggressive and oppressive mechanisms of interference and control in the name of helping the human species increase its chances of survival, of improving its conditions and quality of existence.

With these larger issues in the picture, the controversy over sexuality becomes ever more complicated. Just as it is, for feminist theory, insufficient for sexuality to be understood from within its capacity for infinite differentiations, so too is it inadequate for feminine sexuality, now investigated in historical and institutional detail, to be considered the ultimate horizon of human existence. The question for feminist theory in the twenty-first century is, increasingly, something like the following: how do sexuality and feminine sexuality figure in contexts involving peoples of different races and cultures? This, incidentally, is fully in keeping with feminism's interrogation of sexuality from the beginning; that is, with its ethical insistence not only on the complexity of sexual differentiations but also on the often tragic effects of their social materializations. To put this somewhat differently: whereas, for Freud, the social is from the outset pessimistically analogized to an immovable blockage from which human beings can only seek temporary release through perversions, for feminist theory the social remains a contentious, but not closed, battleground, one in which it is still possible to intervene and, it is hoped, to make transformations. Whereas, for Freud, the social is the horizon to which human beings must learn to submit despite the demands of their own sexuality, for feminist theory the social, including its capacity to reproduce itself through practices and institutions, is something to be seized, so that its (potential) oppressiveness may be subverted.

Arguably, then, it is this commendable reluctance to give up the social, which constitutes feminist theory's conflict with Freud's approach to sexuality in the first place, that inevitably leads, in the light of a larger phenomenon such as bio-politics, to the undoing of the object of feminism, woman, itself. In the place of this object, which tends to be white and middle class, it has become necessary to ask about the presence of other kinds of lives, groups and cultures and their relations to 'woman'.

Consider the prominent issue of global biological reproduction. In Freud's account, human sexuality is not essentially oriented towards reproduction, yet human society systematically channels it in such a manner as to make reproduction the 'happy' ending – ideally, in the form of the woman's birth of a male child in a heterosexual marriage. Reproduction, in other words, belongs in Freud's story on the side of the social imperative, as part of that coercive script that human beings, especially women, have to mimic and learn to 'want' for themselves. Taken radically, Freud's theory implies that biological reproduction, especially in the case of women, can in fact be seen as the ultimate source of social oppression. In her reading of some strands of French feminism and their tendency to valorize the pleasures of motherhood, Gayatri Chakravorty Spivak attributes this imperative of biological reproduction to what she calls a uterine social organization, 'the arrangement of the world in terms of the reproduction of future generations, where the uterus is the chief agent and means of production' (Spivak 1987: 152). Her Marxist alliance with subaltern women in underprivileged parts of the world and her feminist critique of Freud's apparent misogyny aside, Spivak's reading is also, simultaneously, profoundly Freudian in its approach to human sexuality. To denormalize the uterine social organization, she argues, it is necessary to situate it in the economic and cultural, as well as sexual, contexts in which another female genital organ, the clitoris, is consistently effaced as 'the signifier of the sexed subject' (1987: 151). As the organ that 'escapes reproductive framing' (1987: 151), the clitoris and the pleasures women derive from it constitute nothing less than a purposeless 'sexual aberration' that civilized society must suppress.

Feminist theory's attempt to rewrite the social script of sexuality, meanwhile, suggests that the function of reproduction that was at one time the exclusive *telos* of the heterosexual couple is now a democratized ideal to be attainable by all. The empowerment not only of women but also of people of different sexual orientations such as gays, lesbians and transgender persons means that, theoretically speaking at least, all citizens in capitalist societies should have access to sexual reproduction on their own terms, with various advanced techniques of manipulating timing, intervening in infertility, adopting and so forth. Is this multiplication of reproductive possibilities and opportunities, an historical phenomenon so well analysed by Foucault, an optimal advancement made on sexuality's fundamental purposelessness? Or is it further proof of Freud's notion of the ever-expanding reach of human civilization and its programme to direct sexuality into a socially practicable – that is, *reproducible* – end? Is this 'end' an irreversible displacement of compulsory heterosexuality with its vested interests in property ownership and social privilege as much as in biological reproduction – or is it compulsory heterosexuality's most updated version? As Spivak writes, in a society still bound to the nuclear family and its forms of material possession, 'The uterine norm of womanhood supports the phallic norm of capitalism' (1987: 153).

So far, the democratized trajectories for reproduction have moved in consistency with the unequal distribution of the world's material resources. As contraception frees women from the burden of pregnancy and allows them to enjoy sex, materially impoverished women are serving as surrogate wombs for those with means. The babies thus produced, as well as orphaned infants and children in underprivileged nations, are acquired by wealthy single mothers, same-sex partners, heterosexual partners and married couples in Western Europe and North America, who form a fashionable class of new-age parents who can afford to purchase or appropriate other people's reproductive (still by and large uterine) labour in order to experience parenthood. Sexuality is now efficiently managed to the point at which biological reproduction is not only a physical capacity or a cultural option but also a prized commodity available on demand, its products often genetically made to order. However laudable feminism's political goal to help women (as well as those persecuted for their sexual practices) assume control over their reproductive fates might have been, it would be impossible for it to ignore the new world circumstances under which the progressive democratization of sexuality and reproduction, now unstoppable with the collaboration between capitalism and medical scientific technology, stands as a key constituent of the coercion of bio-power and its surveillance over life.

For Further Discussion

The material covered in this chapter is, of necessity, complex and, for a reader coming new to the area, might seem overwhelming. Thus, I want finally to review some of the main issues that have been raised, a review which may serve as a guideline for further discussion.

Sexuality in Freud is an object 'lost and found'. Freud's project may be described as apolitical in the sense of not being centred on the possibility of a political and social transformation of the fundamental conflict between sexuality and human civilization. Instead, he has shown us how sexuality, ever recalcitrant in the face of constraints placed upon it by civilization, seeks out 'perverse' routes of escape. When Freud explains sexuality in terms of the divisions of labour between men and women – that is, processes of sexuation, the production of sexual difference, and the assignment of sexual identities – the problem of the social becomes acute. In his notoriously negative depictions of female sexuality, in particular, we are left with a nagging question: is Freud being descriptive (of an existing state of affairs) or is he further debasing women by being theoretically prescriptive (of the 'inferiority' of female sexuality)?

Foucault's critique of Freudian psychoanalysis by way of what he calls the repressive hypothesis allows sexuality to be explored on explicitly social grounds. Unlike Freud, Foucault argues that sexuality is not the opposite but rather a vehicle and an effect of power. Foucault's intervention brings to a crux the question of differentiation pertaining to sexuality. Between Freud's and Foucault's analyses, we can discern two modes of differentiation and two methodologies of defining an object of enquiry: one consists in (showing) sexuality's infinite mutations, variations and transformations within itself; the other consists in (showing) sexuality's infinite linkages with factors outside it.

Feminism's encounter with Freud is interesting precisely on the difficult issue of the social, which feminist theorists approach in a variety of manners, from revolting against misogyny, to rescuing the object of woman in representational terms, to empowering her as equal to but uniquely different from man. At the same time, feminism's engagement with the social, with the mechanisms of differentiation, and with the hierarchies generated by such differentiations, predestines the necessary problematization – and deconstruction – of its own object (woman) as certain groups of women become socially dominant over other groups. If feminist theory once occupied the position of a special cultural identity that challenged the hegemony of patriarchal society, it finds itself increasingly charged by other cultural groups for failing to include them in its project.

Finally, one of the most important contributions made by Foucault in this context is, arguably, his attempt to place sexuality within the realm of bio-power. Much more work needs to be done in this connection (for an admirable example, see Stoler 1995). In light of Foucault's arguments about bio-power and bio-politics, feminist theory's social agenda to support women's access to and control over their reproductive destinies would likely need to be fundamentally reassessed. For, has not the rewriting of sexuality through female sexuality somehow become complicit with the expansion and explosion of bio-power, with ever more complex ways of exploiting the wretched of the earth?

References and Further Reading

Armstrong, N. (1987) *Desire and Domestic Fiction: A Political History of the Novel*. New York: Oxford University Press.

Brousse, M-H. (1992) Sexuality, trans. M. Whitford. In E. Wright (ed.), *Feminism and Psychoanalysis: A Critical Dictionary*, pp. 406–9. Oxford: Blackwell.

Butler, J. (1990) *Gender Trouble: Feminism and the Subversion of Identity*. New York: Routledge.

Chodorow, N. (1978) *The Reproduction of Mothering: Psychoanalysis and the Sociology of Gender*. Berkeley, CA: University of California Press.

Collins, P. Hill. (1990) *Black Feminist Thought: Knowledge, Consciousness and the Politics of Empowerment*. Boston, MA: Unwin Hyman.

Coward, R. (1983) *Patriarchal Precedents: Sexuality and Social Relations*. London: Routledge and Kegan Paul.

Firestone, S. (1979) *The Dialectic of Sex: The Case for Feminist Revolution*. London: The Women's Press.

Foucault, M. (1980) *The History of Sexuality, Vol. I: An Introduction*, trans. R. Hurley. New York: Vintage.

Freud, S. (1924) The passing of the oedipus-complex. In P. Rieff (ed.), *Sigmund Freud, Sexuality and the Psychology of Love*, pp. 176–82. New York: Collier, 1963.

— (1925) Some psychological consequences of the anatomical distinction between the sexes. In P. Rieff (ed.), *Sigmund Freud, Sexuality and the Psychology of Love*, pp. 183–93. New York: Collier, 1963.

— (1927) Fetishism. In P. Rieff (ed.), *Sigmund Freud, Sexuality and the Psychology of Love*, pp. 214–19. New York: Collier, 1963.

— (1931) Female sexuality. In P. Rieff (ed.), *Sigmund Freud, Sexuality and the Psychology of Love*, pp. 194–211. New York: Collier, 1963.

— (1938) Splitting of the ego in the defensive process. In P. Rieff (ed.), *Sigmund Freud, Sexuality and the Psychology of Love*, pp. 220–23. New York: Collier, 1963.

— (1975) *Three Essays on the Theory of Sexuality*, trans. J. Strachey. New York: Basic Books.

Friedan, B. (1983) *The Feminine Mystique*. Harmondsworth: Penguin.

Gallop, J. (1982) *Feminism and Psychoanalysis: The Daughter's Seduction*. London: Macmillan.

Greer, G. (1971) *The Female Eunuch*. New York: McGraw-Hill.

hooks, b. (1984) *Feminist Theory from Margin to Centre*. Boston, MA: South End Press.

— (1991) *Yearning: Race, Gender, and Cultural Politics*. London: Turnaround Press.

Humm, M. (ed.) (1992) *Modern Feminisms: Political, Literary, Cultural*. New York: Columbia University Press.

Irigaray, L. (1985) *This Sex Which is Not One*, trans. C. Porter and C. Burke. Ithaca, NY: Cornell University Press.

Jackson, S. and Scott, S. (1996) Sexual skirmishes and feminist factions: twenty-five years of debate on women and sexuality. In S. Jackson and S. Scott (eds), *Feminism and Sexuality: A Reader*, pp. 1–31. New York: Columbia University Press.

Kofman, S. (1985) *The Enigma of Woman: Woman in Freud's Writings*, trans. C. Porter. Ithaca, NY: Cornell University Press.

Laplanche, J. (1989) *New Foundations for Psychoanalysis*, trans. D. Macey. Oxford: Blackwell.

de Lauretis, T. (1987) *Technologies of Gender: Essays on Theory, Film, and Fiction*. Bloomington, IN: Indiana University Press.

Marcus, S. (1975) Introduction. In S. Freud, *Three Essays on the Theory of Sexuality*, pp. xix–xli. New York: Basic Books.

Millett, K. (1977) *Sexual Politics*. London: Virago.

Mitchell, J. (2001) Psychoanalysis and feminism at the millennium. In E. Bronfen and M. Kavka (eds), *Feminist Consequences: Theory for the New Century*, pp. 3–17. New York: Columbia University Press.

Moore, H. (1988) *Feminism and Anthropology*. Minneapolis, MN: University of Minnesota Press.

Rieff, P. (ed.) (1963) *Sigmund Freud, Sexuality and the Psychology of Love*. New York: Collier.

Rubin, G. (1984) Thinking sex: notes for a radical theory of the politics of sexuality. In C. S. Vance (ed.), *Pleasure and Danger: Exploring Female Sexuality*, pp. 267–319. London: Routledge and Kegan Paul.

Scott, J. (1988) Gender as a useful category of analysis. In J. Scott (ed.), *Gender and the Politics of History*, pp. 28–52. New York: Columbia University Press.

Spelman, E. V. (1988) *Inessential Woman: Problems of Exclusion in Feminist Thought*. Boston, MA: Beacon Press.

Spivak, G. Chakravorty (1987) French feminism in an international frame. In *In Other Worlds: Essays in Cultural Politics*, pp. 134–53. London: Methuen.

Stoler, A. L. (1995) *Race and the Education of Desire: Foucault's History of Sexuality and the Colonial Order of Things*. Durham, NC: Duke University Press.

Tompkins, J. (1985) *Sensational Designs: The Cultural Work of American Fiction 1790–1860*. New York: Oxford University Press.

Weeks, J. (1986) *Sexuality*. New York: Tavistock and Ellis Horwood in association with Methuen.

Wiegman, R. (1995) *American Anatomies: Theorizing Race and Gender*. Durham, NC: Duke University Press.

Williams, L. (1989) *Hard Core: Power, Pleasure, and the 'Frenzy of the Visible'*. Berkeley, CA: University of California Press (expanded paperback edn, 1999).

6
Subjects
Chris Weedon

The terms 'subject' and 'subjectivity' are fiercely contested in feminist philosophy, social and cultural theory. Competing theories of subjectivity, variously derived from humanism, Marxism, psychoanalysis, post-structuralism and post-colonial theory, have become central to feminist work in literary and cultural studies and they affect how critics view authorship and the production, reception and meaning of texts. Both women's status as subjects and their own subjectivity have long been at the core of feminism. As early as the 1700s, Mary Astell pleaded for women to be seen and treated as rational subjects equal to men. By the 1790s, Mary Wollstonecraft was arguing that femininity was a cultural construct, negatively affected by women's limited access to education and by the social mores of the day. Much feminism in the late nineteenth and early twentieth centuries focused on women's rights as individual subjects and on how the social meanings of sexual difference and femininity affected women's status as subjects.

Second-wave feminism, beginning in the late 1960s, made gendered subjectivity a central focus of feminist politics alongside the struggles for equal pay, education, an end to sexual double standards and the exploitation of women in all areas of life. The feminist rallying cry 'the personal is political' encouraged women to examine how their subjectivity had been shaped by patriarchal relations which determined aspirations, self-worth, the sexual division of labour and patriarchal gender roles. This was the agenda that consciousness-raising groups set themselves. At issue were the nature of woman and the meanings of femaleness and femininity. Competing theories were taken up and developed within liberal, socialist, radical and postmodern feminisms each of which had implications for how one might read cultural texts.

Some Questions of Definition

The term 'subject', like all signifiers, has plural meanings that are context specific. In the definitions of the *Oxford English Dictionary*, a subject is defined as 'a person subject to political rule' and as 'any member of a state other than the sovereign'. Being a political subject with rights and duties comparable to those of men has long been a key feminist issue. In addition to its political significance, the term 'subject' has grammatical meaning in relation to verbs and predicates which has become important in post-structuralist theories of subjectivity where identification with the position of the subject in language constitutes the subjectivity of the individual. In philosophy, the subject is variously defined as 'the thinking and feeling entity, the mind, the ego, the conscious self' (*Oxford English Dictionary*), all of which are important in feminist debates. Subjectivity, as it occurs in feminist theory, variously refers to the conscious thoughts and feelings of the individual, her sense of self and, in psychoanalytic and post-structuralist contexts, it encompasses unconscious meanings, wishes and desires. In addition to 'subject' and 'subjectivity', the terms 'experience' and 'identity' occur regularly in feminist discussion. In experienced-based theories of the subject, a woman's self is formed by her observation of and practical engagement with the world. Identity is used to refer to a woman's conscious sense of who she is.

Feminist discussions of subjectivity have long revolved around the question of whether femaleness and femininity have essential, unchanging characteristics grounded in the female body, psyche or experience or whether they are historically and socially specific. Nineteenth- and twentieth-century scientific and psychological theories of gender difference proposed a distinct female nature, different from that of men, with its origins in women's bodies. At best, women were seen as equal but different, more often as inferior to men. This way of seeing women carried over into the field of literature and the arts. For example, while women could become celebrated actresses portraying the works of men, they were not welcomed as writers for the theatre. In the broader field of literary production, where women writers were prolific, their work was seen as inferior to fiction and poetry by men.

Second-wave feminism set about challenging these long-established patriarchal theories of women's nature, transforming dominant understandings of politics and extending the political to personal life. Previously restricted to the public domains of government and trade unionism, politics was now understood to include areas often regarded as private: the family, sexuality, gender roles and subjectivity itself. Challenging the public/private divide, second-wave feminism re-instated the importance of the body as a site of political oppression and women's exploitation and oppression by patriarchy came to be seen as intrinsic to all elements of contemporary society.

The Liberal-humanist Subject

The various approaches to subjects and subjectivity within second-wave feminism revolve around the meaning of difference: is it natural or cultural? Liberal feminists hold to a view of the subject grounded in humanist ideas of the rational individual, governed by free will. Subjectivity is based on an understanding of reason as universal, transcending gender and race. Humanist ideas about subjectivity privilege the individual, consciousness and lived experience over theories which ground human nature either in biology or social structures. In liberal-humanist thought the subject and subjectivity are assumed to be unified and rational. Governed by reason and free will, the subject is given agency.

A controversial aspect of liberal-humanist ideas of the subject for feminists is that they are founded on a dualist mode of thinking according to which the mind is conceived as distinct from the body and superior to it. This binary opposition between mind and body is the basis on which liberal feminists argue for the non-relevance of gender and race to women's social status as subjects. Since the defining feature of the abstract individual of the liberal tradition is rational consciousness, neither female nor non-white bodies should be used as a basis for excluding any women, or men of colour, from universal human rights. Until well into the twentieth century women faced a continuing struggle for full subjectivity in its liberal guise and for the rights and duties that this subjecthood brought with it. For liberal feminists the key issues remain securing equality of opportunity in education and the workplace as well as equal rights to pay and sexual equality in all areas

113

of life. The liberal principle of individual free choice is paramount. In the realm of cultural production this means an end to discrimination against women in the production and reception of texts.

It was liberal feminism's exclusion of the body and failure to challenge the normative dualism that defines the essence of human beings solely in terms of rationality which helped motivate the development of alternative forms of feminism with different and often more complex understandings of women's subjectivity. Disregard for questions of the body and emotions was perhaps the central focus of critique since, it was argued, to ignore the social significance of bodies for both patriarchy and racism is to fail to address many aspects of women's lives and the structural power relations which continue to govern them. Many of the key areas in which patriarchal power is focused – for example, sexuality and procreation – have the body at their centre. Moreover, to insist on the primacy of reason is to fail to recognize the importance of other dimensions of subjectivity which throw light on women's complicity with patriarchal oppression. Alternative theories of subjectivity were thus developed within socialist, radical and post-structuralist feminisms.

The Subject in Socialist Feminism

Socialist feminists, for whom class is a fundamental dimension of patriarchal forms of oppression, look to Marxist theories of ideology and subjectivity in order better to theorize women's subjectivity. In Marxist theory, history is conceptualized as a series of modes of production (slave-owning, feudal, capitalist) governed by specific forms of class relations. Class is first and foremost an economic category, determined by whether or not an individual has access to control of the means of production, and class position is a crucial determinant in the formation of subjectivity. In modern capitalist states, the relations between capital and labour appear in the form of contracts between apparently free individual subjects – workers and employers. These relations of production are secured by ideology which is embedded in social and cultural practices and which shapes subjectivity.

Early second-wave socialist feminists came to see women as a 'class' oppressed by the structures of capitalist patriarchy. In this context the most readily available and accessible model of subjectivity was that of false consciousness. In Marxism false consciousness is an effect of capitalist ideology which prevents the working class from perceiving and challenging the exploitative nature of capitalist social relations. In its feminist articulations, false consciousness was seen as an effect of patriarchal social relations. For both Marxism and feminism, the key to undermining false consciousness is adequate theory. While for Marxists this meant a grasp of historical materialism, for socialist feminists Marxism needed to be supplemented by a theory of how patriarchy distorts women's consciousness in the interests of capitalism. Feminist cultural criticism that worked with notions of false consciousness sought to uncover how writing or visual media reproduced ideological assumptions about femininity and women's role in society.

Socialist feminists in the 1970s soon moved beyond false consciousness to develop more complex theories of subjects and subjectivity via appropriations of Althusser, Freud and Lacan. The Althusserian model of the subject, sketched in the essay 'On Ideology and Ideological State Apparatuses: Notes Towards an Investigation' (1971), was itself profoundly influenced by Lacanian psychoanalysis. The essay is concerned with what Althusser calls 'ideological state apparatuses' and the role they play in the reproduction of capitalist relations of production via the constitution of subjectivity. These apparatuses, which include, for example, education, religion, the political apparatus, trade unionism, the family, culture and the media, play a central role in the reproduction of a willing workforce and the other social strata that make up society. Unlike the police, the army and the courts – that is, the 'repressive state apparatus' – the ideological state apparatuses 'function massively and predominantly *by ideology'* (Althusser 1971: 158). Ideological state apparatuses operate by 'interpellating' (Althusser's term for the process) individuals as subjects within specific ideologies.

For Althusser, ideology is the precondition of both subjectivity and human sociality and it functions through the category of the 'Subject' which 'is constitutive of all ideology insofar as all ideology has the function (which defines it) of "constituting" concrete individuals as subjects' (1971: 160). Here Althusser draws on Lacan's theory of the mirror phase, a process based on misrecognition. The process of misrecognition enables subjects, interpellated within specific ideologies, to work independently to reproduce capitalist social relations without recourse to the repressive apparatuses. Feminist appropriations of Althusserian theory of the subject sought to make the role and functioning of ideology more complex by adding the dimension of gender to that of class. All cultural texts and practices had a role in this process which feminist criticism sought to identify. Ultimately, it was the inability of feminists to account adequately for all the manifold dimensions of patriarchal oppression in terms of their usefulness to the capitalist mode of production that led many socialist feminists to move beyond Marxism into psychoanalytic and post-structuralist theories of the subject and subjectivity.

The Subject of Radical and Revolutionary Feminisms

Even as socialist feminists were attempting to develop Marxist theory in ways useful for understanding patriarchy, other feminists were developing new forms of radical and revolutionary feminism which privileged what were seen as the universal structures of patriarchy as the primary determinant in women's oppression. Starting from early ideas of women as a 'class', radical feminists evoked a collective subject, women, and sought to identify the shared, global determinants on their lives. They proclaimed ideas of sisterhood, based on shared oppression, which was said to unite women everywhere. In doing so they reinstated the centrality of the body both in women's oppression and in women's subjectivity. Women's bodies, whether conceived in terms of their labour power, procreative power or sexuality, had, they argued, been appropriated by patriarchy in the interests of men. The political objective was to liberate women from patriarchal control of their minds, bodies and subjectivity.

Radical tendencies within second-wave feminism sought to reclaim and revalue the female body and to instate a liberated female subjectivity, undistorted by patriarchy. They often looked to ideas of essential femaleness grounded in women's capacity for motherhood, in female sexuality and in women's experience as the victims of patriarchal power relations (Daly 1979). Men and masculinity were conceived as oppressive, and many radical and ecological feminists argued that women were essentially different from men, possessing qualities which far exceeded those of their male counterparts. Being a woman meant possessing many of those qualities traditionally ascribed to women by patriarchal ideology: intuition, emotion, a caring nature and a greater affinity with the natural world (Griffin 1984). Ecological feminists, in particular, drew parallels between men's exploitative treatment of women and of the natural world. In these approaches to women's subjectivity, femaleness and femininity had authentic, natural characteristics distorted by patriarchy which women must reclaim from the distortions of patriarchy.

116

For many radical and revolutionary feminists in the 1970s, to reclaim women's subjectivity from patriarchy was to uncover a subject who would be lesbian in orientation (Rich 1984). On the one hand, this was the era of the political lesbian when sexual orientation was thought to be a matter of political choice and lesbianism marked a refusal to have anything to do with patriarchal sexuality. On the other, there were those who argued that women – when freed from patriarchal control of their minds and bodies – were naturally 'woman-identified'. Women occupied what Adrienne Rich termed a 'lesbian continuum' which might or might not involve actual sexual relations with other women. In her essay 'Compulsory Heterosexuality and Lesbian Existence', Rich argues that heterosexuality is an institution, imposed on women by patriarchy, that colonizes their minds and bodies. Rich moves beyond what she sees as a limiting definition of lesbianism as merely a form of sexual practice: 'As the term lesbian has been held to limiting, clinical associations in its patriarchal definition, female friendship and comradeship have been set apart from the erotic, thus limiting the erotic itself' (Rich 1984: 228). To make such a move is to open up the possibility of a female erotic, not defined or constrained by patriarchy.

Woman-centred Literary and Cultural Analysis

The influence of radical feminism gave rise to a wealth of woman-centred scholarship on history, society and culture which focused on recovering the history of women and lost or marginalized traditions of female cultural production. Woman-centred research takes woman as both subject and object of knowledge, privileging texts by women. Whereas it began as an undifferentiated project which claimed to take women as its subject, it soon diversified to encompasses work on the history and cultural production of a range of specific groups of women who found themselves excluded from the predominantly white, middle-class, heterosexual and Western focus of initial works of recovery: working-class women, lesbian women, black women, women of colour and Third World women.

In literary and cultural studies, women's writing became a key focus of feminist research. Much archival work was done to find and reclaim lost writers and to produce new editions of their work. Attention was paid to what women wrote about and how they wrote, that is, to an exploration of the difference of women's writing. Critics addressed the

117

questions of whether women artists and writers show evidence of a specifically female aesthetic and how should this could be theorized. The idea that women might have intrinsically different modes of expression led to a focus on three related questions:

1 Do women *naturally* have languages and modes of expression that are different from men?
2 Do women use different modes of representation for social and historical reasons?
3 How can women use existing language to contest and resist patriarchal forms of subjectivity?

In addressing these questions, feminist scholarship falls into two main groups which draw on different concepts of the female subject: first, work concerned with essentially female modes of expression which posits a fixed female subject as author and guarantee of meaning and, second, work concerned with historical specificity and social change where the female subject is socially and contextually produced. Writers in the second group tend to concentrate on historically specific forms of writing and visual representation by women and the constructions of femininity and female subjectivity that go with them. The first group seeks to identify essentially feminine modes of representation. They assume the existence of a naturally different female or feminine language. This language is often rooted in female biology or a female imaginary and it is thought to enable women to articulate an identity freed from patriarchal colonization. In feminist writing influenced by psychoanalysis, for example, this includes the work of Luce Irigaray (1985) on the feminine imaginary and Hélène Cixous's theory of feminine writing, *écriture féminine*, which offers a challenge to the patriarchal symbolic order (Cixous and Clément 1986). Black feminist critics have also been concerned with the question of black female aesthetics. Their approach has been predominantly historical. They have looked to the history of black women since slavery and the influence of transplanted and partially transformed West African cultural forms in their work. Here difference – positively valued and historically produced – is central.

Subjectivity, Psychoanalysis and Feminism

The need to theorize the acquisition of gendered subjectivity led feminists in the 1970s to turn to psychoanalysis. Freud, in his various models of subjectivity, radically decentred the humanist subject, suggesting that rational consciousness is but one dimension of subjectivity that is not master in its own house. The ego, far from being unified and in control, is, for Freud, a product of repression and constantly subject to the laws of the unconscious. Language is motivated by the desire for the power and control that unified sovereign subjectivity promises. If influential writers such as Kate Millett (1971) had rejected Freudian theory on account of its profoundly patriarchal assumptions, other feminists turned to psychoanalysis as a starting-point for more complex theorizations of gendered subjectivity.

The attraction of psychoanalysis lay in its rejection of any simple biological determinism. According to Freud, gender identity is not inborn but acquired through a process of psycho-sexual development and is always precarious because based on repression. Taking the male body as the desirable norm, Freud theorized female subjectivity as governed by lack and the penis envy to which this gave rise. Thus, for example, in his influential and controversial essay of 1925, 'Some Psychical Consequences of the Anatomical Distinction between the Sexes', Freud outlined the varied psychical effects of the absence of a penis in women, which included: the development of a masculinity complex; disavowal of difference, that is, refusal to 'accept the fact of being castrated'; the development of a sense of inferiority; 'the character-trait of *jealousy*'; 'a loosening of the girl's relation with her mother as a love object'; the rejection of masturbation and 'the elimination of clitoral sexuality' which is, for Freud, by definition a 'masculine activity' (1925: 32–3). In attempting to reclaim Freud, feminists sought to re-read the meaning of the penis. For example, Juliet Mitchell in her influential study, *Psychoanalysis and Feminism* (1975), reads it as a symbol of the powerful position occupied by men under patriarchy.

Feminist Object Relations Theory

While the unconscious and the precarious nature of subjectivity were to become central to most feminist appropriations of psychoanalysis, American feminism produced theories of subjectivity based on the development of the ego within the patriarchal nuclear family. Drawing on the work of the American school of object relations theory, Dorothy Dinnerstein (1976), Nancy Chodorow (1978), Jane Flax (1980), Carol Gilligan (1982) and Jessica Benjamin (1988) sought to identify distinctive aspects of femininity, located in the pre-Oedipal and the

119

mother–daughter bond, that gave rise to more fluid ego boundaries and relationally structured identities in women. Perhaps the most influential feminist object relations theorist, Nancy Chodorow, privileges the pre-Oedipal relationship of the infant with the mother and examines the subsequent differential development of girls and boys (Chodorow 1978). Assuming the identification of girls with their mothers, Chodorow argues that daughters develop a stronger bond with the mother than sons. As a result, girls experience a lesser degree of individuation than boys and thus develop more flexible ego boundaries which create the psychological preconditions for the reproduction of women's subordination to men. In the socialization of boys, mothers encourage them to differentiate themselves from their mother enabling them to develop a masculine identity based on their father or father substitute. However, the boy's relation with his father is qualitatively different from the girl's relationship with her mother; it is what Chodorow terms a 'positional identification' brought about by the fact that the father generally plays a lesser role in child care. The difference between personal and positional identification is crucial to Chodorow's account of the differential constitution of femininity and masculinity. In the difficult process of differentiation from his mother, the boy both represses his feminine dimensions and learns to devalue femininity.

Chodorow's theory places the acquisition of gendered subjectivity firmly within the realm of the social, opening up the possibility, at least in theory, of changing gender norms through the transformation of the social organization of family life. Men's greater personal involvement in child care could, for example, transform the psycho-sexual structures governing masculinity and femininity and create the preconditions for the abolition of the sexual division of labour.

Lacanian Models of the Subject

The re-reading of Freud by the French psychoanalyst, Jacques Lacan, has been particularly significant in the development of feminist appropriations of psychoanalytic theory. Privileging one particular emphasis in Freud's work which can be found in texts such as *The Interpretation of Dreams* (1900) and *The Psychopathology of Everyday Life* (1901), Lacan argues that the symbolic order of language, law and meaning is founded on the unconscious which is itself structured like a language. Subjectivity is an effect of language, governed by repression and the realm of the unconscious. The intentional subject is a subject based on a structure of misrecognition, laid down in the mirror stage during which the infant misrecognizes itself as a whole, unified and autonomous being (Lacan 1977). Prior to the mirror stage, the child's pre-Oedipal experience of its body is of being in fragments, lacking a definite sense of a unified self, separate from the world around it. This is compounded by the lack of control over the satisfaction of needs and desire which becomes the motivating force behind language. Governed by a fragmented sense of self and unable to distinguish itself as a separate entity, the infant overcomes its fragmentation by identifying with an 'other', an external mirror image. This process of misrecognition becomes the basis for all future identifications by the subject of itself as autonomous and sovereign once it has entered the symbolic order of language.

In this model, subjectivity is divided and its sense of unity is based on misrecognition. The subject's lack of fullness, lack of self-presence and inability to control meaning motivates language. The process of assuming subjectivity invests the individual with a temporary sense of control and of sovereignty which evokes a 'metaphysics of presence' (Derrida 1973) in which s/he becomes the source of the meaning s/he speaks and language appears to be the expression of meaning fixed by the speaking subject. Yet, in Lacanian-based theories, the speaker is never the author of the language within which s/he takes up a position. Language pre-exists and produces subjectivity and meaning. The subject 'I' is an effect of language and marks the points at which the individual is inserted into the symbolic order of language, law and meaning.

Lacanian theory posits a symbolic order which is patriarchal and which, from a feminist perspective, represses or marginalizes anything other than a male-defined feminine. In the Lacanian order women are essentially objects of exchange in what Luce Irigaray describes as a 'homosexual economy' (1985: 171–2). They are placed both symbolically and socially in relation to men and denied access to what Irigaray calls the 'maternal feminine', a feminine which would allow women to realize their difference from men in positive terms. In post-Lacanian feminist theory, attempts to rethink female subjectivity and the symbolic order in non-patriarchal terms focus on the body of the mother and the maternal feminine.

Under patriarchy the maternal feminine is repressed by the processes of psycho-sexual development which enable the individual to enter the symbolic order as gendered subject. It is further marginalized by the structures of the patriarchal symbolic order which govern the law, culture and sociality. It is exiled from the symbolic order which women inhabit as lack via a patriarchally defined feminine subjectivity. Post-Lacanian feminists have identified the unconscious as the site of the repressed feminine which has its roots in the pre-Oedipal relationship with the mother. Julia Kristeva (1986a) calls this realm the semiotic and in her theory it plays an integral part in the language of the symbolic order. Similarly, Luce Irigaray suggests that, although repressed, the maternal feminine continues to play a role in women's lives. Woman's own desire, 'a desire of which she is not aware, moreover, at least not explicitly . . . [is] one whose force and continuity are capable of nurturing repeatedly and at length all the masquerades of femininity that are expected of her' (1985: 27). As such the maternal feminine is the potential source for resistance and change.

Kristeva rewrites aspects of Lacanian theory concerning the constitution of the individual as gendered subject in the symbolic order, reinstating the importance of the feminine and conceiving of the subject as *in process*. In her work, the Lacanian concepts of the imaginary and the symbolic become two distinct processes, the semiotic and the symbolic, both of which constitute signification. Here the body of the mother plays a central structuring role mediating symbolic law and ordering the semiotic chora where the 'subject is both generated and negated, the place where his [*or her*] unity succumbs before the process of charges and stases that produce him [*or her*] (1986a: 95; my italics). This theory of the subject in process is one of the most influential aspects of Kristeva's work. Challenging the notion of subjectivity as a fixed, humanist essence, Kristeva sees it as constituted in language and subject both to the laws of the symbolic order and the unconscious. Language, with both its masculine (symbolic) and feminine (semiotic) dimensions, becomes a potential site for revolutionary change, an idea most fully developed in Kristeva's *Revolution in Poetic Language* (1984).

Like other theorists whose work has been influenced by post-structuralism, Kristeva emphasizes both process and plurality and resists replacing existing master discourses with alternative grand narratives, be they socialist, feminist or otherwise. In her writing she seeks to disrupt monolithic power structures. Thus, for example, in 'A New Type of Intellectual: The Dissident' (1986b) she develops a critique of the possibility of collective political action of the type widely advocated by feminists, since, as she sees it, the politically active intellectual is caught up in the very logic of power that she seeks to undermine. To speak is to inhabit the kind of discourse permitted by the patriarchal law of the symbolic order: 'A woman never participates as such in the consensual law of politics and society but, like a slave promoted to the rank of master, she gains admission to it only if she becomes man's homologous equal' (1986b: 296). Yet if the feminine is different from and a challenge to existing symbolic language and meaning, it can only be thought within the symbolic which requires radical transformation of its patriarchal structuring of difference and subjectivity.

The transformation of the symbolic order is an idea taken up rather differently by Irigaray whose work is marked by a critique of Western philosophy, rationality and the legacy of the Enlightenment, all of which are seen to be founded on the exclusion of the maternal feminine. Like Kristeva, Irigaray writes in the context of the psychoanalytic and post-structuralist questioning of the primacy of conscious rational subjectivity. Her diagnosis of the existing symbolic order as one in which reason, the subject and language are male, leads her to argue that the West is in fact a monosexual culture in which women are seen as a lesser form of men. In her influential text *This Sex Which is Not One* (1985), she argues that women's difference is not represented by the patriarchal symbolic order, nor are women's interests served by the laws and language of this order. In order to be heard within the symbolic, women have to speak like men. The plural, non-patriarchal feminine remains outside the symbolic order since, under patriarchy, there is only masculine representation.

According to Irigaray, Western thought is founded on the exclusion of the maternal feminine. This exclusion is the precondition for language and subjectivity. Patriarchal reason denies feminine otherness, reconstituting it as male-defined. This results in the denial of subjectivity to non-male-defined women. A subjectivity founded on the maternal feminine would, she argues, enable women to step outside patriarchal definitions of the feminine and become subjects in their own right. Whereas the unconscious in Freud and Lacan lays claim to fixed universal status, for Irigaray, its form and content is a product of history. Thus, however patriarchal the symbolic order may be in Lacan, it is open to change. The question is how this change might be brought about. For Irigaray, the key to change is the development of a female imaginary. This can only be achieved under patriarchy in a fragmented way, as what she terms the excess that is realized in margins of the dominant culture. The move towards a female imaginary would also entail the transformation of the symbolic which would enable women to assume subjectivity in their own right. For Irigaray, the male-to-male, homosexual economy, in which women become mere objects of exchange with no subjectivity of their own, reduces relations between women to a status equivalent to male homosexuality. They are based on masquerade and motivated by penis envy. The masquerade of 'acting like a man' is, for Irigaray, a serious distortion of the potentially transformative role of relations between women which are the precondition for women's escape from the male-defined feminine imposed by patriarchy.

Masquerade as a way of theorizing gender has been taken up and developed particularly in the work of feminist queer theorists. In this approach, subjects are constituted in often ritualized performance. In some respects this work looks back to an essay by the psychoanalyst Joan Riviere published in the *International Journal of Psychoanalysis* in 1929. The essay, entitled 'Womanliness as a Masquerade', was written at a time when social attitudes to gender included the assumption that intellectual pursuits were 'masculine'. While the essay reaffirms Freud's notion that masculinity in women is related to penis envy, it is interesting for present-day theory for the general conclusion that it draws about femininity, namely that it *is* masquerade and that there is no essential or true female subjectivity.

Riviere argues that women who are active in male spheres 'put on a mask of womanliness to avert anxiety and retribution feared from men' (1986: 35). Her argument is based on case studies of women who are successful, particularly, in intellectual pursuits. In one case a successful professional woman activist, with a good marriage and proficient skills as a housewife, suffers anxiety after every public lecture and seeks reassurance in the form of sexual advances from father figures, although 'often not persons whose judgement on performance would in reality carry much weight' (1986: 36). Riviere comments that 'the extraordinary incongruity of this attitude with her highly impersonal and objective attitude during her intellectual performance, which it succeeded so rapidly in time, was a problem' (1986: 36). It pointed to anxiety over the transgression of femininity. Riviere concludes that 'Womanliness therefore could be assumed and worn as a mask, both to hide the possession of masculinity and to avert the reprisals expected if she was found to possess it' (1986: 38). She refuses to draw a distinction between 'genuine womanliness' and the 'masquerade', arguing that they are the same thing (1986: 38).

Post-structuralist Approaches to the Subject

A major site for the contestation of humanist models of language, the subject and subjectivity has been linguistics. Two theorists, in particular, have been influential in the formation of alternative post-structuralist ideas of subjectivity: the French linguist Emile Benveniste and the Swiss linguist Ferdinand de Saussure. Benveniste takes as his starting-point Descartes's famous premise *cogito, ergo sum* ('I think, therefore I am') according to which the act of thinking points to the existence of the subject as the source and guarantee of meaning. Benveniste challenges and complicates this model by insisting on the distinction between the subject of the enunciation and the subject of the enounced (a distinction that is also important in Lacanian psychoanalysis). According to Benveniste, the subject who says 'I think' should be held distinct from the subject whose existence is assumed in the act of thought. Thus the subject can no longer be seen as unified and the source of knowledge. It is the very structure of language that points to the implausibility of such models of subjectivity.

Saussure, a structuralist linguist who is seen as the founder of semiology (the study of signs), does not directly address the question of subjectivity, yet his theory has had profound implications for post-structuralist theories of language and subjectivity. In a series of lectures, published posthumously in 1916 as *Cours de linguistique générale* (*A Course in General Linguistics*, 1974), Saussure breaks with reflective theories of language according to which words label meanings that already exist in the external world. Saussure suggests that language, far from being a set of labels for already given meanings, is a system of differences. Individual signs in the language system are composed of sound or written signifiers and signifieds (meanings). The link between signifiers and signifieds is a conventional effect of language which has no external guarantee in the world of referents beyond language. In post-structuralist appropriations of this theory, it is read as having profound implications for how subjectivity is conceived. Since there is no longer fixed meaning in the world which the knowing subject perceives, the subject no longer controls meaning but is an effect of it.

The terms subject and subjectivity are central to post-structuralist theories as developed in the work of Derrida, Lacan and Foucault. Derrida has been important both for his critique of the self-present, humanist subject and his deconstructive approach to language. Lacan has been important for his theory of the split subject laid down in the mirror phase, for his conception of the symbolic order and for feminist appropriations of his work. Foucault is best known for his theory of subjectivity, discourse and power (Foucault 1980).

In post-structuralist models, language constitutes rather than reflects or expresses the meaning of society, experience and the individual's sense of self. Post-structuralism takes issue with the Cartesian subject, theorizing subjectivity (defined as our conscious and unconscious sense of self, our emotions and desires) as an effect of language. Rational consciousness is only one dimension of subjectivity. It is in the process of using language – whether as thought or speech – that we take up positions as speaking and thinking subjects. Language exists in the form of many competing and often contradictory discourses. For Foucault, discourses constitute our subjectivity for us through material practices that shape bodies as much as minds and involve relations of power. Some discourses, and the subject positions and modes of subjectivity that they constitute, have more power than others. For Foucault, power is a relationship, not something held by a particular group, though as a relationship which inheres in discourses (economic, media, familial and so on) it serves particular interests and functions through the discursive constitution of embodied subjects. Discourses produce subjects within relations of power which potentially or actually involve resistance. The subject positions and modes of embodied subjectivity constituted for the individual within particular discourses allow for different degrees and types of agency both compliant and resistant. The discursive field, which produces meanings and subjectivities, is not homogeneous; rather, it includes discourses and discursive practices which may be contradictory and conflicting and which create the space for new forms of knowledge and practice. While there is no place beyond discourses and the power relations that govern them, resistance and change are possible from within.

Subjectivity as Embodied Performance

A range of post-structuralist feminist theorists, influenced to different degrees by Foucault, Lacan and Irigaray, have sought to theorize the body and its relation to difference and gendered subjectivity. Examples of this development can be found in the work of Jane Gallop, Elizabeth Grosz and Judith Butler. Gallop (1988), for example, challenges the culture–biology opposition as a restatement of traditionally oppressive binary oppositions in which women are placed outside culture. She argues that it is not biology itself but rather the ideological use made of biology that is oppressive. Like Irigaray, she uses psychoanalysis to develop a different understanding of corporeality in which the female body is a site of resistance to patriarchy, but one which is refused representation by the patriarchal symbolic order. Grosz (1994, 1995) is critical of analyses of the representation of bodies which disregard their materiality, thereby enabling the dominance of reason. Grosz concludes that 'sexual differences, like those of class and race, *are* bodily differences' and that 'the body must be reconceived, not in opposition to culture but as its pre-eminent object' (1995: 32). Moreover, a new language is needed to articulate women's specific difference.

In the work of Judith Butler (1990, 1993) an attempt is made to theorize the ways in which 'bodies are materialized as sexed' in the light of a critique of heterosexism. Starting from the premise 'that bodies only appear, only endure, only live within the productive constraints of certain highly gendered regulatory schemas' (1993: xi), Butler suggests a way of theorizing these schemas through the concept of performativity. In other words, gendered subjectivity is acquired through the repeated performance by the individual of discourses of gender. Butler argues that 'there is no gender identity behind the expressions of gender . . . Identity is performatively constituted by the very "expressions" that are said to be its results' (1990: 24–5). This 'performativity must be understood not as a singular or deliberate "act", but, rather, as the reiterative and citational practice by which discourse produces the effects that it names' (1993: 2).

Butler's appropriation of Foucauldian theory involves a decentred notion of the subject and of agency:

> [T]he agency denoted by the performativity of 'sex' will be directly counter to any notion of a voluntarist subject who exists quite apart from the regulatory norms which she/he opposes. The paradox of subjectivation (*assujetissement*) is precisely that the subject who would resist such norms is itself enabled, if not produced, by such norms. Although this constitutive constraint does not foreclose the possibility of agency, it does locate agency as a reiterative or rearticulatory practice, immanent to power, and not a relation of external opposition to power. (1993: 15)

Here Butler, following Foucault, locates resistance and the possibilities of transformation within the discursive field which produces both existing power relations and forms of subjectivity. While this model does not allow for either fully autonomous subjectivity or a space beyond power from which to act, agency can transform aspects of material discursive practices and the power relations inherent in them.

In bringing Foucault to bear on feminist and queer theory, Butler challenges those distinctions between sex and gender which see sex as the biological basis on which gender is inscribed. Sex is as much a matter of culture as is gender and the very distinction between the two is 'the effect of the apparatus of cultural construction designated by gender' (1990: 7).

The challenge to the subject has become a site of opposition to post-structuralist feminism. Nancy Hartsock, for example, asks:

> Why is it that just at the moment when so many of us who have been silenced begin to demand the right to name ourselves, to act as subjects rather than objects of history, that just then the concept of subjecthood becomes problematic? Just when we are forming our own theories about the world, uncertainty emerges about whether the world can be theorized. Just when we are talking about the changes we want, ideas of progress and the possibility of systematically and rationally organizing human society become dubious and suspect? (1990: 164)

These objections rest on the assumption that to question the Western Enlightenment category of the subject is to undermine the possibility of subjecthood. They are shared by many feminist writers who advocate the importance of identity politics and they highlight a fundamental question in post-structuralism about the relationship between a deconstructive approach to subjectivity and the question of agency. While it is the case that some versions of post-structuralism show little interest in the question of lived subjectivity or agency, this has not been the case in many feminist appropriations of Foucault, Derrida, Irigaray and Kristeva. Here agency is seen as discursively produced in the social interactions between culturally produced, contradictory subjects. Subjecthood is necessary to communication and action in the world and social change requires visions of how societies could be different which are often produced by marginalized groups. Subjectivity and agency are not, however, fixed prior to language and the discursive practices in which individuals assume subjectivity.

The Death of the Author

A key implication of post-structuralism for feminist textual analysis concerns authorship, particularly – to use the title of Roland Barthes's essay – 'The Death of the Author' (1977). In this essay Barthes argues that the process of writing displaces the author's control over meaning and the author becomes an instance of writing, just as the subject 'I' is an instance of saying 'I'. In his autobiography, *Roland Barthes by Roland Barthes* (1991), Barthes attempts to explore this idea textually by dispersing his subjectivity across a range of voices.

The post-structuralist critique of the subject as unified author of meaning has profound implications for both feminist works of recovery and feminist criticism that attempts to identify a female aesthetic grounded in unproblematized assumptions about authorship. Foucault identifies the conception and role of the author in much mainstream criticism as follows:

> The author explains the presence of certain events within a text, as well as their transformations, distortions and their various modifications (and this through an author's biography or by reference to his [*or her*] particular point of view, in the analysis of his [*or her*] social preferences and his [*or her*] position within a class [*or gender*] or by delineating his [*or her*] fundamental objectives). (1977: 128; my italics)

These assumptions about authorship have been put into question both by the post-structuralist critique of the rational, self-knowing subject as the author of meaning and the Derridean theory of meaning as plural, unfixed and subject to constant deferral. In 'The Ear of the Other' (1988), for example, Derrida offers a deconstructive approach to autobiography which problematizes the idea of author as referent external to the text. In the light of this critique, biography and autobiography become textual constructs and feminist cultural analysis can no longer assume that the author intentionally controls the meaning of a text or that she or her life explains it. From this perspective, the author herself becomes a social and textual construct, which Foucault calls the 'author function': 'the function of an author is to characterize the existence, circulation and operation of certain discourses within a society' (Foucault 1977: 124). Authorship does not have a singular function but varies between discourses, as can be seen in the different types of feminist criticism that have developed since the late 1960s. Among them are attempts to develop a middle position between essentialism and deconstruction that does not see the author as purely textual nor as a simple referent. Liz Stanley (1992), for example, argues for an author that is not a unique self but rather a fictive truth, shaped by the relationship between cultural conventions and the material reality of the life in question.

Chris Weedon

The Eurocentric Subject and the Third World Woman

The debates about the subject and subjectivity outlined above, both within feminism and beyond, have been conducted within the broad framework of Western philosophical assumptions about the rational subject which they have sometimes affirmed and often challenged. A fundamental critique of aspects of this whole debate has come from Third World feminists who do not accept the primacy of Western traditions of thought which they see as eurocentric in their assumptions. Both liberal and radical feminisms in the West have been criticized for their assumptions about women, the subject and women's subjectivity and their claims to speak on behalf of all women (Spivak 1988; Mohanty 1991; Narayan 1997). Critics argue that this often involves a denial of the specificity of the varied positions of women in the Third World, a reading of them through a Western gaze that victimizes them and denies them agency, and an 'othering' that renders them silent. Post-structuralist theory, with its socially constructed and historically specific subject, has been taken up as a more useful analytical tool than other Western models by some Third World women. The liberal-humanist subject, however, remains important in the struggle for human rights.

References and Further Reading

Althusser, L. (1971) On ideology and ideological state apparatuses: notes towards an investigation. In *Lenin and Philosophy*, trans. Ben Brewster, pp. 121–73. London: New Left Books.
Barthes, R. (1977) The death of the author. In *Image–Music–Text*, trans. S. Heath, pp. 142–8. London: Fontana (first published 1968).
— (1991) *Roland Barthes by Roland Barthes*. Berkeley, CA: University of California Press.
Benjamin, J. (1988) *The Bonds of Love: Psychoanalysis, Feminism and Problems of Domination*. New York: Pantheon.
Benveniste, E. (1971) *Problems in General Linguistics*. Miami: University of Miami Press.
Butler, J. (1990) *Gender Trouble: Feminism and the Subversion of Identity*. New York: Routledge.
— (1993) *Bodies that Matter: On the Discursive Limits of 'Sex'*. New York: Routledge.
Chodorow, N. (1978) *The Reproduction of Mothering: Psychoanalysis and the Sociology of Gender*. Berkeley, CA: University of California Press.

Cixous, H. and Clément, C. (1986) *The Newly Born Woman*, trans. B. Wing. Minneapolis, MN: University of Minnesota Press (first published as *La jeune née* 1975).

Daly, M. (1979) *Gyn/Ecology*. London: The Women's Press.

Derrida, J. (1973) *Speech and Phenomena*, trans. D. Allison. Evanston, IL: Northwestern University Press.

— (1988) *The Ear of the Other: Otobiography, Transference, Translation Texts and Discussions with Jacques Derrida*, ed. C. McDonald. Lincoln: University of Nebraska Press.

Dinnerstein, D. (1976) *The Mermaid and the Minotaur: Sexual Arrangements and Human Malaise*. New York: Harper Row.

Flax, J. (1980) Mother–daughter relationships: psychodynamics, politics, and philosophy. In H. Eisenstein and A. Jardine (eds), *The Future of Difference*, pp. 20–40. New Brunswick, NJ: Rutgers University Press.

Foucault, M. (1977) What is an author? In D. F. Bouchard (ed.), *Language, Counter-memory, Practice: Selected Essays and Interviews*, pp. 113–38. Ithaca, NY: Cornell University Press.

— (1980) *The History of Sexuality, Vol. I: An Introduction*, trans. R. Hurley. Harmondsworth: Penguin.

Freud, S. (1900) *The Interpretation of Dreams*. Harmondsworth: Penguin, 1976.

— (1901) *The Psychopathology of Everyday Life*. Harmondsworth: Penguin, 1975.

— (1925) Some psychical consequences of the anatomical distinction between the sexes. In J. Strouse (ed.), *Women and Analysis: Dialogues on Psychoanalytic Views of Femininity*, pp. 27–38. New York: Dell, 1975.

Gallop, J. (1988) *Thinking Through the Body*. New York: Columbia University Press.

Gilligan, C. (1982) *In a Different Voice: Women's Conceptions of the Self and Morality*. Cambridge, MA: Harvard University Press.

Griffin, S. (1984) *Woman and Nature: The Roaring Inside Her*. London: The Women's Press.

Grosz, E. (1994) *Volatile Bodies: Towards a Corporeal Feminism*. Bloomington, IN: Indiana University Press.

— (1995) *Space, Time and Perversion*. New York: Routledge.

Hartsock, N. (1990) Foucault on power: a theory for women? In L. Nicholson (ed.), *Feminism/Postmodernism*, pp. 157–75. New York: Routledge.

Irigaray, L. (1985) *This Sex Which is Not One*, trans. C. Porter and C. Burke. Ithaca, NY: Cornell University Press.

Kristeva, J. (1984) *Revolution in Poetic Language*, trans. M. Waller. New York: Columbia University Press.

— (1986a) *The Kristeva Reader*, ed. Toril Moi. Oxford: Blackwell.

— (1986b) A new type of intellectual: the dissident. In *The Kristeva Reader*, ed. Toril Moi, pp. 292–300. Oxford: Blackwell.

Lacan, Jacques (1977) The mirror phase as formative of the function of the I. In *Écrits*, trans. A. Sheridan. London: Tavistock.

Millett, K. (1971) *Sexual Politics*. London: Rupert Hart-Davies.

Mitchell, J. (1975) *Psychoanalysis and Feminism*. Harmondsworth: Penguin.

Mohanty, C. T. (1991) Under western eyes: feminist scholarship and colonial discourses. In C. T. Mohanty, A. Russo and L. Torres (eds), *Third World Women and the Politics of Feminism*, pp. 51–80. Bloomington, IN: Indiana University Press.

Narayan, U. (1997) *Dislocating Cultures: Identities, Traditions and Third World Feminism*. New York: Routledge.

Rich, A. (1984) Compulsory heterosexuality and lesbian existence. In A. Snitow, C. Stansell and S. Thompson (eds), *Desire: The Politics of Sexuality*, pp. 212–41. London: Virago.

Riviere, J. (1986) Womanliness as a masquerade. In V. Burgin, J. Donald and C. Kaplan (eds), *Formations of Fantasy*, pp. 35–61. London: Methuen (first published 1929).

Saussure, F. de (1974) *A Course in General Linguistics*. London: Fontana (first published as *Cours de linguistique générale* in 1916).

Spivak, G. Chakravorty (1988) Can the subaltern speak? In C. Nelson and L. Grossberg (eds), *Marxism and the Interpretation of Culture*, pp. 271–313. London: Macmillan.

Stanley, L. (1992) *The Auto/biographical I: The Theory and Practice of Feminist Auto/biography*. Manchester: Manchester University Press.

7

Language

Sara Mills

Dominance or Difference?

In this chapter, I examine the complex relationship between gender and language, so that the common-sense nature of each of the terms and their relation to each other are troubled. I also analyse the way in which stereotypes of femininity play a major role in informing our beliefs about women, men and language and I suggest how we can consider the relationship between language, gender and other variables more productively.

Feminist language research in the 1970s focused on the question of male dominance and female deference in conversation (Lakoff, R. 1975; Spender 1980). It criticized both the social system, which it viewed as patriarchal and as forcing women to speak in a subservient way, and also individual males who were seen to violate the rights of their female interlocutors. Robin Lakoff's polemical analysis of what she considered to be female language patterns was one of the first feminist linguistic analyses that made a clear connection between the social and political oppression of women as a group and their linguistic behaviour. This subordinated status was displayed in the language patterns which she describes as 'talking like a lady' (Lakoff, R. 1975: 10). She gives, as an example, two statements which, she suggests, characterize the difference between women's subordinated language and men's dominant language:

1   Oh dear, you've put the peanut butter in the refrigerator again.
2   Shit, you've put the peanut butter in the refrigerator again. (Lakoff, R. 1975: 10)

The first, Lakoff asserts, is women's language and the second is men's language; this distinction is made primarily on the basis of perceptions that (1) is more polite than (2) because of the 'softer' expletive which mitigates the force of the utterance and therefore is less of a challenge to the interlocutor's face. Lakoff makes a connection between seemingly stronger expletives and stronger positions in relation to power. As she argues:

> [I]f someone is allowed to show emotions, and consequently does, others may well view him as a real individual in his own right, as they could not if he never showed emotion . . . the behaviour a woman learns as 'correct' prevents her from being taken seriously as an individual, and further is considered 'correct' and necessary for a woman precisely because society does not consider her seriously as an individual. (1975: 11)

Thus, within the work of early feminist linguistic theorists like Lakoff, femininity and femaleness are elided and powerlessness is seen as a major factor in the constitution of femininity.

Lakoff and also Dale Spender (1980) argued that women's language style was characterized by the use of elements which signalled subordination. These features consist of: mitigating statements, hedges, tag questions and elements which signal indirectness, tentativeness, diffidence and hesitation. In contrast to this, male speech was characterized as direct, forceful and confident, using features such as interruption. As a polemic, this early feminist research was extremely important, since it challenged the assumption that certain males were sanctioned to act linguistically in ways which could disadvantage women and it made those linguistic acts seem less 'natural' or 'common sense'. Many women also questioned their own deferent linguistic behaviour as 'natural', as just part of being a woman. Thus, this consciousness-raising research, which was very widely read by people outside academic circles, made a major impact on many women, forcing them to reflect on language use as an indicator of power relations and, indeed, encouraging them to make metalinguistic comments on language use. Perhaps one of the most important aspects of this work is that women felt that they could comment on an interruption by a male interlocutor and, rather than dismissing such behaviour as solely due to the particular chauvinism of that individual, they could relate it to wider societal structures which made available to men privileged positions which it did not provide for women.

However, critics have noted that this type of analysis seemed to be focused on the stereotypical language usage of a very small group of women, that is middle-class, white Anglo-Americans. It was not based on the examination of any data but rather on personal anecdotes which seemed to uphold a stereotype of submissive women, without any counter-examples being considered. In the 1980s and 1990s many feminist linguists, such as Deborah Tannen and Jennifer Coates, rather than analysing dominance, as such, since it was clear that the nature of power relations between women and men were being fundamentally changed at this time, turned to an analysis of the socially constructed differences between women and men's language. They saw these differences as akin to dialects spoken by different groups, rather than seeing them as indicating dominant and dominated groups (Coates and Cameron 1988; Tannen 1991; Coates 1996). This female and male linguistic difference, Tannen argued, developed because women and men are largely socialized in single-sex groups where they develop different language preferences and styles. Women and men have different aims in conversation which lead to breakdowns in communication or misunderstandings. This is because women are concerned, in the main, to establish rapport between members of a group and to ensure that conversations go smoothly (rapport talk), whilst men are concerned to establish their place in the pecking order and use the production of information as a tool to move up the hierarchy (report talk). Although Tannen claims that men can also do 'rapport talk' and women may do 'report talk', she argues that generally such is not the case. Moreover, she believes, use of these diametrically opposed styles is what leads to misunderstanding between men and women.

This focus on difference has been widely criticized by Troemel-Ploetz (1998) and Cameron (1998a) for its reactionary political stance and for its failure to acknowledge the inequality that persists in many relations between women and men. Furthermore, Troemel-Ploetz argues that women and men do not, in fact, grow up in homogeneous and separate linguistic communities but actually spend a great deal of their time in mixed-sex environments, whether in the school, the home or at work. What Troemel-Ploetz is most concerned about is the erasure of the factor of power difference in the analysis of interaction between women and men and although she, as other feminist linguists, does not wish to characterize all women's language as subordinate, the effacing of power from feminist analysis is a worrying trend. Cameron goes further than Troemel-Ploetz in critiquing Tannen's work in particular, since she argues that 'power relations are *constitutive* of gender differentiation as we know it' (Cameron 1998a: 438).

The positive aspects of the 'difference' type of feminist analysis is that it generally calls for a re-evaluation of the styles that are associated with women; thus, Coates (1996) argues that we should revalue what has been classified as gossip and cooperative strategies/rapport talk, in general, and Holmes (1995) argues that what she claims are women's styles of politeness are, in fact, more productive for debating issues than masculine styles of speech. This re-evaluation of women's speech styles has made an important impact in certain areas. For example, in the evaluation of oral performance in secondary schools in Britain, it is generally those aspects of speech associated with 'feminine' speech styles (rapport/cooperative talk) that are most highly evaluated. This would include supportive comments, minimal responses, concern for others in the group and so on. This is a significant shift from other ways of assessing oral performance which are more concerned to evaluate aspects such as rhetorical skill and confidence. Cameron has suggested that the view that women are more cooperative than men, that their language is concerned with establishing rapport rather than with dispensing information, based as it is on stereotypes of women's speech, has also led to the widespread employment of women in the communications industries, such as call-centres (Cameron 2000; Walsh 2001). The so-called 'feminine' skills of communication, however, are not highly valued and workers in call-centres generally receive low salaries.

Thus, whilst this process of re-evaluation of what has been considered to characterize women's speech has been of great value, it cannot make up for the fact that, in general, the shift in the way that women really speak and are evaluated when they speak has been in the direction of women adopting wholesale what are seen to be masculine ways of speaking in the public sphere (and sometimes being negatively evaluated for using this type of language). Thus, assertiveness-training programmes developed for women in the 1980s and 1990s often focused on changing language styles so that, instead of displaying deference and indecision, the woman speaker projects a confident image of herself through her language. There are obviously problems with the type of language advocated for women in some of these programmes since it relies on a number of systematized routines, as Cameron has noted, but as a strategic intervention which enables women in the public and private spheres to assert themselves linguistically, it is clear that such training has a particular value (Cameron 1995). However, the assumption behind these programmes is that masculine speech is the appropriate form of expression in the public sphere.

Despite the value of this early focus on women and men as different speech communities, Bing and Bergvall (1996: 18) remark:

> It would be ironic if *feminists* interested in language and gender inadvertently reinforced gender polarisation and the myths of essential female–male difference. By accepting a biological female–male dichotomy, and by emphasising language which reflects the two categories, linguists may be reinforcing biological essentialism, even if they emphasise that language, like gender, is learned behaviour.

Cameron (1998a) argues that the focus on difference-versus-dominance approaches to the analysis of gender and language, with the dominance analysts being criticized for problems with their analytical procedures and difference theorists being critiqued for their political shortcomings, leads to a lack of real debate, since theorists have tended simply to set up camps and defend their own position. She suggests instead that dominance theorists should develop more thorough analytical procedures and focus, not on a simplistic notion of dominance as such, but on conflict. Thus, rather than assuming that breakdown in communication between males and females occurs because participants do not understand the intentions of the other speaker, she argues that perhaps it is not misunderstanding which is at issue but conflicts of interest, conflict over increasingly diminishing resources and power, or conflict over perceptions of the position from which the speaker is/or should be speaking.

Within language and gender research, there has been a wealth of research working within either the difference or dominance frame of reference which has aimed empirically to demonstrate that women or men use a particular feature. The one striking overall assessment which can be made of nearly all of the research done on language and gender differences is that the research is contradictory. The hypotheses are generally very clear, usually taking the format: 'in what way does women's use of such and such an element differ from men's use of the same element, when other variables are kept constant?' However, whichever research article seems to prove that women's language use does differ from men's language use – for example, that women interrupt less, that they are interrupted by men more, that they use tag questions more, or directness less – there is generally another piece of research which proves that, in fact, in other contexts, men use that same element to the same extent or more than women. For example, Chan (1992) discusses studies which contradict each other: Zimmerman and West's study in 1975 suggests that men interrupt women more, whereas Smith-Lovin and Brody's study in 1989 suggests a slightly more complex situation where men interrupt the most but women interrupt men just as much as they interrupt other women; Chan's research seems to find that there are no differences whatever which can be wholly attributed to sex difference alone (1992). This is not to say that empirical research should be completely discarded but it does suggest that other factors than gender may be playing a role in the way that people behave linguistically. It also suggests that language and gender research must move beyond the binary oppositions of male and female.

Beyond Binary Thinking

In recent years, gender has begun to be theorized in more productive ways, moving away from a reliance on binary oppositions and global statements about the behaviour of all men and all women to more nuanced and mitigated statements about certain groups of women or men in particular circumstances who reaffirm, negotiate with and challenge the parameters of permissible or socially sanctioned behaviour (Coates and Cameron 1988; Bing and Bergvall 1996; Johnson and Meinhof 1997). Rather than seeing gender as a possession or a set of behaviours which is imposed upon the individual by society, as many essentialist theorists have done so far (see, for an overview, Fuss 1989; Butler 1990), many feminists have now moved to a position where they view gender as something that is enacted or performed and, thus, as a potential site of struggle over perceived restrictions in roles (Crawford 1995).

Coates and Cameron's edited collection *Women in their Speech Communities* (1988) was one of the first attempts to analyse the specificity of the production of speech by particular groups of women, in particular communities, at specific locations and times. For example, the language of older white women in a Welsh mining community and that of British black women in Dudley are analysed. Other researchers started to turn to this type of 'punctual' analysis – one which is focused on a specific linguistic community at a particular moment – because the generalizations that had characterized feminist analyses of language in the past were considered untenable. The essays in the collection edited by Johnson and Meinhof (1997) on masculinity and language also signalled a change in the focus of language and gender research so as to analyse women's and men's speech production in relation to each other, rather than in isolation.

Bing and Bergvall's essay, 'The Question of Questions: Beyond Binary Thinking', and the collection which they edited, *Rethinking Language and Gender Research* (1996), of which the essay is a part, is an important move forward in language and gender research. It draws together a number of discontents which had been surfacing in the research literature and which centred precisely on the difficulty of making generalizations about women as a homogeneous group. They call for a questioning of the clear-cut divisions that researchers had made between the linguistic behaviour of males and females, arguing that the boundaries between women and men are fuzzy. They draw an analogy with racial categorization and argue that, particularly in American society, it has become possible to acknowledge the diversity within 'racial' groups and, at the same time, it has become difficult to assert that there is a clear-cut biological basis for the category 'race' at all. They also draw attention to the variety of sexual identifications that cross the binary divide between female and male, such as hermaphrodite, trans-sexual, transgendered individual, androgyne, and they thus assert: 'the simple belief in "only two" is not an experiential given but a normative social construction' (1996: 2).

In relation to the previous research in language and gender difference, they feel it necessary to ask the following questions:

1   Why are the questions that strengthen the female–male dichotomy so frequently asked, while those that explore other types of variation evoke much less interest?
2   How much of this apparent dichotomy is imposed by the questions themselves? (1996: 3)

Their argument revolves around a dilemma within linguistic research: if you analyse data asking the question 'In what ways do men and women speak differently?', then that is all that you will find. Similarities between the linguistic behaviour of women and men will be ignored in the interpretation of the results and differences among women in the study will be minimized. Bing and Bergvall note that few features if any can be said exclusively to index gender.

They also criticize the way in which statistical averages are used to generalize about women's linguistic behaviour, arguing that 'one obvious oversimplification is that of using statistical differences between two groups as proof that all members of one group have characteristics shared by no members of the other group (and vice versa)' (1996: 15). The problem for them is not with difference as such but with gender polarization. As Bem argues:

> [I]t is thus not simply that women and men are seen to be different but that this male–female difference is superimposed on so many aspects of the social world that a cultural connection is thereby forged between sex and virtually every other aspect of human experience, including modes of dress and social roles and even ways of expressing emotion and experiencing sexual desire. (Bem, 1993: 2, cited in Bing and Bergvall, 1996: 16)

Research in gay and lesbian language and in Queer theory has made gender and language researchers question the seeming stability of the term 'woman' or 'women'. Although early research in this area seemed to be trying to prove the difference between lesbian and straight women, more recent work has questioned the assumption that one can generalize about the linguistic behaviour of lesbians (Wittig 1992). In the essays in the collection *Queerly Phrased*, edited by Livia and Hall (1997), the very notion of a lesbian language is at once posited and held under erasure. Furthermore, in collections of essays, such as Leap's (1995) *Beyond the Lavender Lexicon*, the notion of a gay language or a lesbian language has been subject to careful scrutiny. Queen (1997) asserts that such notions of a lesbian language are a strategic construction by lesbians drawing on ironized stereotypes of straight feminine and masculine speech together with stereotypes of gay and lesbian speech. There has been an interrogation within Queer linguistics research of the existence of a set of linguistic signs which could be interpreted as signalling to others that one is gay or lesbian (gaydar) and also of the existence of a set of linguistic patterns used uniformly by gay and lesbian people. This challenging of the existence of a gay and lesbian 'language' has also led to a questioning, in language and gender research as a whole, of a similar sort of difficulty in the analysis of women's language and men's language in general and heterosexual women's and men's language specifically.

Many feminist theorists have turned to Judith Butler's work on gender and performativity. She argues that gender is a repeated performance of a range of behaviours associated with a particular sex: 'The materiality of sex is constructed through a ritualised repetition of norms' (Butler 1993: x). Thus, gender is not a given, a possession, but rather a process which one constantly has to perform. Crawford (1995) suggests that, rather than seeing gender as a noun, we should see it as a verb. The stress on performance does not suggest for Butler that one can be anything that one decides to be:

> if I were to argue that genders are performative, that could mean that I thought that one woke in the morning, perused the closet . . . donned that gender for the day, and then restored the garment to its place at night. Such a willful and instrumental subject, one who decides *on* its gender, is clearly not its gender from the start and fails to realise that its existence is already decided *by* gender. (Butler 1993: x)

However, perhaps, both the disjuncture between the 'self' and this gendered identity and the process model of gender identity developed by Butler are positive, productive elements which can be drawn on by those who aim to resist the way that women are generally encouraged to behave according to restricting gender norms. For, as Butler suggests, 'That this reiteration is necessary is a sign that materialization is never quite complete, that bodies never quite comply with the norms by which their materialization is impelled' (1993: 2). This model draws attention to the instability and fragility of gender difference and suggests that, although the individual is not entirely in control of the production of her/his gender identity, there is the possibility of some measure of agency, resistance and hence change.

This important questioning of the notion of gender does not mean that the category of gender is empty or that there is no such thing as gender difference. As Freed (1996) has argued, for example, the fact that the category 'woman' is not one which is coherent does not prevent people classifying you as a woman and making judgements about you on the basis of that classification. What has to be reconsidered is the simple binary division between female and male and also the way in which gender operates at the level of a system which has been institutionalized rather than as something which functions solely at the level of the individual.

141

Gender and Other Variables

As I mentioned earlier, one of the problems with early feminist research was that it often focused exclusively on the language usage of white, middle-class women and then made generalizations about all women. Many studies have since shown that groups of women behave in different ways depending on variables of context, class, race, education and so on. In some ways it could be argued that gender itself in isolation does not exist, but only gender as it is raced and classed (McClintock 1995).

Perhaps one of the most difficult variables to analyse for feminist linguists has been power. As I stated above, essential to feminist thinking about gender difference has been a particular model of power relations. Much early feminist thought presupposed that there was a more or less simple correlation between males and power and females and powerlessness. Whilst Foucault's formulation of power relations has been influential in this area and many feminists have urged that we need to think through power relations in a more complex manner to avoid such a simple binary opposition, there remains little work which details how to analyse seemingly endemic structural inequalities and at the same time individual transgressions and contestations of those inequalities (Foucault 1978; Diamond and Quinby, 1988). If we consider Foucault's notion of the dispersion of power – that is, the spread of power throughout a society, rather than the holding and withholding of power by individuals – we can move towards an analysis which will see language as an arena whereby power may be appropriated, rather than societal roles being clearly mapped out for participants with language reflecting those roles (Mills 1997). In engaging in interaction, we are also at the same time mapping out for ourselves a position in relation to the power relations within the group and within society as a whole. This is what I call 'interactional power', to differentiate it from those roles which may or may not be delineated for us by our relation to institutions, by our class position and so on (Mills, forthcoming c.). It is possible for someone who has been allocated a fairly powerless position institutionally to accrue to themselves, however temporarily, a great deal of interactional power by their verbal dexterity, their confidence, their linguistic directness (those more stereotypically masculine/competitive/report talk attributes) as well as through the use of the seemingly more feminine linguistic display of care, concern and sympathy, which we noted earlier as cooperative strategies or rapport talk.

It may be argued that since power and masculinity are correlated (however complex that relation is), interactional power can only be achieved by using masculinist strategies in speech; however, one's position within a speech community may be advanced by using a range of different strategies, including the seemingly more cooperative/rapport ones, depending on the community of practice. Competitive talk is not always valued by communities of practice which may code it as too direct, bullying and overbearing. For example, Adams (1992) remarks on the way in which the discourse norms associated with a particular context – in the case of her research of the broadcast television interview – play a major role in determining what styles and strategies are viewed positively. Her article questions the notion that an aggressive style in debate (a stereotypically masculine style) is necessarily seen as most effective by participants and observers alike; she notes that those candidates who observe the rules in terms of turn-taking, what she terms 'accruing power by obeying rules', in short, behaving in a more feminine way, also bring benefits to themselves in terms of how they are judged by the audience (1992: 9). A further example of the complexity of the relation between power and gender can be seen if we consider that a female secretary in a university department may be able to use a fairly direct form of address to those in positions of power over her because of her access to information upon which they depend; conversely, lecturers who need this information and who are reliant on her, will need to employ politeness forms which would normally signal deference (Mills 1996). Thus, positions of power mapped out by one's role in an institution may not relate directly to the interactional power that one may gain through one's access to information, one's verbal skill or one's display of care and concern for other group members.

O'Barr and Atkins, in their paper ' "Women's Language" or "Powerless Language"?' (1980) argue that there is a confusion between the language features that are determined by gender and those determined by a position of lesser power. Through their analysis of the type of speech that is produced by female and male witnesses in a court-room setting, they suggest that powerless men seem to produce speech which exhibits the same features that, as Lakoff (1975) argued, women in general use. They also show that not all women use to the same degree the features that Lakoff stated were indicative of women's language. Thus, they argue that 'so-called "women's language" is neither characteristic of all women nor limited only to women' (O'Barr and Atkins 1980: 102). All of the women using relatively few of the 'powerless', 'feminine' features described by Lakoff were of high status, primarily middle class and professional, and the men who used high numbers of seemingly 'feminine' features were low status, mainly working class, and were unused to court-room protocol.

O'Barr and Atkins's article suggests that power relations play a more important role than gender as such in the production of certain types of language; however, even this statement must be treated with some caution. It is clear that power, however we define it, is part of the way in which gender as a whole is defined; therefore power cannot be entirely disentangled from gender. Nor can power be considered in isolation from other variables such as race, gender and class. As O'Barr and Atkins (1980: 111) remark, 'It could well be that to speak like the powerless is not only typical of women because of the all-too-frequent powerless social position of many American women, but is also part of the cultural meaning of speaking "like a woman". Gender meanings draw on other social meanings.' Thus, what we need to move away from is the sense that all women are powerless and all men are powerful and we also need to question the way in which we define power. Cameron argues that a more useful approach to the analysis of power and gender focuses less on unchanging, unequal relations between men and women and more on the resources available to speakers in particular positions to draw upon strategically. I quote at some length to illustrate how her approach:

> treats the structural fact of gender hierarchy not as something that must *inevitably* show up in surface features of discourse, but as something that participants in any particular conversation may, or may not, treat as relevant to the interpretation of utterances. Furthermore, it insists that where assumptions about gender and power are relevant, they take a form that is context-specific and connected to local forms of social relations: however well founded they may be in structural political terms, global assumptions of male dominance and female subordination are too vague to generate specific inferences in particular contexts, and thus insufficient for the purposes of discourse analysis. (Cameron 1998a: 452)

Strong Women Speakers

As I have argued so far, for many feminist linguists, female speech is powerless speech but it is clear that, because of changes in the way in which many women perceive themselves and the employment of women in the public sphere, this is no longer the case for all women

(Mills 1998, 1999). Thus, there are a great number of women whose linguistic behaviour does not appear deferent and submissive, and indeed submissive speech by women is now generally derided. On the radio and television, we frequently hear women ministers, presenters and spokespersons speaking confidently and competently, using direct forceful language (for example, Condoleezza Rice, Claire Short, Sara Cox). Rather than seeing the speech of women in positions of power within the public sphere simply as an appropriation of masculine speech, however, Webster (1990) has shown that the speech of former British Prime Minister Margaret Thatcher mixes features associated with the stereotypical language of both women and men, sometimes within a single utterance. Thus, for a complex range of motivations and judgements made about her audience and her own standing, Thatcher seemed to be drawing strategically on both masculine and feminine speech elements. Because of the planning that goes into the production of the speech of the Prime Minister in Britain, as Fairclough (2000) has shown in his analysis of the speech of Tony Blair, it is fair to assume that the production of Thatcher's speech cannot be assumed to be typical of other women's speech. However, this mixing of feminine and masculine styles has been noted of women's speech in other public spheres (Walsh 2001).

We might also consider here the linguistic behaviour of Ann Widdecombe, a British Conservative member of parliament, who seems to have developed a particular speech style for herself which is masculine, combative, direct, and forceful. The British press variously describe her and her speech style in both positive and negative terms, either as too forceful or as sufficiently statesman-like. Since Thatcher, it does seem to be the case that it is slightly more acceptable for women in Britain to be forceful verbally in public life and this is in large measure because of the number of women in high-profile public positions, in the media, business and politics, and because those women who are in these positions have adopted, more or less wholesale, the speech styles of the men who still dominate in these public positions. However, Walsh has noted that those women who have entered into male-dominated professions and have either changed the dominant ethos of the organization through their language use, or who have simply adopted the masculinist norms, have all been very negatively viewed by others within that domain (Walsh 2001). For example, the presenter Anne Robinson's aggressive, humiliating language behaviour on the television quiz show, *The Weakest Link*, has been widely criticized in the British media, whereas aggressive tactics by male presenters such as Jeremy Paxman, have not been criticized in such personal and damning terms (Braid 2001).

What we can draw from Webster's (1990) analysis is the fact that the situation in which the speech is to be produced and the expectations of that role by both the speaker and her/his assessments of audience are crucial in determining the type of speech which will be produced in a situation. Gender may be a factor in the assessment of the appropriate language for a particular situation but there is nothing to suggest that it is the only factor that is salient, nor that it is a simple variable to analyse. Thus, if the situation is one in which masculine speech norms have been prevalent over a period of time, it is likely that women who work within the environment will adopt those norms if they are to be seen as professional. Alice Freed suggests in her analysis of the types of speech that are produced by close friends that certain styles of interaction are coded by the participants as feminine or masculine; thus, because of the context and the perception that intimate conversation is feminine, the males in her study seemed to be behaving like stereotypical females (Freed 1996). This does not seem entirely satisfactory since it is clear that some males would perhaps see this as an occasion to mark their speech in hyper-masculine ways. Furthermore, not all linguistic communities would code this type of relaxed conversation as feminine. However, the notion of gendered domains is important here in being able to describe the way in which gender impacts at the level of the setting and context, rather than simply at the level of the individuals involved in the interaction.

It is clear that context, broadly speaking, is important in terms of the production of speech and in the assessment of what types of language and speech styles are appropriate. Take, as an example, McElhinny's (1998) analysis of the language of women police officers in Pittsburgh where she demonstrates the ways in which stereotypical masculine practices have been adopted in order for these women to appear professional and credible to the wider community. She suggests that:

> institutions are . . . often gendered in ways that delimit who can properly participate in them and/or how such participation can take place . . . Workplaces are gendered both by the numerical predominance of one sex within them and by the cultural interpretation of given types of work which, in conjunction with cultural norms and interpretations of gender, dictate who is understood as best suited for different sorts of employment. (McElhinny 1998: 309)

Because police officers often have to deal with trauma on a daily basis, they generally adopt a particular range of linguistic expressions and stance indicative of affectless behaviour. Women police officers, thus, have to adopt this style of response to situations which seem to many prototypically masculine but:

> because masculinity is not referentially (or directly) marked by behaviours and attitudes but is indexically linked to them (in mediated non-exclusive probabilistic ways) female police officers can interpret behaviours that are normatively or frequently understood as masculine . . . as simply 'the way we need to act to do our job' in a professional way. (McElhinny 1998: 322)

Where many studies falter in the analysis of the relation of power and gender is in the assumption that there is a simple relation between them. Although there are clearly generalizations which can be made about the types of language that will be produced when there are differences of power and status, there is no simple link. If we assume that asymmetrical power relations determine different styles of linguistic performance and that gender difference is enmeshed with power difference in intricate ways, then we should be led to believe that women speaking to men will produce different styles of language from men speaking to men or women speaking to women. This assumption would only hold if there were a clear correlation between gender and power, which there is not.

Gendered Stereotypes

Stereotypes can be usefully thought of as hypothesized scripts or scenarios (sets of features, roles and possible narrative sequences) which take some extreme aspect of an out-group's perceived behaviour and generalize that feature to the group as a whole. In this sense, the stereotype is based on a feature or set of behaviours which does occur within that community but the stereotype is one noticeable form of behaviour which is afforded prototypical status, backgrounding all of the other, more common, and in a sense the more defining, forms of behaviour (Lakoff G. 1987; Mills 1995). This notion of the prototype is important, since stereotypes often inform judgements made about male and female linguistic behaviour and set for us, often unconscious, notions of what is appropriate. The notion of the prototype allows us to acknowledge that stereotypes of femininity which circulate within British or US society now may have originally been fairly accurate descriptions of certain aspects of white, middle-class women's behaviour within a certain era, but that even within that class, at that time, there were other forms of behaviour which conflicted and challenged them.

To give an example of stereotypical assumptions, let us consider the analysis of an anecdote by Cameron (1998a). A friend's father, when he sits down to eat his dinner, always asks his wife: 'Is there any ketchup, Vera?' and this indirect question is interpreted by all as a request by the father for his wife, Vera, to fetch him the ketchup. Conservative stereotypes of the role of wives in relation to husbands, which here are shared by both the man and the woman, lead to both interpreting this as a request for the ketchup to be brought rather than as a request for information about the availability of ketchup.

Stereotypes of gender, as I have shown above, are very powerful in our assessment of language both as interactants and as analysts. However, that is not to say that there is only one stereotype of women's behaviour. If we consider the stereotypes of the nagging woman and the gossip, these can be seen to coexist with other stereotypes of women, for example, the stereotype of the over-polite woman who is concerned only with the surface appearances or the stereotype of the woman who is silenced by a dominating male partner. As Liladhar (2001) has shown in her work on femininity, feminist analyses of femininity have changed markedly over the past ten years, so that femininity is no longer seen as a set of negative behaviours which keep women in a subordinate position; now feminists are beginning to see the potential play within the behaviours which have traditionally been seen as denoting powerlessness, particularly when they are used ironically as in the demeanour of the Soap Queen and the Drag Queen (see also Whelehan 2000).

Cameron (1998a: 445) asserts: 'Information about who someone is and what position she or he speaks from is relevant to the assessment of probable intentions. Since gender is a highly salient social category, it is reasonable to assume that participants in conversation both can and sometimes (perhaps often) do make assumptions in relation to it.' But, as Cameron makes clear in her work, whilst we may be making assumptions about gender in our interactions, stereotypes of gender may not be shared. Indeed, conflict in conversation often occurs when assumptions about gender are not shared by participants and this is not a conflict that is restricted to a struggle between women and men as the dominance theorists assumed but can be a conflict between women, where some hold a more traditional view of what women should do and how women should speak, whilst others aim to challenge that stereotype.

We should not assume that stereotypes are permanent, unchanging discursive structures. They tend to change fairly rapidly, leaving certain aspects behind in stereotypes which are anachronistic but which can still be called upon by certain speakers. Discursive structures, by their very nature, because they are constantly being challenged and used in new ways by speakers and texts, are in a process of continuing change; yet, there are certain of these structures which seem as if they are more stable because they have endured over a relatively long period of time (Mills 1995). I would argue, however, that it is perhaps the community's view of these seemingly more stable stereotypes and discursive structures in general which changes and thus colours a speaker's use of them as part of his/her linguistic resources or assumptions. Stereotypes of gender, developed in the society as a whole or in the specific communities of practice, inform individual choice of linguistic style, strategy and content, either in terms of reaffirming or challenging those stereotypes in relation to one's own linguistic production or in relation to someone's assumptions about one's own gendered identity.

Conclusion

In Western societies, women's position has changed enormously in recent years, perhaps not as much as many of us would have liked but nevertheless we have to recognize that great changes have taken place in terms of women's participation within the public sphere. These changes have been largely due to campaigns by feminists on a wide range of issues (equal pay, equal employment rights, birth control, sexual harassment) which have become part of the common-sense expectations of many women, who would not necessarily identify as feminists, and have been instrumental in major changes in the number of women in employment. However, whilst these changes have meant that there has been a radical shift in women's expectations and their actual linguistic behaviour, there has been a slight tendency for anachronistic discourses of femininity to remain in circulation. Thus, whilst women are either using the same sort of language as men within the public sphere or are modifying the type of language which is thought appropriate in masculinist work environments, there are stereotypes of femininity which classify their language use as aberrant. Thus, the problem posed for language and gender research is how to deal with the great variety of positions which it is possible for women and men to take up in language, whilst at the same time being aware of the force of stereotypes in terms of the way in which linguistic behaviour is judged. We are no longer able to make generalizations about the way women or men speak, nor are we able to assume that stereotypes work in the same way in all situations. Instead, we need a complex, finely tuned system of analysis which is sensitive to the specificities of the context and which can describe the way in which gender operates as a system.

Acknowledgement

Some material from sections of this chapter will appear in a revised form in a chapter in *Rethinking Gender and Politeness* (Cambridge University Press, forthcoming).

References and Further Reading

Adams, K. (1992) Accruing power on debate floors. In K. Hall, M. Bucholtz and B. Moonwomon (eds), *Locating Power: Proceedings of the Second Berkeley Women and Language Conference*, Vol. I, pp. 1–11. Berkeley, CA: University of California Press.

Bergvall, V., Bing, J. and Freed, A. (eds) (1996) *Rethinking Language and Gender Research: Theory and Practice*. London: Longman.

Bing, J. and Bergvall, V. (1996) The question of questions: beyond binary thinking. In V. Bergvall, J. Bing and A. Freed (eds), *Rethinking Language and Gender Research: Theory and Practice*, pp. 1–30. London: Longman.

Braid, M. (2001) Cruella of prime time. *Independent*, 10 March: 5.

Butler, J. (1990) *Gender Trouble: Feminism and the Subversion of Identity*. New York: Routledge.

— (1993) *Bodies that Matter: On the Discursive Limits of 'Sex'*. New York: Routledge.

— (1997) *Excitable Speech: A Politics of the Performative*. New York: Routledge.

Cameron, D. (1995) *Verbal Hygiene*. London: Routledge.

— (1997) Performing gender identity: young men's talk and the construction of heterosexual masculinity. In S. Johnson and U. Meinhoff (eds), *Language and Masculinity*, pp. 86–107. Oxford: Blackwell.

— (1998a) 'Is there any ketchup, Vera?': gender, power and pragmatics. *Discourse and Society*, 9 (4): 435–55.

— (ed.) (1998b) *The Feminist Critique of Language: A Reader*, 2nd edn. London: Routledge.

— (2000) *Good to Talk? Living and Working in a Communication Culture*. London: Sage.

Chan. G. (1992) Gender, roles and power in dyadic conversation. In K. Hall, M. Bucholtz and B. Moonwomon (eds), *Locating Power: Proceedings of the Second Berkeley Women and Language Conference*, Vol. I, pp. 57–67. Berkeley, CA: University of California Press.

Coates, J. (1996) *Woman Talk*. Oxford: Blackwell.

— and Cameron, D. (eds) (1988) *Women in their Speech Communities*. London: Longman.

Crawford, M. (1995) *Talking Difference: On Gender and Language*. London: Sage.

Diamond, I. and Quinby, L. (eds) (1988) *Feminism and Foucault: Reflections on Resistance*. Boston, MA: Northeastern University Press.

Fairclough, N. (2000) *New Labour, New Language*. London: Routledge.

Foucault, M. (1978) *The History of Sexuality Vol. 1: An Introduction*, trans. R. Hurley. Harmondsworth: Penguin (first published 1976).

Freed, A. (1996) Language and gender research in an experimental setting. In V. Bergvall, J. Bing and A. Freed (eds), *Rethinking Language and Gender Research: Theory and Practice*, pp. 54–76. London: Longman.

— (1999) Communities of practice and pregnant women: is there a connection? *Language in Society*, 28 (2): 257–71.

Fuss, D. (1989) *Essentially Speaking: Feminism, Nature and Difference*. London: Routledge.

Hall, K., Bucholtz, M. and Moonwomon, B. (eds) (1992) *Locating Power: Proceedings of the Second Berkeley Women and Language Conference*, Vol. I. Berkeley, CA: University of California.

Holmes, J. (1995) *Women, Men and Politeness*. London: Longman.

Johnson, S. and Meinhof, U. (eds) (1997) *Language and Masculinity*. Oxford: Blackwell.

Lakoff, G. (1987) *Women, Fire, and Dangerous Things: What Categories Reveal about the Mind*. Chicago: Chicago University Press.

Lakoff, R. (1975) *Language and Woman's Place*. New York: Harper and Row.

Leap, W. (ed.) (1995) *Beyond the Lavender Lexicon: Authenticity, Imagination and Appropriation in Lesbian and Gay Languages*. Luxembourg: Gordon and Breach.

Liladhar, J. (2001) Making, remaking and unmaking feminity. Unpublished PhD thesis, Sheffield Hallam University.

Livia, A. and Hall, K. (eds) (1997) *Queerly Phrased: Language, Gender and Sexuality*. London: Routledge.

McClintock, A. (1995) *Imperial Leather: Race, Gender and Sexuality in the Imperial Contest*. London: Routledge.

McElhinny, B. (1998) 'I don't smile much anymore': affect, gender and the discourse of Pittsburgh police officers. In J. Coates (ed.), *Language and Gender: A Reader*, pp. 309–27. Oxford: Blackwell.

Mills, S. (1995) *Feminist Stylistics*. London: Routledge.

— (1996) Powerful talk. Unpublished discussion paper, Loughborough University, Loughborough.

— (1997) *Discourse*. London: Routledge.

— (1998) Post-feminist text analysis. *Language and Literature*, 7 (3): 235–53.

— (1999) Discourse competence: or how to theorise strong women speakers. In C. Hendricks and K. Oliver (eds), *Language and Liberation: Feminism, Philosophy and Language*, pp. 81–9. Albany, NY: State University of New York Press.

— (forthcoming a) Rethinking politeness, impoliteness and gender identity. In J. Sunderland and L. Litoselliti (eds), *Discourse and Gender Identity*. Amsterdam: John Benjamins.

— (forthcoming b) *Beyond Sexism*. Cambridge: Cambridge University Press.

— (forthcoming c) *Rethinking Gender and Politeness*. Cambridge: Cambridge University Press.

O'Barr, W. and Atkins, B. (1980) 'Women's language' or 'powerless language'? In S. McConnell-Ginet, R. Borker and N. Furman (eds), *Women and Language in Literature and Society*, pp. 93–110. New York: Praeger.

Queen, R. (1997) I don't speak Spritch: locating lesbian language. In A. Livia and K. Hall (eds), *Queerly Phrased: Language, Gender and Sexuality*, pp. 233–42. London: Routledge.

Skeggs, B. (1997) *Formations of Class and Gender: Becoming Respectable*. London: Sage.

Spender, D. (1980) *Man Made Language*. London: Routledge.

Tannen, D. (1991) *You Just Don't Understand: Women and Men in Conversation*. London: Virago.

Troemel-Ploetz, S. (1998) Selling the apolitical. In J. Coates (ed.), *Language and Gender: A Reader*, pp. 446–58. Oxford: Blackwell.

Walsh, C. (2001) *Gender and Discourse: Language and Power in Politics, the Church and Organisations*. Harlow: Longman/Pearson.

Webster, W. (1990) *Not a Man to Match Her*. London: Women's Press.

Whelehan, I. (2000) *Overloaded: Popular Culture and the Future of Feminism*. London: Women's Press.

Wittig, M. (1992) *The Straight Mind and Other Essays*. Hemel Hempstead: Harvester Wheatsheaf.

8

Literature

Mary Eagleton

Writing in 1986 an essay on feminist literary theory, Toril Moi concludes:

> [W]e can now define as *female*, writing by women, bearing in mind that this label does not say anything at all about the nature of that writing; as *feminist*, writing which takes a discernible anti-patriarchal and anti-sexist position; and as *feminine*, writing which seems to be marginalised (repressed, silenced) by the ruling social/linguistic order. (1986: 220)

These definitions, useful and widely held as they have been, nevertheless generate queries, as Moi herself realizes. For instance, she points out that we cannot presume that female writing – that is, writing by women – is necessarily feminist writing. There are many women writers who are indifferent to feminism and, indeed, a tradition of women making lucrative livings out of castigating other women. Occasionally, despite all evidence to the contrary, the most unlikely women are reclaimed for feminism. Thus, at a conference at the University of London in 1999, Elaine Showalter commended Natasha Walter's description of former British Prime Minister Margaret Thatcher as an unsung heroine of British feminism and was greeted by a chorus of gasps from her audience. One quakes at the thought of the collected works of Margaret Thatcher featuring on future bibliographies of British feminism alongside Mary Wollstonecraft, the Pankhursts and Virginia Woolf. This would be evidence of a dangerous conflation between 'female' – or, rather, 'powerful female' – and 'feminist'. Or, to pose the problem in another way, we need to be clear about the distinction between 'being' a feminist (which Margaret Thatcher clearly is not) and producing feminist effects (which Margaret Thatcher – inadvertently, unwillingly and in restricted areas – has done). Lest anyone misinterprets me here, I have to add immediately that she has also produced lots of anti-feminist effects, not to mention lots of policies that adversely impacted on women. At the same time, it is still the case that simply to name women is interpreted, often rightly, as a feminist gesture. Thus to set up a series of lectures on women explorers or to advertise an evening of women's music will, like it or not, be framed by the discourse of feminism which, over the past thirty years, has made such events possible.

If female writing and feminist writing are not synonymous, can we say that women are irrelevant to feminist writing and, to continue the bibliography example, that a course on feminist literary studies could consist entirely of male-authored texts? Theoretically such a course could exist since men have made a sufficient number of significant interventions; politically it should not and to design such a course would give a distorted impression of feminist literary history. The presence of women and the experience of women are necessary to feminism, however difficult the terms 'presence', 'women' and 'experience' might be, and it is an indication of how far the postmodernist turn has gone that one has to make that obvious point. Tania Modleski provocatively entitled her 1991 book *Feminism Without Women* and explained that the title 'can mean the triumph either of a male feminist perspective that excludes women or of a feminist anti-essentialism so radical that every use of the term "woman", however "provisionally" it is adopted, is disallowed' (1991: 15). The frequent use of inverted commas in such debates indicates the degree to which previously self-evident categories have become ironized or contested. At the same time, it has been vital to ask the questions 'which women?' and 'whose experience?' Feminism, constructed on the narrow basis of white, middle-class, Anglophone or Francophone women, has, at best, a partial relation to other women; at worst, it actively oppresses them. It is not just that black women did not feature much during the late 1970s and into the 1980s in either the theory or practice of feminism, but that the actual conceptualizing of femininity and feminism is intrinsically deficient if black women and women of colour are excluded. Moreover, constructions of femininity, black or white, are internally diverse and variously constituted in different cultures and periods. Just as there is no single femininity so there is no single white femininity or single black femininity.

The links between female and feminine, and feminist and feminine, are as uncertain as those between female and feminist. In *Thinking About Women* (1968), Mary Ellmann lists the following as common feminine stereotypes: 'formlessness, passivity, instability, confinement, piety, materiality, spirituality, irrationality, compliancy' and names 'two incorrigible figures: the shrew and the witch' (1968: 55). Similarly, in *The Newly Born Woman*, Hélène Cixous notes as the feminine side of a series of binary pairings: 'passivity, moon, nature, night, mother, emotions, sensitive, pathos' (Cixous and Clément 1986: 63). In patriarchal thinking there is an unquestioned linkage between 'female' and 'feminine'. Feminine characteristics are viewed as natural to the female and are largely inferior to the masculine characteristics linked to the male. So, for example, if you want to climb the corporate ladder, you had better show rationality rather than irrationality and activity rather than passivity. I say 'largely inferior' since, even within this paradigm, women are allowed pockets of influence – in their supposed piety and moral status, for instance – and they are ascribed attributes which are at once recognized by and deeply troubling to patriarchy: the maternal or women's association with the natural world. Feminists have responded in a number of ways to this situation. We may deny the position of inferiority and insist that women are just as capable as men and, hence, deserve equal opportunities; or we may valorize the subordinated term and claim that sensitivity and an emotional responsiveness is life-affirming and more socially productive than brash self-centredness; or we may, as Cixous does, question the very nature of binary thinking and in a deconstructive reading dismantle the hierarchies; or we may, opportunistically, use different responses at different times for feminist purposes.

At the same time, feminine characteristics as marks of inferiority are not unique to women but are often attributed to other oppressed groups. So the racist and the colonizer will see the non-white male as uncivilized but also as child-like and effeminate. Ellmann picks up this point when commenting on a Mary McCarthy short story which ascribes to Jewish men not only a self-indulgent vanity usually applied to women but also the feminine virtues of 'unusual intuitive powers, sympathy, loyalty, tenderness, domestic graces and kindnesses unknown to the Gentile' (1968: 57). As Cixous tells us, there has to be an inferior category to keep the superior snugly in place: 'There has to be some "other" – no master without a slave, no economico-political power without exploitation, no dominant class without cattle under the yoke, no "Frenchmen" without wogs, no Nazis without Jews, no property without exclusion – an exclusion which has its limits and is part of the dialectic' (Cixous and Clément 1986: 71). The 'other' is sometimes female but always feminine.

Both Ellmann and Cixous also complicate the link between female and feminine with respect to writing. Ellmann suggests that the authoritative mode of writing might, in the past, have been more associated with men and the expression of sensibility more with women, but it is no longer possible to make that equation. Thus, in Simone de Beauvoir, Ellmann discovers an adherence to the tone of authority which disappoints her, while in that most macho of writers, Norman Mailer, she finds a delightful, exhilarating abuse of it. Indeed, Ellmann suggests, literature's rejection of the voice of authority in the contemporary period marks an opportunity for women. (Remember that her book was published in the revolutionary year of 1968.) In like manner, when Cixous talks of *l'écriture féminine* she does not necessarily mean writing by women and she certainly does not mean writing that is girlish and gushing or a high-falutin version of Harlequin or Mills and Boon. For Cixous, feminine writing is a practice that 'can never be theorized, enclosed, coded' (1981: 253) and hence cannot be tied to any precise gender definition. In writing, Cixous feels that she escapes prescriptiveness and becomes 'a feminine one, a masculine one, some? – several, some unknown' (Cixous and Clément 1986: 86) and, though 'it is much harder for man to let the other come through him' (1986: 85), it is not impossible. In short, the author could be a male feminine writer. Furthermore, if we think back to Moi's definitions of these three terms, there is a connection between the feminine and the feminist since giving voice to the 'marginalised (repressed, silenced)' might well lead to 'a discernible anti-patriarchal and anti-sexist position'. The author, then, could also be a male feminist writer – a position which, as Modleski's comment indicates (1991: 15), might sound alarm bells.

Thus we have reached a situation where women may or may not be feminine – either in terms of patriarchal conventions or in terms of a practice that exceeds the bounds of the *status quo* – and they may or may not be feminist. Men have possibilities for being both feminine and feminist, though the psychic and social positions of men and women mean that it is more likely that women rather than men should be feminine and feminist. Just when things seem complicated enough, we need to remind ourselves that this feminine, feminist female is also constituted in other ways and that class, race, sexuality (and other power relations) will be, on occasions, as important as or more important than gender and always interrelating with gender in complex formations. As David Glover and Cora Kaplan (2000: 9) neatly put it, we could view femininity 'as a part-time occupation for full-time humans'. In the rest of this chapter I want to look more closely at three key areas of literary production: the notion of a literary tradition or canon; the roles of the author and the reader; and recent developments in genre and literary form. Threading their way throughout will be these problem terms – female, feminine, feminist.

Literary Traditions

For feminist literary criticism from the late 1960s and into the 1970s, the issue was both 'female' and 'male', that is the inadequacy – indeed, misogyny – of representations of women in male canonical texts. But, increasingly, a much stronger impulse in feminist literary criticism gained ground, a concern not with the male author but the female, who was often referred to as 'lost', 'silenced', 'hidden', a victim of male-establishment 'gate-keeping'. Thus, in *A Literature of their Own* (1978), Elaine Showalter complains that 'in the atlas of the English novel, women's territory is usually depicted as desert' (1978: vii), but then, more optimistically, affirms that 'the lost continent of the female tradition has risen like Atlantis from the sea of English Literature' (1978: 10). Tillie Olsen's study of the difficulties women writers have had in getting into literary production is actually called *Silences* (1980); Sandra Gilbert and Susan Gubar, in *The Madwoman in the Attic* (1979), refer to women's texts as 'palimpsestic', containing hidden depths of rage and desire beneath a more socially acceptable surface. More than half a century after Virginia Woolf lamented in *A Room of One's Own* (1929) the empty shelves where women's writing should be found, feminist critics were still struggling to explain the absences, to discover the forgotten texts and to decode their meanings. Undertaking this project would at the very least, it was thought, challenge the male domination of the literary canon, revive forgotten writers of significance and might redraw our literary history.

Showalter named the first response 'the feminist critique' and saw it as focused on the woman as reader and her uncomfortable relation to literary tradition; she coined for the second response the term 'gyno-criticism', that is 'concerned with *woman as writer* – with woman as the producer of textual meaning, with the history, themes, genres, and

157

structures of literature by women' (Showalter 1979: 128). From this perspective, women writers were not simply a few inexplicable and isolated geniuses but part of what Showalter called 'a subculture within the framework of a larger society . . . unified by values, conventions, experiences, and behaviours impinging on each individual' (Showalter 1978: 11). To substantiate that claim has involved literary feminists in extensive work in retrieval, finding the women who had fallen out of literary history and the network of connections to which they may have belonged, and work in re-evaluating those writers in terms of their literary significance. Though some critics have tried to construct a 'matrilineage' of women's writing in opposition to the dominant 'patrilineage', Showalter has always been cautious about that project, pointing to the 'holes and hiatuses' (1978: 11) that undermine the notion of an unbroken tradition.

By the second half of the 1980s, however, the whole 'tradition approach' was under much more fundamental attack from three main groups: first, from feminists influenced by post-structuralism. Not only can the notion of a woman's tradition suggest a false coherence across history and cultures but also, it was argued, it rests on an inadequate response to the constitution of female subjectivity – that problem word 'female' again. The debate takes two classic forms. Either the attempt to find the unity of 'values, conventions, experiences, and behaviours' that Showalter spoke of, necessitates women authors being so tightly scripted that they all become little more than 'exceptionally articulate victims of a patriarchally engendered plot' (Jacobus 1981: 522); or the attempt to give witness to the diversity of women's subjectivity results in collections of writing without *any* apparent commonality, let alone anything specific to women. What remains unclear is the basis for this identity as 'female' or as a collectivity, 'women'. Post-structuralism has also questioned the nature of the relationship between author, text and reader. The author can no longer be seen as fully present in her text, in control of her meanings and transmitting those meanings, in explicit or coded ways, through the tool of language to a responsive and equally coherent reader; rather, all these concepts around the subjectivities of the author and the reader, language and meaning, and objective reality are radically in doubt. Far from texts telling 'the truth about women's experience' – an oft-repeated demand in the early days – they can offer only 'representations' or 'social constructions' of women and uncertain links between author, reader and character. Those who hope for 'positive images' or for direct lines of communication, a woman learning from a woman what it means to be a woman, are confronted with the shiftiness and instability of textuality. I shall return to the problem of the gendered author and reader in the next section.

Secondly, while post-structuralism was philosophically undermining the concept of a female tradition, a more direct, political assault was coming from black women and lesbians. This conjuncture is no mere coincidence. Critics such as Elizabeth Abel (1993) have indicated how, on issues of race for instance, white feminism may turn to black feminism to re-politicize a white feminist agenda under attack from post-structuralism. A similar relationship can be discerned between heterosexual feminists and lesbians. In ground-breaking essays by, among others, Deborah McDowell (1980), Adrienne Rich (1980), and Bonnie Zimmerman (1981), the case was put for the difference of black women's and lesbian experience, about the notable absence of these women from the female tradition under construction, about their relegation to the marginal in the odd paragraph or, as Trinh T. Minh-ha says, 'a special Third World women issue' (1989: 79). Collections of essays, exploring a diversity of white, heterosexual feminist experience, would feature a single black woman as somehow 'representative' of a whole history (Lim 1993: 240); or 'the production of the "Third World Woman" as a singular monolithic subject' would enable Western feminism to 'appropriate and colonize the constitutive complexities which characterize the lives of women in these countries' (Mohanty 1988: 61, 63). We need to be aware, says Chela Sandoval, of 'the official stories by which the white woman's movement understands itself and its interventions in history' and how these stories serve to 'legitimize certain modes of culture and consciousness only to systematically curtail the forms of experiential and theoretical articulations' permitted to others (1991: 5–6). In traditional literary history, women have been the discredited 'other' to the sovereign man – few in number, deemed limited in ability and restricted in scope. Black feminism and lesbianism, though not deliberately discredited by the dominant discourse of white heterosexual feminism, have often been positioned in ways that reinforce hierarchies, exclusions, 'otherness'. Even in the most egalitarian of political movements, relations of inequality alarmingly re-emerge.

To some extent inclusiveness in literary representation has increased; from another perspective it remains inadequate, partial and insecure. We have seen over the past thirty years a publishing explosion in women's writing, driven by the establishment of feminist publishing companies (The Feminist Press, des femmes, Virago, The

Women's Press, Attic Press, Spinifex) and having consequences in mainstream and academic publication, in education and the media and for 'the common reader'. Books of and about 'women's writing' as a unified category were soon joined by books focusing on particular periods or forms of writing. In terms of the representation of difference, specific racial, ethnic, national and sexual identities continue to be highlighted. However, this proliferation – important though it is – is only partially adequate as a political strategy since representation cannot in itself solve the structural problems of racism, ethnocentricism and heterosexism; a widening of representation does not have any necessary political effects. It is partial in that any diversity of representation is unevenly spread in the culture. So, for example, in Irish bookshops one finds, cheek by jowl, excellent Attic Press books of and about women's writing and a popular postcard, entitled 'Ireland's Writers', which illustrates twelve writers from Swift to Beckett – all male. It is insecure in that the norms of representation are resistant to change. New categories may add, enhance, complicate, on occasions substitute. The new category unsettles demarcations between the included and the excluded, central and peripheral and, inevitably, questions how literary history has been constructed and the cultural values operating. But, at the same time, for each new category the supplementary position renders it vulnerable, never firmly in place, always surplus and in danger of slipping out of the reckoning. Thus Kate Muir recounts in her column in *The Times*:

> I haven't had time to visit the feminist theory shelves since I had three children, so I go over to my huge local Books etc. to investigate. I find Gay Writing and Black Writing, but I have to ask for Women's Writing.
> 'Umm,' says the teenage assistant. 'Never seen that. Women's stuff is under Popular Culture now.' (*The Times*, 24 November 2001: 7)

Within the female tradition, too, these problems are endemic. No matter how many groups one includes, there is always an excess; all-inclusiveness is a fantasy. Thus, even when Afra-American writing is joined by Asian-American, Native American and Chicana, the sum falls far short of the full ethnic diversity of the US. And these new groups will, in another context, obliterate other groups equally worthy of being heard. What we see at such moments is the collision of different discourses. It is hard to tease apart the effects of large-scale philosophical and political problems about representation and the hard economic facts of book marketing. For instance, how do we interpret the huge recent success of Arundhati Roy and Zadie Smith – a sign of a significant cultural shift in race and gender or a smart marketing ploy? It is certainly the second; one just hopes it might also contribute to the first.

A third form of critique has come from feminists influenced by socialism and Marxism and has questioned the privileging involved in tradition-making (see the work of Michèle Barrett and Janet Wolff). Materialist feminists have not been the only ones suspicious of the 'disinterestedness' of established aesthetic judgement, which rationalizes its elitism and masks its ideological investment and its self-serving avoidance of questions about cultural production and access to cultural capital. But, more emphatically than liberal feminists, they have questioned the politics of aesthetic value. Since women have historically 'failed' in terms of traditional aesthetic values, rarely reaching what is deemed the highest standard, associated with the minor arts rather than the major, imitative rather than innovative, either the obstacle or the muse for the male genius but never the genius themselves, they may have little to gain from trying to co-opt those values for the benefit of feminism. To construct a female tradition, then, can reinforce the canonical view which looks upon literary history as a continuum of privileged names. The selective approach, which has always found women writers lacking, is sometimes transposed uncritically to a separate female tradition and the liberal-humanist ethic which supports that approach is accepted as basically valid, merely in need of extending its franchise.

We can see how the arguments so far work across three key activities: the making of a canon, the exploration of a literary tradition and matters of aesthetic value. It is not helpful that these activities have often been presented as synonymous. Researching and evaluating a literary history, the contexts of writing and the interconnections between writers are not of necessity part of a canonical undertaking. Indeed, as the work of Margaret Ezell indicates, literary history can be very questioning of canon formation. She examines the tendency of feminist literary criticism to read early women's writing through the lens of the nineteenth century and, thus, impose on earlier periods not only a nineteenth-century model of narrative historiography but also 'strong preconceptions about genre, gender, and authorship' (Ezell 1993: 38). Though somewhat relegated to the margins in the late 1980s and 1990s through the impact of successive waves of theory, there is clearly much to be done within the field of feminist literary history. A quick glance through reference books on women's literature readily reveals scores of under-researched names, periods, movements. Janet Todd's call in 1988 for an 'historically specific, archival, ideologically aware but still empirically based enterprise, using a sense of specific genre as well as notions of changing female experience' (1988: 7) remains to be answered.

Along the way literary feminism *has* created its own canon: *Jane Eyre*, *The Yellow Wallpaper*, *A Room of One's Own*, *The Colour Purple*, *Beloved* are some of the iconic texts that feature frequently on courses of women's writing and have been at the centre of feminist critical debates. We have created also our own canon of feminist critics, and collections of feminist critical essays repeatedly cover the same names. Despite feminists' rhetoric about difference, plurality and equality, the institutions of education and publishing and the social practices we are involved in of studying, teaching and writing constantly involve us in processes of prioritizing and containment. These processes inevitably endow certain names and texts with significance and neglect others. To devise a course, produce a book list, write this chapter, are expressions of that selection process. Curiously, even that which is deemed most 'transgressive', 'subversive', 'uncodified' can be marketed as a commodity, the latest cutting-edge title or contained within increasingly phallocentric and 'managerialized' institutions. In a rather jaundiced mood I once wrote: 'For what it's worth I'm now adept at translating the concepts of *l'écriture féminine* into four neat learning outcomes, three modes of assessment and a near-guaranteed twenty credit points' (Eagleton 1996: 6). The most anti-canonical authors can find themselves stars in an alternative firmament; the most questioning of theorists are firmly ensconced at the heart of the academy. Hence there is a need for a continued interrogation of value – aesthetic and otherwise – and its relation to social structures, institutions and distributions of power. It is in this context that Rita Felski (1989, 1995) talks of getting 'beyond feminist aesthetics', whether that be defending a female 'great tradition' (the aesthetics side of feminist aesthetics) or celebrating in a non-evaluative way the diversity of women's cultural production (the feminist side of feminist aesthetics). Both those responses remain within the known: the first reproduces a selective aesthetics; the second 'often leads to a direct reversal of traditional hierarchies of evaluation' (Felski 1995: 434).

Authors and Readers

The year 1977, which saw the publication of the first US edition of Showalter's *A Literature of their Own*, was also the year that Barbara

Smith did 'something unprecedented, something dangerous, merely by writing about Black women writers from a feminist perspective and about Black lesbian writers from any perspective at all' (Smith 1977: 168). Despite her sense of insecurity, of stepping into the unknown, Smith began the production of another important 'literature of their own', that of black women and black lesbians. But 1977 was also the year when Roland Barthes's highly influential essay, 'The Death of the Author', reached a large new audience in both the US and the UK through the publication of *Image–Music–Text*, Stephen Heath's edited selection of Barthes's essays. What irony that at the very moment feminism, black and white, is declaring the re-birth of the woman author, post-structuralism is marking her 'death'. 'Writing', Barthes tells us, is 'that neutral, composite, oblique space where our subject slips away, the negative where all identity is lost, starting with the very identity of the body writing' (1977: 147). If this is true, then it does not matter if the author is female. What is the point of looking for lost women authors or forming a female literary history? On the other hand, one can argue that Barthes's challenge to the author, as the conceptual, moral and legal controller of the text, its source and limit, is to the advantage of the woman author and other under-represented groups. If the traditional, authoritative author, the DWM (dead, white, male), is divested of his power, then there should be possibilities to create new meanings and functions for the author that encourage greater diversity.

Feminism has generally had problems with notions of authority and control since women have often been on the receiving end of them. Far from being the controlling author, the woman writer has, until very recently, according to Sandra Gilbert and Susan Gubar, experienced an 'anxiety of authorship', the product of the 'complex and only barely conscious fears of that authority which seems to the female artist to be by definition inappropriate to her sex' (1979: 51). During periods of intense feminist activity, a vein of prescriptive thinking can emerge which looks to literature to fulfil specific political objectives: for example, to inspire and sustain women, to be immediately relevant to them, to provide role-models. For even the most sympathetic creative writer, this can seem like an irritating change of role from 'writer' to 'agent of the movement'. However, while the prescriptive author is certainly controlling and determining of the text, this impulse does not spring from any sense of supremacy. Rather, it was a feminist sense of both a disabling lack of such authority and an urgency to make political advances that, in the 1970s and early 1980s, fuelled such demands.

Barthes ends his essay with the assertion that the death of the Author is the price to pay for the birth of the reader, and we could say that the pressing question for feminism is not what *is* a feminist text or what *is* a feminist author but how to produce feminist readings of any texts by any authors. As Judith Fetterley has suggested, the feminist reader may be a 'resisting reader' (1978), who challenges the anti-women positions that much canonical literature offers her. She could be involved in 'polar reading' as 'a method particularly appropriate to lesbian readers and others whose experience is not frequently reflected in literature' (Kennard 1986: 77) or she could be an 'appropriating reader', garnering for feminism not only the male literary tradition but the theoretical masters, Marx, Freud, Lacan, Derrida and others. To put together the two words 'woman' and 'reading' necessitates both a theory of reading as in 'reading woman' and a theory of woman as in 'woman reading' (Jacobus 1986: 5). Who is this subject reading, what are the practices of the reading subject and how is that reading affected by gender?

We have already seen in work on the female literary tradition how one strategy for knowing the woman author has come from literary and social history. The same is true with respect to the woman reader. The more sociological aspect of this work is seen in studies on the composition and reading material of reading groups (Hartley 2001). A more textual approach is evident in, for example, Kate Flint's study (1993) of the Victorian and Edwardian woman reader as a site of ideological struggle about authority, legitimacy and propriety. Paintings of languorous women, lost in reading and unaware of the male gaze, the discourse on reading for women as dangerous – either over-extending the mind or over-exciting the sensations – the need for a specialist reading for women, offering them prudent advice, all testify, as Flint indicates, to 'the proximity of textuality and sexuality' during that period (1993: 4). Since then the issues Flint identifies have been reformulated but have not disappeared. For instance, the attitude of suffrage women, who looked to reading as revelatory, inspirational, educative for the struggle, has been equally strongly expressed in the context of the current women's movement, as we have seen. However, the ease with which suffrage women turned to the male author to fulfil these roles would be cautiously framed in the contemporary period. More common in Anglo-American feminism has been a response of suspicion towards the male-authored text, indulgence towards the female and the woman reader is advised to monitor her reading just as the author was exhorted to circumscribe her writing.

From this perspective, the best the woman reader can offer male-authored texts is 'a dual hermeneutic: a negative hermeneutic that discloses their complicity with patriarchal ideology, and a positive hermeneutic that recuperates the utopian moment' (Schweickart 1986: 43), while in a trusting, non-critical way the female-authored text is offered 'a positive hermeneutic whose aim is the recovery and cultivation of women's culture' (1986: 51).

A second response, springing from post-structuralism and psychoanalysis, has been less confident that we can 'know' the woman author or reader. Peggy Kamuf (1980) argues with respect to the woman author: 'If the inaugural gesture of this feminist criticism is the reduction of the literary work to its signature and to the tautological assumption that a feminine "identity" is one which signs itself with a feminine name, then it will be able to produce only tautological statements of dubious value: women's writing is writing signed by women' (1980: 285–6). Kamuf's essay, from which this comment comes, is called 'Writing Like a Woman'. Three years after its publication, Jonathan Culler published 'Reading as a Woman' (1983). Showalter subsequently suggested that Culler would better read 'as a man and a feminist' (1987: 126). Meanwhile, Robert Scholes writes 'Reading Like a Man' (1987), Modleski asserts the necessity of reading as a 'female feminist' (1986: 134) and Diana Fuss entitles her essay, 'Reading Like a Feminist' (1989). In this flurry of identities – man, woman, feminist, female – we are obviously back to the problems of terminology with which the chapter started, but note also the play on the prepositions, 'as' and 'like'. For Kamuf, identity is so uncertain that the word has to go in inverted commas. For Culler, the woman reader is 'a role she constructs with reference to her identity as a woman, which is also a construct' (1983: 64). There is no 'real' woman. We cannot read or write 'as' anything. Instead we read and write 'like', taking up positions with respect to the text, positions which are not given but varied and changing and produced in the process of reading and writing.

Those who have been most critical of this analysis point out that it can underplay the power differentials between men and women. Scholes (1987: 217) wittily writes of Culler's position:

> Can Mary actually read *as* a woman because she *is* a woman, or can she only read *like* a woman because no individual can ever be a woman? To put the question still another way, can John read *as* a woman or only *like* a woman? If neither John nor Mary can really read *as* a woman, and either can read *like* a woman, then what's the difference between John and Mary?

The proposition could extend further if we introduced other possibilities. John could also read 'like a lesbian' and Mary 'like a gay'; John and Mary, though white, could read 'like blacks'. Not only are the assertions beginning to sound like some awful mathematical problem (if Jane is twice the age of Bill and Bill is half the sum of Ann and James, how many oranges have I got?), but also the real effects of difference might be eradicated. This is Nancy Miller's point with respect to the woman author when she takes Kamuf to task. Miller insists that paying attention to the woman author makes visible 'the marginality, eccentricity and vulnerability of women' and challenges 'the confidence of humanistic discourse as *universality*' (1988: 74). Given that the historical position of women has been different, the arrival of the woman author on the literary stage will have different effects and, in Miller's view, it is too precipitate to dispense with the notion of female authorship since to do so 'will reauthorize our oblivion' (1988: 69). As with the author, the subject position of the reader is crucial. For a woman to read 'like a man' can be a pleasure or part of a liberating play of subject positions but, as Fetterley (1978) has pointed out, it can also be an unwelcome textual and political obligation. Subordinated groups learn to read the dominant group as a survival strategy. Black people know how to read situations of racial threat; similarly women with violent partners and the signs of impending violence. For a man to read 'like a woman' or 'like a feminist' might risk the charge of effeminacy but it might also earn him political and intellectual kudos and it might be a way of displacing or containing feminism.

To secure feminism as a viable political project without, on the one hand, essentializing woman or, on the other, deconstructing her out of existence has been a central debate for the past fifteen years. There is a lot of ground between the patently ludicrous suggestions at either extreme that all women write the same and read the same or that the sex of the author and reader is irrelevant. The arguments about positionality we discussed above have been fruitful with respect to both reader and author. Other strategies have also been proffered; let us consider just two. Elizabeth Grosz makes use of Derrida's work on 'the trace'. She suggests that 'there are ways in which the sexuality and corporality of the subject leave their traces or marks on the texts produced, just as . . . the processes of textual production also leave their trace or residue on the body of the writer (and readers)'. In this scenario the author neither determines the text nor exists outside the text but also is neither invisible nor unimportant in the text; the relation between text and author is 'more enfolded, more mutually implicating' (Grosz 1995: 21). Secondly, Spivak's deployment of 'strategic essentialism' (1987) with reference to subaltern studies has had a wider currency. The belief in an essential subject, such as 'we women' or 'women authors' or 'female readers', might be theoretically 'impure' but politically expedient and acceptable if employed with a clear-eyed understanding of political contexts and effects.

Genre and Literary Form

It is not surprising in a period so preoccupied with subjectivity that some of the most vibrant writing has been autobiographical or has incorporated the autobiographical within other forms. What better subject to look at than oneself? The author, it appears, is not quite as 'dead' as we thought but resurrected in this particular literary form. Nor is it surprising that the history of feminist work on autobiography has followed a familiar trajectory: concern about the absence of women autobiographers, the construction of a new canon, questions of gender difference, the positing of a subjectivity which is multiple and mobile. Domna Stanton's essay, 'Autogynography: Is the Subject Different?' (1984), illustrates an engagement through autobiography with a whole feminist literary history. She casts herself in an ersatz Woolfian position and, using the same literary devices as Woolf, asks with respect to women's autobiography all the questions Woolf asks in *A Room of One's Own* (1929) about women's literary production generally. But, at the same time, the term, 'autogynography', which Stanton glosses as 'autobiographical writing by women' (1984: 5), constitutes a nod at Showalter and her coinage 'gynocriticism', while Stanton's conclusion that the gender of the author does make a difference and that women should not abandon the notion of 'self-possession' (1984: 15) is footnoted with reference to Miller. Autobiography has turned out to be women's 'flexible friend', featuring not only in relatively 'straight' form in autobiographies such as Lorna Sage's *Bad Blood* (2000) but in autobiographical novels, for example, Maxine Hong Kingston's *The Woman Warrior* (1975) and Margaret Drabble's *The Peppered Moth* (2000). The degree of autobiographical content, the relation between the autobiographical and the fictional and the reading effects produced have been much debated in the criticism of these texts.

Hong Kingston calls her writing 'memoirs'. One could also apply to her text Audre Lorde's description of her autobiography, *Zami* (1982), which she calls a 'biomythography', a productive welding of life (*bio*), myth and writing (*graphe*). For Hong Kingston and Lorde, this form allows them to introduce narratives from other cultures and periods into the twentieth-century US in a way that is politically challenging. Both the range of political causes and the forms that such writing has taken are interestingly varied. Sidonie Smith talks of 'autobiographical manifestos', 'self-consciously political autobiographical acts' in which it is possible to 'lay out an agenda for a changed relationship to subjectivity, identity, and the body' (1993: 157). For other writers responding to memories of the Holocaust or the Gulag, the political impetus may not be towards an agenda but to witness and testimony. One of Smith's examples, Gloria Anzaldúa's *Borderlands/La Frontera: The New Mestiza* (1987), demonstrates the deeply suggestive way in which this form can develop, embracing autobiography and politics but, in addition, poetry, myth, cultural criticism and history. The title of the book with its two languages, the dividing line, the reference to the *Mestiza* (that is the woman of mixed race) graphically demonstrates some of the borders – geographical, cultural, linguistic – that Anzaldúa crosses. Elsewhere she talks of the border crossings between race, class, sexuality and within the psyche. The movement of diasporic peoples and the creation of what in post-colonial studies would be referred to as a new hybridity are explored in Anzaldúa's work in a way that illustrates both the painfulness and the hopefulness of the process. The form of the writing struggles to encompass the complexities and the contradictions.

A further hybrid form is in the crossing of autobiography and theory. In 'Me and My Shadow', Jane Tompkins castigates theory as 'one of the patriarchal gestures women *and* men ought to avoid' (1989: 122). Tompkins recognizes in herself not only the two personas, 'me and my shadow', but also two voices, one which is professional and critical and another which 'wobbles, vacillates back and forth, is neither this nor that' (1989: 126). Writing her essay between 1987 and 1989, she cannot find any satisfactory way to incorporate the feeling, autobiographical voice alongside the academic. Toril Moi returns to Tompkins's essay in her 1999 study *What is a Woman?*, agrees that she has identified an important problem but rejects what she sees as an anti-intellectual stance and affirms that women do not have to choose between theory and autobiography or theory and the personal. Indeed, between 1989 and 1999 there have been a number of interesting examples of a new cross-form which, at once, is intellectually searching and yet retains a strong sense of the embodied author. What has been termed 'French

feminism' provides the most striking illustration. Rejecting a theoretical stance which has false claims to objectivity and impersonality, the
style of such writing is often impassioned, poetic, utopian, hyperbolic
or declamatory. Yet, at the same time, the writing is certainly not anti-
theoretical; it is fully engaged in a dialogue with 'high' theory and the
'I' who emerges is not a plain-speaking everywoman but a complex,
multi-layered figure. The personal turns out to be not only just as complicated as the theoretical but also not separate from the theoretical;
each term is infused with the force of the other.

While subjectivity might be at the centre of contemporary readings
of autobiographical and biographical writing, it has not been entirely
at the expense of a concern with social class. In a period of proliferat-
ing differences, the one that has been consistently overlooked is economic difference. When difference has often been represented as
malleable and playful there seems no place for the intractable misery
of poverty. Hence, attempts to recover working-class voices have been
extremely significant. We see this work in, for example, Reginia
Gagnier's study of Victorian and Edwardian working-class autobiography (1991) or in reflections on one's own working-class history such
as Carolyn Steedman's influential *Landscape for a Good Woman* (1986)
with its exploration of a period in which austerity is both material and
psychic. Once again, the autobiographical novel has been productive
in, for instance, Jeanette Winterson's *Oranges Are Not the Only Fruit*
(1985) and the writing of Buchi Emecheta. Steedman's more recent
work takes a different tack on the question. She sees the working class,
from the seventeenth century onwards, as increasingly involved in the
production of 'enforced narratives' (2000: 25), subject to an 'autobiographical injunction' (2000: 28) from a state developing its administrative apparatus. These accounts are far removed from any
self-initiated desire to explore one's experiences and inner thoughts.
Rather, they are the product of 'a history of expectations, orders and
instructions' (2000: 28) relating often to settlement or bastardy exam-
inations. Steedman also notices how in the middle-class novel the
working-class narrative of selfhood is expropriated in the construction
of 'the modern bourgeois suffering self' (2000: 37). She uses as
her two examples Daniel Defoe's *Moll Flanders* (1722) and Mary
Wollstonecraft's *Maria, or, The Wrongs of Woman* (1798).

This expropriation of other people's experience for one's own
purpose without thought of the power relations involved is, as we saw
earlier, precisely the complaint that women have made against men
and black feminists have made against white. Steedman actually

quotes bell hooks to this effect: 'Re-writing you I rewrite myself anew. I am still author, authority. I am still coloniser, the speaking subject, and you are now at the centre of my tale' (2000: 36). Thus, the issue is not simply who gets represented but who gets represented by whom, how, within what discourses and distributions of power and with what consequences. Moreover, to talk about an ever-widening representation of various groups in literature, as authors or characters, suggests an open field on which, in time, all will be appropriately placed. It is salutary to remember, then, that Virginia Woolf's questions about unequal access to literary production and consumption are still demanding a remedy. At the beginning of the twenty-first century, working-class people are, by and large, neither the authors nor the readers of feminist literature and feminist literary criticism or, one could add, feminist thought generally. That truth must have serious implications for the political project of feminism.

References and Further Reading

Abel, E. (1993) Black writing, white reading: race and the politics of feminist interpretation. *Critical Inquiry*, 19 (3): 470–98.

Anzaldúa, G. (1987) *Borderlands/La Frontera: The New Mestiza*. San Francisco, CA: Aunt Lute Books.

Barrett, M. (1999) *Imagination in Theory: Essays on Writing and Culture*. Cambridge: Polity Press.

Barthes, R. (1977) The death of the author. In *Image–Music–Text*, trans. S. Heath, pp. 142–8. London: Fontana (first published 1968).

Cixous, H. (1981) The laugh of the Medusa, trans. K. Cohen and P. Cohen. In E. Marks and I. de Courtivron (eds), *New French Feminisms: An Anthology*, pp. 245–64. Brighton: Harvester (first published as *Le rire de la méduse* in 1975).

— and Clément, C. (1986) *The Newly Born Woman*, trans. B. Wing. Manchester: Manchester University Press (first published as *La jeune née* in 1975).

Culler, J. (1983) *On Deconstruction: Theory and Criticism after Structuralism*. London: Routledge.

Eagleton, M. (1996) Who's who and where's where: constructing feminist literary studies. *Feminist Review*, 53: 1–23.

Ellmann, M. (1968) *Thinking About Women*. New York: Harcourt Brace Jovanovich.

Ezell, M. J. M. (1993) *Writing Women's Literary History*. Baltimore, MD: The Johns Hopkins University Press.

Felski, R. (1989) *Beyond Feminist Aesthetics: Feminist Literature and Social Change*. Cambridge, MA: Harvard University Press.

— (1995) Why feminism doesn't need an aesthetic (and why it can't ignore Aesthetics). In P. Zeglin Brand and C. Korsmeyer (eds), *Feminism and Trad-*

ition in Aesthetics, pp. 431–45. Pennsylvania: Pennsylvania State University Press.

Fetterley, J. (1978) *The Resisting Reader: A Feminist Approach to American Fiction*. Bloomington, IN: Indiana University Press.

Flint, K. (1993) *The Woman Reader 1837–1914*. Oxford: Oxford University Press.

Fuss, D. (1989) *Essentially Speaking: Feminism, Nature and Difference*. London: Routledge.

Gagnier, R. (1991) *Subjectivities: A History of Self-representation in Britain, 1832–1920*. Oxford: Oxford University Press.

Gilbert, S. and Gubar, S. (1979) *The Madwoman in the Attic: The Woman Writer and the Nineteenth-century Literary Imagination*. New Haven, CT: Yale University Press.

Glover, D. and Kaplan, C. (2000) *Genders*. London: Routledge.

Grosz, E. (1995) *Space, Time, and Perversion: Essays on the Politics of Bodies*. New York: Routledge.

Hartley, J. (2001) *Reading Groups*. Oxford: Oxford University Press.

Jacobus, M. (1981) Review of *The Madwoman in the Attic*. *Signs*, 6 (3): 517–23.

— (1986) *Reading Woman: Essays in Feminist Criticism*. London: Methuen.

Kamuf, P. (1980) Writing like a woman. In S. McConnell-Ginet et al. (eds), *Women and Language in Literature and Society*, pp. 284–99. New York: Praeger.

Kennard, J. E. (1986) Ourself behind ourself: a theory for lesbian readers. In E. A. Flynn and P. P. Schweickart (eds), *Gender and Reading: Essays on Readers, Texts, and Contexts*, pp. 63–80. Baltimore, MD: The Johns Hopkins University Press.

Lim, S. Geok-lin (1993) Asians in Anglo-American feminism: reciprocity and resistance. In G. Greene and C. Kahn (eds), *Changing Subjects: The Making of Feminist Literary Criticism*, pp. 240–52. London: Routledge.

McDowell, D. E. (1980) New directions for Black feminist criticism. In E. Showalter (ed.), *The New Feminist Criticism: Essays on Women, Literature and Theory*, pp. 186–99. London: Virago, 1986.

Miller, N. (1988) *Subject to Change: Reading Feminist Writing*. New York: Columbia University Press.

Modleski, T. (1986) Feminism and the power of interpretation: some critical readings. In T. de Lauretis (ed.), *Feminist Studies: Critical Studies*, pp. 121–38. Bloomington, IN: Indiana University Press.

— (1991) *Feminism Without Women: Culture and Criticism in a 'Postfeminist' Age*. New York: Routledge.

Mohanty, C. T. (1988) Under western eyes: feminist scholarship and colonial discourses. *Feminist Review*, 30: 61–88.

Moi, T. (1986) Feminist literary criticism. In A. Jefferson and D. Robey (eds), *Modern Literary Theory: A Comparative Introduction*, pp. 204–21. London: Batsford.

— (1999) *What is a Woman? And Other Essays*. Oxford: Oxford University Press.

Olsen, T. (1980) *Silences*. London: Virago.

Rich, A. (1980) Compulsory heterosexuality and lesbian existence. In *Blood, Bread, and Poetry: Selected Prose 1979–1985*, pp. 23–75. London: Virago, 1987.

Sandoval, C. (1991) US Third World feminism: the theory and method of oppositional consciousness in the postmodern world. *Genders*, 10: 1–24.

Scholes, R. (1987) Reading like a man. In A. Jardine and P. Smith (eds), *Men in Feminism*, pp. 204–18. London: Methuen.

Schweickart, P. P. (1986) Reading ourselves: toward a feminist theory of reading. In E. A. Flynn and P. P. Schweickart (eds), *Gender and Reading: Essays on Readers, Texts, and Contexts*, pp. 31–62. Baltimore, MD: The Johns Hopkins University Press.

Showalter, E. (1978) *A Literature of their Own: British Women Novelists from Brontë to Lessing*. London: Virago (2nd edn, 1999).

— (1979) Toward a feminist poetics. In E. Showalter (ed.), *The New Feminist Criticism: Essays on Women, Literature and Theory*, pp. 125–43. London: Virago, 1986.

— (1987) Critical cross-dressing: male feminists and the woman of the year. In A. Jardine and P. Smith (eds), *Men in Feminism*, pp. 116–32. London: Methuen.

Smith, B. (1977) Toward a Black feminist criticism. In E. Showalter (ed.), *The New Feminist Criticism: Essays on Women, Literature and Theory*, pp. 168–87. London: Virago, 1986.

Smith, S. (1993) *Subjectivity, Identity, and the Body: Women's Autobiographical Practices in the Twentieth Century*. Bloomington, IN: Indiana University Press.

Spivak, G. Chakravorty (1987) *In Other Worlds: Essays in Cultural Politics*. London: Methuen.

Stanton, D. C. (1984) Autogynography: is the subject different? In D. C. Stanton (ed.), *The Female Autograph*, pp. 3–20. Chicago: University of Chicago Press.

Steedman, C. (1986) *Landscape for a Good Woman*. London: Virago.

— (2000) Enforced narratives: stories of another self. In T. Cosslett, C. Lury and P. Summerfield (eds), *Feminism and Autobiography: Texts, Theories, Methods*, pp. 25–39. London: Routledge.

Todd, J. (1988) *Feminist Literary History: A Defence*. Cambridge: Polity Press.

Tompkins, J. (1989) Me and my shadow. In L. Kauffman (ed.), *Gender and Theory: Dialogues on Feminist Criticism*, pp. 121–39. Oxford: Blackwell.

Trinh, T. Minh-ha (1989) *Woman, Native, Other: Writing Postcoloniality and Feminism*. Indianapolis, IN: Indiana University Press.

Wolff, J. (1990) *Feminine Sentences: Essays on Women and Culture*. Cambridge: Polity Press.

— (1993) *The Social Production of Art*, 2nd edn. Basingstoke: Macmillan.

Woolf, V. (1993) *A Room of One's Own* (1929). In M. Barrett (ed.), *A Room of One's Own and Three Guineas*. Harmondsworth: Penguin.

Zimmerman, B. (1981) What has never been: an overview of lesbian feminist literary criticism. In E. Showalter (ed.), *The New Feminist Criticism: Essays on Women, Literature and Theory*, pp. 200–24. London: Virago, 1986.

9

The Visual

Griselda Pollock

Those who have no country have no language. Women have no imagery available – no accepted public language – with which to express their particular point of view. And, of course, one of the major elements involved in any successful language system is that it can be easily under-stood, so that its tropes have a certain mobility and elasticity, as it were – they can rise from the lowest levels of popular parlance to the highest peaks of great art. (Nochlin 1972: 11)

Feminist theory radically changed art, art history and film studies, opening onto the anti-hierarchical approach of 'visual culture' (Carson and Pajaczkowska 2001). The focus is now on 'image', 'representa-tion', 'the gaze', 'identification', 'spectatorship', while psychoanalyti-cal theory has added terms like 'voyeurism', 'fetishism' and 'scopophilia'. In anguished interaction with theorists of class and race, feminist theory has forged terms that enable us to see 'the power of the image' (Kuhn 1985) and to acknowledge 'the power of discourses to "do violence" to people, a violence which is material and physical, although produced by abstract and scientific discourses as well as dis-courses of the mass media' (de Lauretis 1987).

Following industrialization and urbanization, images proliferated as part of nineteenth-century economies of entertainment, shopping and commerce, advertising, illustrated newspapers and magazines. By the mid-twentieth century, this huge increase in visual images demanded theoretical analysis. The power and ubiquity of the image in modern cultures required a new tool kit to grasp its meanings, the economies, regimes and systems, and the effect of these images on those to whom they were directed. The domain of the visual is no longer dismissed as the cultural icing on the socioeconomic cake. With digitalization and satellite, it is one of the major global economies at the intersection with the cultural: where meanings are produced and, as importantly, where 'subjects' of those meanings – we – are formed and constantly reshaped. We are consumers of modern cultures because we are spectators, viewers and users of images.

Roland Barthes, applying semiotics – the study of signs and meanings – in essays on contemporary cultural imageries from the face of Greta Garbo to the Citroën car, menus and travel guides, identified ideology at work in what he called the 'rhetoric of the image' (Barthes 1977a). Barthes created a systematic approach to 'reading' an image: each element is a sign composed of a signifier (sounds, marks, colours, shapes) and a signified (the mental concept). At first reading, we decipher a literal meaning, 'denotation'. But these first-order signs then interact to form larger visual sentences, themselves comprising a whole as complex as a book. Barthes named the second level, 'connotation' or 'myth' because the ensemble of signs is impregnated by social and cultural meanings that serve to create an ideological picture of the world. Barthes swiftly discovered that images are always polysemic, contingent, dynamic and historically situated, serving class or national interests. Semiotics shows that images are never innocent visual reflections of the world; nor are they merely the artist's or maker's intentions directly expressed. They are mediated representations open to varied, unstable, contested readings, and images work on us to convince us that their 'vision' is real, true, natural. Images, therefore, need to be deciphered in relation to cultural practices, social histories and the interests of the dominant class, race, gender and sexuality.

Feminist theory uses a new tool bag but attends to gender and sexual difference – always in a complex, asymmetrical relation to class, race and sexuality – in ways to which founding masculine theorists of these new theories and methods often remained blind. Feminists have transformed these terms of analysis by asking: who is represented and who does the representing? Who is seen and who is looking? Whose interests does an image encode, whose eroticism and desire? Who becomes the object or sign of that desire? The first work is to deconstruct existing regimes of representation: identifying the dominant 'story' allows us to determine what it excludes so as to discover how a phallocentric culture does not represent women, feminine desire(s) and difference(s). The premise that images are not reflections of a world but constructions of meaning not only implies the critique of stereotypes that show limited aspects of women's lives and experiences, it also means that what we take to be common definitions of femininity are themselves already part of this fabrication. 'Feminine' here is not the conventional idea of what women are or should be, but invokes the potential of a 'different difference' that as yet lies unacknowledged in current regimes of visual representation. We do not yet know, fully, if at all, what 'woman' wants.

Cultural Sniping

One form of feminist work on the image is the critique of representation. Jo Spence, Mary Kelly, Carrie Mae Weems and Lorna Simpson are examples of visual artists doing this work and inventing other ways of representing and looking. Feminist theory of the visual cannot be separated from art practice. In *The History Lesson* (1982), Jo Spence and Terry Dennett radically exposed some of what we take for granted in the visual images we receive through the media and art history. In *Colonization* (figure 9.1), Jo Spence stands in the doorway of a brick terrace house. Two bottles of milk are on the doorstep. She holds a broom. She is wearing glasses and thus is not glamorized. These signs signify a modern, Western city, but in a poor, working-class area. The woman with broom signifies housewife. It seems like the stuff of classic documentary photography: the caring, middle-class visitor finds the dignity of domestic labour in the desolate backstreets of the metropolis. But, Jo Spence, the artist, is also the figure in the picture and she is dressed unusually. Naked from the waist up, she is wrapped in a rough sarong and wears a string of beads around her neck. These signs evoke Gauguin's paintings of Polynesian women or news and travel photographs of African women who are also 'housewives' and 'workers' but their semi-nakedness is circulated in images for the touristic Western male audience as 'exotic' and 'erotic'. Jo Spence's staged photograph slams two traditions into each other, exposing the class and racializing foundations of two visual traditions normalized as 'modern art' or 'documentary photography'. Her deconstructive reconstruction makes us see the otherwise invisible ideology of the colonial and classist culture we inhabit. Jo Spence called her work *Cultural Sniping* (1995).

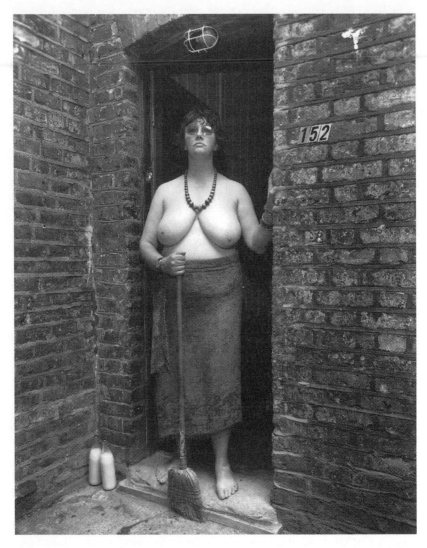

Figure 9.1 Jo Spence and Terry Dennett, *Colonization*, 1982, from *Remolding Photo History*. © Jo Spence Archive, London, 2002.

Looking and Being Looked At

Ideology has the force of common sense, treated as a fact of nature when it is in fact a product of a politics and power. Structures of looking are not natural, but historical. Any regime, such as the 'natural' assumption that men look at women, and women watch themselves being looked at (Berger 1972), has specific effects that are not the reflection of a given difference between men and women: gender. Looking contributes to the way in which the hierarchy of gender is fabricated and maintained. I am looked at not because I am a woman; I learn femininity as that repeated experience of being subjected to being looked at, appraised, accosted, commented upon and so on that will agonize my teenage years and cause older women to want their faces to be cut up in order to maintain the beautiful appearance.

In November 1970, feminists demonstrated against the Miss World competition in London and 'struck a blow against this narrow destiny, against the physical confines of the way women are seen and the way they fit into society . . . against passivity that we all felt in ourselves' (Mulvey 1989: 3). The beauty pageant is still a major rite of passage for many young women in the advanced world; in India in 2000 Indian women protesting against the degrading event threatened mass suicide. Commercializing and commodifying a convention that runs back to the legend of the judgement of Paris, the beauty contest confirms that women are valued for face and figure according to what is both a heterosexist and a eurocentric scale. Women are particularly disciplined by the visual, by how they look to others, how attractive they are within a heterosexual system. They learn this 'fact' by its repetition in all forms of visual representation from Barbie dolls to make-up ads in teen magazines. 'Woman' is, in semiotic terms, a signifier of 'to-be-looked-at-ness'. Since the majority of women do not by genes, age, work, health, even culture, conform to the ideal of that signifier, there is a massive industry that sells us the commodities by means of which we will in vain struggle to approximate to the delusory appearance of visual perfection offered by a tiny, mostly Caucasian, minority, whose professional success depends upon appetite-inhibiting drugs, excessive exercise or sheer chance in the genetic draw. These women model for the cosmetic and fashion adverts and for the animated versions called movies, creating in every woman the internal division between a sense of self generated through an inner range of abilities, characteristics, desires and thoughts, and this 'mask', this external visual image that is offered to us through the vast array of visual representations of 'woman' that are manufactured through complex technologies of highly manipulated photography and cinema, lighting, cosmetics, surgery, and what we can politely call 'body sculpture'. Woman is not only image but surface. Beauty, however, veils a threat, hence the complementary fantasy of the *femme fatale*.

177

The visual sign 'woman' does not describe female people with changing bodies, intellects, desires, capacities. 'Woman' as icon is the work of masculine fantasy/dread. It is neither natural nor viable. It is clearly historical/political. Contrast, for instance, the idealized body and facial types of traditional Indian, Chinese, African and European art to see a vast and changing range of 'ideals', or consider the radical shift from the substantial Marilyn Monroe to Julia Roberts and Kate Moss. We must ask why late capitalist Western society, which over-produces vast quantities of food in a world of near starvation for millions, elsewhere favours as its idealized image of the feminine the adolescent, anorexic body from which almost all traditional signs of femininity – breasts, thighs, hips, flesh – have been systematically and often technologically erased? If we were to compare an infamous 1999 'Accent' advertisement for a wristwatch, which ran the caption 'Put some weight on' under the image of an emaciated model with an upper arm so thin you could hang the wristwatch from it, to the statue of a substantial mature female form, known as the 'Venus of Willendorf', dating to 25,000 BCE, we could justifiably begin to speculate about the difference between the ways in which each society valued its female members as encoded in its imagery.

We may surmise that women's socioeconomic and cultural role in the society that produced the Willendorf statue will be related to the value and reverence it had for creativity, production and responsibility of the mature, maternal feminine. In a society in which the pre-vailing images present the feminine body as a starved, adolescent, an almost boyish spectre, or as a near-skeletal support for a mask of cosmetically fabricated, eroticized, emaciated beauty, we can deduce a very different, even aggressively negative valuation of women's place and meaning that has little to do with the full range of women's experiences or desires.

The Phallocentric Order: Feminism and Psychoanalysis

The words/signs/visuals 'man' and 'woman' are not spontaneous descriptors of male and female persons. They signify according to values created by a social/ideological system, just as 1 and 2 and 3 have no intrinsic meaning but acquire a value relative only to the scale we call numbers. However, 'phallocentric' describes a cultural system premised, paradoxically, on *one* sex and its negative: man (human) and non-man (woman). The organizing symbol of this One is called the phallus. Under the *phallo*centric order, there is the One, identified with or appropriated by the masculine, and what is not-man, deemed damaged, reduced, unfit for full participation, weaker, a mere vessel, the object not the subject of desire, the seen and not the see-er, the spoken and not the speaking. Phallocentric cultures cannot conceive two sexes, or even sexual differences. Under this regime, the feminine is a negative space, not a source of supplementary or differential meanings for an expanded, differentiated concept of humanity.

In 1973, Laura Mulvey reviewed an exhibition by pop artist Allen Jones which had attracted the rage of the emergent women's movement because he exhibited casts of women in tight-fitting leather or metallic restricting costumes and stiletto heels, in humiliating postures that served as chairs, tables, hat stands. Feminists denounced the degrading 'images' of women. Laura Mulvey, however, responded by saying: 'You Don't Know What is Happening, Do you, Mr Jones?' (1989). Laura Mulvey linked Jones's fine art with popular comics and cult films like *Barbarella*, as well as with classic pornographic images of bondage and sadism to disclose a common psychic structure, first defined by Freud: fetishism. Fetishism is a minority sexual perversion. Freud, however, defined fetishism structurally as a widespread defence against anxiety that holds two contradictory beliefs at the same time. 'I know and yet . . .'. The anxiety against which the defence emerges concerns the presence or absence of the phallus. Why does the idea of the male organ have such importance, particularly in infancy or early childhood? We must keep in mind the key argument of semiotics: language produces meanings only through a play of differences. There are no positive terms. For there to be meaning, there must be at least two terms, in which one is *not* the other. Meaning works by what we call a negative difference.

The phallocentric system depends on the presence or absence of this signifier, the phallus, that determines the pattern of meaning. If the phallus – the abstract idea of presence, power, the positively valued and, paradoxically, the idea of lack – comes in fantasy to be associated with a small piece of male flesh which grows and deflates and is involved in procreation and narcissistic pleasure, then its absence on a differently configured anatomy will read – to the masculine subject – as a distressing absence. The male child, endowing in fantasy its own flesh with positive meaning, will view this absence as a *nothing to see*. Remember, by contrast, the Neolithic sculptures that enlarged the thighs, swelled the belly and filled the breasts in order to make visible as an external sight the imagined invisible interiority of the feminine body that was endowed with mysterious power and value. In the phallocentric regime, *nothing to see* means not only the absence of the valued term, but also the dreadful possibility of its disappearance: castration. Thus the sight of female difference does not register as a different, equally interesting and self-pleasuring anatomy, with an invisible sexual specificity. It acquires in fantasy the double load of both absence and the threat of absence; it 'reads' as both castrated and castrating. Fetishism, however, allows the masculine subject to maintain contradictory ideas. Imagine the little fellow: 'I have discovered that the mother's body lacks a penis, but I re-endow her with that penis through a substitute, that will, however, ironically always remind me of the lack the substitute or fetish tries to cover up.'

Far from seeing fetishism as the 'private taste of an odd minority', Mulvey suggests that it is widespread in visual culture. First, we are all fetishists in relation to the image. I know that the image is not real, yet I respond to what is represented as if it were. But it goes further, and has specific gender connotations. Woman is not naturally lovely, we know. The image-woman is fabricated according to certain conventions that make a visually pleasurable spectacle. One convention – the soft pornography that Allen Jones plays with – involves strapping women into tight clothing and high heels. The effect is to show us 'woman' as lack and as threat, while also making her a fetish for what she lacks, remodelling her whole form as itself 'phallic'. But these visual dramas are never about women. They stage the psychic fantasies of men. Laura Mulvey concludes, therefore:

> The message of fetishism concerns not woman, but the narcissistic wound she represents for man. Women are constantly confronted with their own image in one form or another . . . Yet, in a real sense, women are not there at all. The parade has nothing to do with woman, everything to do with man . . . Women are simply the scenery onto which men project their narcissistic fantasies. (Mulvey 1989: 13)

Feminist Theory and the Cinematic Spectator

In 1975, Laura Mulvey wrote the most famous text of feminist visual theory. As an avant-garde film-maker adoring classic Hollywood cinema, Mulvey took the cinema to be the most pervasive and most industrially and technologically developed apparatus of phallocentric visual culture, now shaped by the effects of capitalism and its key term, the commodity. Woman signifies lack and thus by that lack 'produc[es] the phallus as symbolic presence' (Mulvey, 1989: 14). Mulvey adds that the feminine also echoes in masculine fantasy as a memory of maternal plenitude. Images of the feminine oscillate between a promise of lost archaic pleasure and its reminder of lack and loss.

In reality no one is castrated. Women lack nothing, at this level. And yet we are all 'castrated', masculine and feminine alike, by language as a symbolic system that obliges us all to give up the bodily intensities of our earliest sensations and become social subjects by using substitutes: signs. The fact that we are speaking subjects and become capable of communication and self-reflection through language, cuts us off from the primordial intensities of bodily sensation and affect. Prior to language, energy flows unregulated through a not yet patterned or remembered field that will slowly become organized as the imagined body that houses our subjectivity. The phallocentric structure is not just the result of what little boys 'see' or even imagine they 'see'. It involves the projection by the masculine subject of his *symbolic* castration, lack as a result of access to language and to the Symbolic order, onto the image of the feminine body (Silverman 1988). It is only within social and cultural framing that the feminine becomes a masculine fetish: in fact, disguising *his* lack, while marking the site and, therefore, generating a compulsively repetitious culture of excessive exposure of a feminine body, constantly refashioned to accommodate contradictory impulses and anxieties.

I have just leapt a theoretical fence from classic Freudian theory to the work of a (post)-structuralist psychoanalyst, Jacques Lacan. Lacanian theory considers human beings as 'subjects'. The subject is not the same as the individual and is not determined by its body precisely because the psycho-symbolic subject is split, sexed and speaking. The subject is split because we are divided by the unconscious, which itself determines much of what we do and say without our ever knowing it. We are 'sexed'. That means we are not born with a sexuality or even what most of us think of as a sex; sexuality is an effect of the process of psychic formation that translates intensities and impulses, sensations and pleasures into aims, objects, zones and practices. These are never natural or anatomically predetermined: just think of the variety of ways in which humans derive sexual pleasure and the ways in which what heterosexist societies call the normal outcomes can be deflected through fetishism, for instance, or voyeurism: 'sexuality in the field of vision' (Rose 1986).

Voyeurism involves using sight as a sexual activity. It reveals that the eye itself can become an eroticized if not a fully sexual organ.

181

Voyeurism occurs when a typical stage of psycho-sexual formation becomes arrested but its trace is present in most adults. Babies are pretty helpless but from eight days old they can see. To compensate for the complete lack of self-sufficiency, the baby invests in seeing. It likes to see and imagines that it can have some kind of power over what it sees. The baby also takes pleasure in *being seen*. Folding itself into the look of its mother or carer, it associates being looked at with nourishment and nurture, with utter contentment and passive enjoyment. Passive scopophilia will later give rise to exhibitionism, to attempts to attract the look of others and taking pleasure in being the object of that look. As the infant develops, another psychic formation takes hold: narcissism and a fascination and identification with likeness. We need to pose the question: why do we like looking at images of other human beings? Lacan formulated his now famous hypothesis of the mirror phase (see Silverman 1988) to begin to answer this perplexing issue. An image of another or even ourselves might have no meaning or actually threaten us. There must be a reason for and a mechanism by which we delight in images, especially those that are 'like' us, human images. Lacan suggests that between six and eighteen months, the infant, still underdeveloped in motor skills, glimpses itself, sometimes literally, sometimes figuratively, in the mirror – a real mirror or the regard of those around the child who mirror it back to itself in looks and handling. What it garners from the others who surround it is an image, that of a coherent, boundaried body, a co-ordination of limbs and an ordering of head, body and so on. This image is filled with fantasies because, outside language, the child does not check what it *imagines* against generally held perceptions and interpretations.

The image that comes back to it cannot be grasped as a reflection of an existing self for, without this image as an internal structure to organize its incoherent energy flows and sensations, it cannot locate a discrete space or entity to call a self, an ego, an 'I'. The mirror phase is fundamentally a misrecognition. In the reflection that is the space of an Other, the child is apt to imagine a more coherent, well-organized and functioning imago, an ideal self that it then incorporates. The effect of identifying with this imago involves spatializing hitherto uncoordinated sensations within a body-schema; it involves territorializing a body experienced only in bits and pieces and focalizing its pleasures and sensations in a here/there, me/other dialectic. A self cannot exist without the internalization of this imago as both its housing and as its internal psychic skeleton. During the mirror phase the child internalizes an alien image around which it fashions its potential sense of a distinct self that is always also idealized. What becomes the core of a self is borrowed from the Other; that is, from its culture mediated by parents and carers. It is an alien implant and its translation into the becoming subject involves the mechanism of identification, a taking in of something alien to which the emergent self makes itself correspond. Herein lies the crucial insight. We are not merely influenced by images; we exist as their effect. Beyond the mirror phase of formation in infancy, cultural systems of images replay a comparable process to us, consolidating and refashioning the very sense of what a self is through repetition and remodelling. We are constructed by identification with the image from the space of the Other, from culture and society.

This phase also traumatically involves a less pleasant realization. If the image shows a baby and its Other – for instance, the mother holding up the baby to the mirror – the image actually makes visible the separateness from the Other through whom the baby has dependently survived. The terrible cleft that opens up between emergent self and its big m/Other can be covered over, however, by the fantasy of identification: 'I may be separate from the m/Other, but I am *like* her/him.' So in addition to a narcissistic identification with the image that becomes the idealized imago for the subject, there is an identification with the anthropomorphic, with the human form and the scale and space of its operations. Again we can detect the latent structures that will flower into visual culture and specifically the cinematic form, with its stories, its realism, its anthropomorphism and we can explain why we continue to be fascinated with looking at idealized stars who act out in their perfect bodies and beautiful looks these dramas that narratively echo the very processes of our own psychic formation. The Imaginary is a phase in our formation but it is also a register that remains within the human subject. The Imaginary is a complex of several not necessarily compatible processes: the archaic fascination with looking or with finding ourselves embraced within the mother's gaze collides with the emergent sense of separateness, the possibility of distinguishing 'I' from you. The cinema is the magical machine that replays our fascination, our visual pleasure and manages its anxieties through the star system and narrative realism.

But, the subject is also a speaking subject. This takes us from the Imaginary to the Symbolic, in Lacan's formulation, since language is the system of symbols, substitutes. The formative moments are mechanisms not yet organized into a meaning system. I have already proposed that we live in a meaning system and one that is phallocentric. Under phallocentric logic, which is inscribed through cultural laws and which is, above all, signified through language, masculine and feminine have different values. They are plus and minus, presence and absence. It is language that performs the final separation, installing in the place of our archaic and chaotic sensations and intensities, a symbolic structure imbued with social, historical and cultural meanings.

The Symbolic, as a symbolic cutting us off from archaic bodilyness, also coincides with a moment in the formation of sexuality and sexed identities. (These are distinct since I can adopt a feminine sex position and sexually love women. Sexuality and gender position do not structurally coincide even if it is the ideological work of culture to attempt convergence.) The identification with the Other of the Imaginary moment involves a dyad: the infant and its Other. Sexualization and identity are the effects of the triangular Oedipalizing moment; the Oedipus complex confronts a further fantasmic anxiety as the child has to accommodate to the fact that it must identify with one when it comes from two. Signified as the heterosexual familial terms, Father and Mother, sexual difference confronts the child with a terrible choice. It cannot identify with both. There is a price. At this point what I call the m/Other is formally divided and signified as different terms. What was until this moment the powerful figure of Nurture and Life, the Mother, becomes relativized by the emergence of the Third Term, named the Father, who is the representative of the Law of culture that forbids the child sexual access to its parents. To break the profound bond between child and primary carer is the work of the incest taboo that must redirect its sexual desire laterally, breaking the vertical chain of the mother/child dyad. The triangular Oedipal structure retrospectively determines that what was 'seen' on the body of the mother/woman signifies a deficiency and hence becomes also the site of threat. Thus the meaning of an image of the feminine will oscillate between dread and desire, threats of future danger and memories of lost pleasure. This instability, as well as the fact that human subjectivity is an effect of so dramatic and traumatic a process, means that sexuality and sexual identity are never fully accomplished, stable or predictable. Culture has continuously to work on us and never more acutely than in societies where the traditional social mechanisms are relaxed as in modern, urban societies. Hence the intense visuality and massive industrial and political investment in visual culture in modern societies. Hence 'the power of the image'.

If we go back for a moment to looking and being looked at, narcissistic identification, we find that, under a phallocentric Symbolic, these mechanisms are reshaped within a sexual division of labour. Since phallocentrism is a world ordered by sexual imbalance and asymmetry (not two sexes but man and not-man), we find active looking, mastery and control have become identified with the plus term, masculinity, and passive, 'being-looked-at-ness', exhibitionism, is equated with the feminine. Because this is structural matter, it is effective whether the actor or the character or the model is a man or a woman. To be exhibitionist or looked at feminizes, if not downright 'castrates', a male character. (This device often works to signify the class or race position of a subaltern male.) So far so good. But what of castration anxiety generated by the visual discovery of feminine difference?

Here is the crisis: looking at the image of the feminine arouses the anxiety of castration. So the classic visual language of cinema can be read for the deformations it must perform to get around that double bind of phallocentrism; the feminine is made to bear the burden of exhibitionism yet the wounded woman is an intolerable spectacle, becoming the silenced/beautified image onto which the masculine psyche projects its contradictory fears and fantasies. As in pornography, we will find a sadistic fetishism rampant in the costuming, framing and photographing of the female form. Narrative is also significant and, whatever the plot, it is the woman who is investigated, punished, killed or tamed. Hitchcock's films would serve as the exemplary case. In *film noir* and modern thrillers, this trope still recurs from *The Big Sleep* to *Klute* to *Fatal Attraction*. But we also find *fetishistic scopophilia*, building up the visual beauty of the represented female face or form to such an extent that it acquires an unearthly, unreal, abstract beauty that itself becomes the distracting and compensating fetish.

Spectatorship

What is happening on the screen – the representation of the male and female characters, the framing, the alternations between movement though space and the arrested moment of the icon, the relations, therefore, between form and content – symptomatically rehearses the structuring formations of the subjects who are lured to its screening and sit captivated by its magic as the destination of its ideological work.

The spectator is not just the individual man or woman, straight, lesbian or gay, black or white, African, Indian, Muslim, Jewish or Christian person sitting in the audience, full of social reality and diversity. I will come back to such differences in a moment. *The* spectator is an ideal projected by the cinema, one with which we tend to identify in the imaginary misrecognition of which I wrote earlier. It is the ideal, the Other, that culture projects at us indifferent to our particularity. *The* spectator is an ideological position from which sense can be made of the sequence of images that flows before its visual apprehension and visually cued fantasy. *The* spectator is the industrially, technologically and ideologically fashioned intersection of scopophilia, fetishism and voyeurism pre-shaped by the Imaginary; it is the white, capitalist site of exploitation of a heightened and overstimulated visual erotics that is, none the less, over-determined by a phallocentric logic. This point is important and so easily misunderstood.

The spectator seems a dangerously out-of-date concept in a world made politically aware of the vital significance of our many differences. 'What "we", white man?', as Tonto said so tellingly to the Lone Ranger. What 'the' do I speak of as a white-woman-feminist-theorist? Of course, in our social realities of class, culture, gender and ethnicity we read films in unpredictable ways, feeling included, alienated or outraged. As bell hooks (1992) argues in her essay, 'The Oppositional Gaze', African-American women search in vain in Hollywood cinema for any representation that mirrors their desires, thoughts, experience and beauty back to them. But cinema has worked not only to find a structure to maximize its audience; Hollywood has also used this structure ideologically to mask the political nature of the pictures of the world it peddles. Is the spectator male/white? Is the gaze male/white?

We need to distinguish audience or viewers and the manifold ways they actually read or resist visual texts and images and the hegemonic way in which the dominant cultural systems operate to perform the exclusions and the normalizations against which any of us in our outraged particularity may protest (Stacey 1994). So, if Laura Mulvey talks of *the* spectator and it is presumed to be male, she appears to be privileging gender over other equally important social factors such as race, class and sexuality. But in her politically motivated use of psychoanalysis as her instrument for deconstructing visual pleasure in the cinema, Laura Mulvey asked: is the gaze as active mastery of a visual field and as allegory of desire positioned as 'masculine' according to the phallocentric system Hollywood cinema so perfectly came to mimic? Mulvey identified the logic for a whole apparatus and representational system that produces the terms in which the socially and culturally varied audience experience their social exclusion or the repression of their difference according to the logic of see-er/seen, desiring subject/object of desire, maker of meaning/passive cipher of meaning, power/lack.

Imitation of Life was made in the 1930s by Irving Stahl and again in 1959 by Douglas Sirk. The story concerns two mothers, one black and one white, who help each other. Each has a daughter. The black woman has a pancake recipe that makes the white woman a fortune. The black woman, however, remains the subservient, large, black mammy servant below stairs, while the now rich, white woman's love life and difficult motherhood are the narrative core of the film. The black daughter can, however, pass for white and she desires to escape, to have what white women take for granted. Stahl's film never questioned the conventions of its moment; the Sirk film, however, reworked the story to interrupt the dominant stereotypes, forcing the spectator through manipulations of identification to experience emotionally the pain of the black subject in a racist world. Writing of the Stahl version, bell hooks recalls the effect of Peola, the rebellious black daughter:

> You were different. There was something scary in this image of young sexual sensual black beauty betrayed – that daughter who did not want to be confined by blackness, that 'tragic mulatto' who did not want to be negated . . . I will always remember that image. I remember how we cried for her, for our unrealized desiring selves. She was tragic because there was no place in cinema for her, no loving pictures. She too was an absent image. It was better then, that we were absent, for when we were there it was humiliating, strange, sad. We cried all night for you, for the cinema that had no place for you. And like you, we stopped thinking it would one day be different. (hooks 1992: 122)

The anguish bell hooks speaks underlines the negative effect on the spectator for whom white cinema proffers no idealizing and confirming mirror image. It does, however, work negatively, marking the gap between the ideal imago and the sense of self that does not correspond to it. It negates any possibility of valorization save that of the fabricated image of white femininity as the icon of desirability. The effect is a kind of psychic castration: blackness is recast as lack, deficiency and deformity *vis-à-vis* the white female star, just as femininity appears as deformity and lack in relation to the phallus. Seeking alternatives, bell hooks turned to independent and European cinema but here she had to learn other modes of spectatorship of films choreographed by a different cinematic system – subtitles, long takes, a poetics of film rather than narrative realism. For those African-American women film-makers like Julie Dash (*Illusions* and *Daughters of the Dust*) who aim to create the cinema of black feminine desire that bell hooks missed in the cinema of her childhood, their interventions have operated precisely at the level of the cinematic. They use different kinds of shot, never isolating a figure or a part of a body, always using middle distance to encompass the group, using long takes and other such technical non-voyeuristic devices whose effects are not at the level just of story or character. They work also on changing the nature of our gaze, our visual interface with the meanings created in a political poetics for bodies in space.

Director Sheila McLaughlin intervened into this dominant cinematic system from the position of a white lesbian film-maker in her film, *She Must be Seeing Things* (1987). Teresa de Lauretis writes of this important work and the transformation that is needed not to put lesbians positively on display but to change radically the forms of spectatorship and hence the modes of desire that cinema can inscribe. Jo is a Marilyn Monroe blonde who is a film-maker. Agatha is her South American lover who is a high-level professional in an aid agency. Agatha, constantly paranoid about Jo and men, suffers visual hallucinations. She gives Jo a sexy piece of lingerie and Jo performs a mock reverse striptease, a scene that caused a lot of anxiety in lesbian audiences for seeming to replay the stereotype of woman as erotic object:

> By calling up this iconographic and cultural history, in conjunction with current lesbian practices of both reappropriation and resignification of what is and is not our history, *She Must be Seeing Things* asks what in feminist film culture is clearly a rhetorical question: what are the things Agatha imagines seeing and those Jo 'sees' in her film if not those very images . . . that our cultural imaginary and the whole history of cinema have constructed as the visible, what can be seen *and eroticised*? Namely, the female body displayed as a spectacle for the male gaze 'to take in', to enter it or possess . . . and above all, what can be seen or eroticised – though not actually imaged or represented, but only figured, implied in the look – is the gaze itself, the phallic power of the gaze invested in the

male look as figure and signifier of desire ... the originality of
McLaughlin's film consists in foregrounding that frame of reference, in
making *it* visible, and at the same time, shifting it, moving it aside,
enough to let us see through the gap, the contradiction; enough to create
a space for questioning not only what *they* see but also what *we* see
in the film: enough to see ourselves seeing, and with what eyes.
(de Lauretis 1994: 113)

As lesbian or straight, as black or white, as working class or middle
class, we are subject to comparable structures of psycho-symbolic
formation, formed in fantasy and desire around the structures of
presence and absence and therefore each social exclusion or negation
is experienced also at a *psychic* price. Feminist theory is a complex of
theorizations of class, race, gender, sexuality, ability, generation and
geography. What marks the feminist dimension of discussions of race
or sexuality or class is the way in which this structure of the production of sexual difference, desire and fantasy inhabits and forms all subjectivities, and at a certain specific level: the psycho-symbolic, between
fantasy and language, qualifies the way we experience what we name
as class or race.

The Eye of Power

I have focused first on psychoanalytically informed feminist theories
of cinematic visuality. But we must draw a distinction between
psychoanalytical concepts of the gaze and the notions of the gaze as
'the eye of power' elaborated by Michel Foucault (1980). Foucault
noted an historical shift at the beginning of modernity towards a
society that exercises power not by sudden spectacular acts of violence
but by continuous regulation and discipline that involve a pervasive
watching which ultimately individual subjects internalize, 'surveilling'
and disciplining themselves. There were key sites for this new
disciplinary model of power. The prison where Jeremy Bentham
invented a panopticon was a large circular building with backlit cells
opening inwards, allowing a central observation tower to monitor all
inmates, who would be visible at any time to this invisible watcher. In
streets and shopping centres perpetually monitored by CCTV, with
innumerable computer-linked records, all citizens are now managed
through this kind of disciplinary visibility. Foucault also identified
power effected through the specialist medical gaze of a doctor on a

passive patient, and the family, where what many might consider the most private of activities, sexuality and sexual pleasure, became not a privatized and repressed secret but the object of an immense web of discourse. The body in its pleasures and the social functions of those pleasures were the target of an extensive apparatus that monitored children, women and those designated as perverse adults, homosexuals. At the heart of this new regime of sexuality was the feminine body idealized in its maternal function and medically scrutinized for its dysfunctions, notably hysteria. Photography, invented around 1839, rapidly became a crucial tool of this surveillance and investigative discipline.

Hysteria and the Visual Image

The doctor most associated with the medical study of hysteria, Jean-Marie Charcot produced a photographic iconography of the hysterical attack. The female patients' theatrical and often anatomically distorted poses provided a whole new visual iconography of the female body which we find constituting the novelty of the artistic movements we identify as Modernism. Degas' tortured bodies of bathers and dancers through to Picasso's remodelled sexual anatomies can be traced back to this visualization of female hysteria. The stylistic break of modern art inscribes the hystericization of femininity in an endless parade of intensely sexualized, fragmented, opened, exposed, expressionistically primivitized female bodies that litter the modernist studio and this vocabulary now underpins contemporary advertising and the covers of romantic fiction (Kelly 1996).

The hystericization of the female body works at the intersection of two regimes. The female is identified as only a body, determined from within by sexual anatomy that then exhibits the pathology of this sexuality in external deformation. Woman shows herself, again. This passive, mindless 'showing' sets up as 'knowing' what this mute body cannot understand or speak, namely the gaze of the specialist Other, the doctor, the psychologist, the artist. The visibility of feminine hysteria was contested by Freud who interpreted the affliction psychologically and semiotically, treating it as a radical doubt about the nature of identity and sexuality, a view that links back to both what I have said about identity being built around an image and to sexuality as always incompletely constructed. The feminine becomes, in hysteria *par excellence*, the place to ask the question: what am I? Man or

Woman? Thing or Person? Alive or Dead? It is for this reason that feminist critics have been so interested in the work of American Cindy Sherman. Using herself as model, she produced in the 1980s a series of photographic set-ups that perfectly mimicked the extensive array of femininities offered through cinematic and media images. On the one hand, Sherman's series of *Untitled Film Stills* were read as a critical glossary of types, which the artist herself convincingly recreated and thus effectively revealed as fabrications. Thus her work was treated as a critique of representation of the feminine in American culture, especially since the 1950s. On the other hand, Sherman's later work used high-gloss colour photography to parody soft porn but increasingly it parodied all conventions, becoming darker in mood and ultimately unravelling the inside/outside dialectic. That is to say, if fashion imagery stresses woman as beautiful surface, glossy, shiny like a commodity, denaturalized and perfected (fetishistic scopophilia), the whole regime of phallocentric visual pleasure will unravel if the image of woman becomes wet, abject, physical, revealing intestinal, bloody interiors, decaying food, vomit, bodily fluids and wastes. Does Sherman's 'ugly' phase instate women's internalized misogynist revulsion? Is it aimed at culture's repressions or the whole structure of feminine masquerade? Does it inscribe a new moment, a postmodern sense of the body that oscillates between horror and frankness about mutability, mortality, dreaming of an escape from the disciplining of bodies into conventional sexualities, genders, identities (Bronfen 1998)?

Feminist Theory and Painting

Where has this postmodern critique of representation left traditional art practices such as painting, the very signifier of high art? Almost overwhelmed by the force of feminist critique of the history of representations of the female nude, of the institutionalization of a privileged masculine viewer, of the modernist idealization of the artist as sexually potent Man, painting seemed beyond feminist recuperation both theoretically and practically during the 1970s and 1980s. An exhibition in 1980, 'Women's Images of Men', tried the strategy of reversing the gaze, only to expose its difficulties even in showing such an interesting array of work by women that explored their own desires and anger. While the majority of artwork that has attracted and refracted feminist theoretical attention has been conceptual, photographic, installation or cinematic over the past thirty years, painters have continued painting, even while theorization has lagged behind. There was an interesting debate in the later 1980s with thoughtful writing on the ways in which women painters were exploring aspects of femininity and the body through that medium (Pollock 2000). The privileging of a feminist critique of representation left much of the core activity of painting without its new vocabulary. But once the parameters of the analysis became sharper, parameters I have tried to map here as a theoretical/political structure, we could return to painting as a fascinating site of feminist interventions and effects.

Let us review where we have come from and where we might go. I have set up a central insight: men look; women watch themselves being looked at to expose an historically, ideologically and psychically constructed hierarchy with real effects. I have tried to relate the role of the image to the constructions of identity, sexuality and social relations of difference and power. I have examined two different concepts of the gaze (desire/power) and shown how we have moved from a connoisseur's admiration of an art object to the psycho-semiotic reading of a visual text. Finally, by discussing hysteria, I have reintroduced the inside/outside, surface/interior dialectic as it relates to the anxiety around the representation of the feminine body in phallocentric culture.

Painting is a physical practice, involving concrete materials and active gestures while creating an imaginary space on the canvas. This can be representational or non-figurative. It affects us as viewers not merely by offering a spectacle but by calling upon sympathetic responses that engage our bodies' memories of space, colour and, importantly, touch. If we theorize the gaze, not merely as the 'eye of power' but as a kind of erotic aerial (Lichtenberg Ettinger 1995) that uses seeing to contact sensations, memories, associations, dimensions that are themselves not visual, we can begin to see how potent painting might be for feminist work. It can help discover the country of feminine desires, bodies, fantasies and forge a practice in which the image and the body enter into a productive covenant that allows us to discover what phallocentric culture has repressed: the sexual difference of the feminine. There is still much to be done. But there are now substantial theoretical resources. Feminist theory of the visual has not only made a difference within its own intellectual and practical community. It has also created a paradigm shift that decisively changes the terms of art history, fine art practice and the analysis of all aspects of visual culture.

References and Further Reading

Bal, M. (1992) *Reading Rembrandt: Beyond the Word Image Opposition*. Cambridge: Cambridge University Press.

— (1996) Reading art? In Griselda Pollock (ed.), *Generations and Geographies in the Visual Arts: Feminist Readings*, pp. 25–41. London: Routledge.

Barthes, R. (1977a) *Image–Music–Text*, trans. S. Heath. London: Fontana (first published 1968).

— (1977b) *Mythologies*, trans. A. Lavers. London: Paladin (first published 1957).

Berger, J. (1972) *Ways of Seeing*. Harmondsworth: Penguin.

Bronfen, E. (1998) Beyond hysteria: Cindy Sherman's private theater of horror. In E. Bronfen, *The Knotted Subject: Hysteria and its Discontents*. Princeton, NJ: Princeton University Press.

Carson, F. and Pajaczkowska, C. (2001) *Feminist Visual Culture*. New York: Routledge.

Duncan, C. (1993) *The Aesthetics of Power: Essays in Critical Art History*. Cambridge: Cambridge University Press.

Foucault, M. (1980) The eye of power. In C. Gordon (ed.), *Power/Knowledge 1972–1977*. Brighton: Harvester Press.

hooks, b. (1992) *Black Looks: Race and Representation*. London: Turnaround Press.

Kelly, M. (1996) *Imaging Desire*. Cambridge, MA: MIT Press.

Kuhn, A. (1985) *The Power of the Image: Essays on Representation and Sexuality*. London: Routledge.

de Lauretis, T. (1987) *Technologies of Gender: Essays on Theory, Film, and Fiction*. Bloomington, IN: Indiana University Press.

— (1994) *The Practice of Love: Lesbian Sexuality and Perverse Desire*. Bloomington, IN: Indiana University Press.

Lichtenberg Ettinger, B. (1995) *The Matrixial Gaze*. Leeds: Feminist Arts and Histories Network.

Mulvey, L. (1989) *Visual and Other Pleasures*. London: Macmillan.

Nead, L. (1992) *The Female Nude: Art, Obscenity and Sexuality*. London: Routledge.

Nochlin, L. (1972) Eroticism and female imagery in nineteenth-century art. In T. B. Hess and L. Nochlin (eds), *Woman as Sex Object: Studies in Erotic Art 1730–1970*, pp. 8–15. New York: Newsweek Inc.

Pollock, G. (1988) *Vision and Difference: Feminism, Femininity and Histories of Art*. London: Routledge.

— (1999) *Differencing the Canon: Feminist Desire and the Writing of Art's Histories*. London: Routledge.

— (2000) *Looking Back to the Future: Essays on Art, Life and Death*. London: Routledge.

Pribham, D. (ed.) (1988) *Female Spectators: Looking at Film and Television*. London: Verso.

Rose, J. (1986) *Sexuality in the Field of Vision*. London: Verso.
Silverman, K. (1988) *The Acoustic Mirror: The Female Voice in Psychoanalysis and Cinema*. Bloomington, IN: Indiana University Press.
Spence, J. (1995) *Cultural Sniping: The Art of Transgression*. London: Routledge.
Squiers, C. (1999) *Overexposed: Essays on Contemporary Photography*. New York: The New Press
Stacey, J. (1994) *Star Gazing: Hollywood Cinema and Female Spectatorship*. London: Routledge.

10

Feminist Philosophies

Rosi Braidotti

If as late as the mid-1980s the critical overviews, anthologies and reference texts dealing with feminist philosophy were so few as to constitute collectors' items, by the dawn of the new millennium the feminist philosophical community could pride itself on monumental reference works such as *A Companion to Feminist Philosophy*, edited by professional philosophers of the calibre of Allison Jaggar and Iris Young (1998). As Linda Alcoff put it: 'There is now a generation of fully mature thinkers, a considerable body of work, fully developed sub-areas, and even a bit of recognition. Jürgen Habermas has to respond to Nancy Fraser, Jacques Derrida to Judith Butler and John Rawls to Susan Moller Okin' (2000: 841). It is therefore quite a daunting task to try to sum up the state of this field, considering its vitality, diversity and dynamism.

The very question of the criteria of organization and classification of the different schools of feminist philosophy is so complex that it would deserve a study apart. It is effectively a philosophical issue in itself, which deals with the problems of the indexation and canonization of a rich and varied tradition. For instance, nationally oriented systems of indexation are often used to make sense of this wide field of feminist knowledge production. I did so myself (Braidotti 1994) by drawing an operational distinction between the German-inspired, the French-oriented, the Anglo-American and other traditions within the field broadly known as 'Continental' philosophy. More recently, Claire Colebrook (2000) has made a robust claim for a distinctive Australian tradition of feminist philosophy. This principle of organization offers the clear advantage of highlighting relatively less-known traditions of feminist thought, especially non-European ones and, thus, can contribute to a less ethnocentric approach: the section in Jaggar and Young's *Companion* (1998) entitled 'Africa, Asia, Latin America and Eastern Europe' illustrates the strategy. It is also useful to bring to our attention philosophical movements that occur in languages other than dominant standard English (Nagl-Docekal and Klinger 2000). None the less, I have grown dissatisfied with this nationalistic system of indexation which is not the best way to comprehend and organize the vitality of feminist philosophy. Especially in the context of the contemporary world where nationalism and xenophobia are on the rise, I would prefer to avoid such an approach and to 'nomadize' instead the different categories, so as not to compartmentalize them excessively. To 'nomadize' categories of thought means to dislodge them from their often implicit attachment to the humanistic vision concerning the autonomous, liberal individual so as to open them towards other modes of thinking about the structures of the self and the interrelation to others.

Ever mindful of Mary Eagleton's lesson on the importance of situating our narratives (Eagleton 1996), I would stress the messy, ad hoc and often simply erratic nature of a great deal of the formidable developments that have made feminist philosophy in the past thirty years. Emphasizing the non-linearity of this process is not a way of diminishing its value or significance, but rather it is a way to give back to the philosophical enterprise its adventurous and partial nature, writing it back into women's own experience. Some common features can in fact be detected and it is to these that I will turn first, to establish a sort of indexical system.

The Bond to the Women's Movement

The foundational value of Simone de Beauvoir's work (1953) for feminist philosophy cannot be overstressed. Not only did Beauvoir's phenomenological approach emphasize the need to think through existence and experience but she also stressed the structural value and the structurally discriminatory force of the concept of 'difference'. Beauvoir calls for a Hegelian-inspired overcoming of the dialectic of domination which elevates the Self or the Same to the rank of a sovereign subject and reduces the other/s to a hierarchically inferior category. In order to overthrow this dialectical scheme, Beauvoir posits as a necessary condition a bond of solidarity between herself and all other women, which lays the philosophical foundations for the feminist theory of political sisterhood. Moreover, Beauvoir brings to the fore the fake universalism of philosophical thinking which has passed off reason as a generic human trait, while allowing it to be colonized by masculinity, in dialectical opposition to his 'others'.

Feminist theories start from the assumption that 'the personal is the political' and that all theories about women and gender need to be checked against real-life experiences. This appeal to 'the politics of experience' originated in the 1960s from Marxist epistemology: it means that you have to trust the evidence of real-life women, that real-life conditions are the most important indicator of the status of women. The appeal to 'experience' plays a foundational role also in terms of the feminist critique of what was first called bourgeois-patriarchal ideology (in the Marxist phase) and, later on, under the influence of psychoanalysis and post-structuralism, the phallologocentric regime. *A Concise Glossary of Feminist Theory* (Andermahr et al. 1997) provides a useful introduction to these key feminist concepts. Following Beauvoir, the anchoring point and ground of validation for feminist philosophy remains the politics of location and experience with a privileged bond to the embodied self. Adrienne Rich (1985) re-examines this idea and redefines it in the light of new evidence brought into feminism by women of colour and lesbians. By emphasizing the differences that exist among women, especially on the grounds of race and sexual orientation, Rich diversifies the foundational category of 'experience' and proposes to replace it with a more complex framework of analysis where diversity and multiple power locations play a central role. The materialism of the early appeals to 'real life' is made more complex. With the politics of locations, a feminist critique of power is offered that confronts the many power differences and is based on accountability for our locations. This in turn means that 'we women' are all in it, though in very dissymmetrical and uneven ways.

In fact, a 'location' is not a self-appointed and self-designed subject position. It is a collectively shared and constructed, jointly occupied spatio-temporal territory. Consequently, the politics of location refers to a process of consciousness-raising that requires a political awakening (Grewal and Kaplan 1994) and hence the intervention of others. Politics of locations are cartographies of power which rest on a form of self-criticism, a critical, genealogical self-narrative; they are relational and outside-directed. This means that 'embodied' accounts

197

illuminate and transform our knowledge of ourselves and of the world. Thus, black women's texts and experiences make white women see the limitations of our locations, truths and discourses. Feminist knowledge is an interactive process that brings out aspects of our existence, especially our own implication with power, that we had not noticed before. It estranges us from the familiar, the intimate, the known and casts an external light upon it; in Foucault's language, it is micropolitics, and it starts with the embodied self. Feminists, however, knew this well before either psychoanalysis or post-structuralism theorized it in its philosophy.

Thus, feminist theory is about multiple and potentially contradictory locations and differences among, but also within, different women (Braidotti 1994). To account for them, locations are approached as geo-political, but also temporal zones, related to self-reflexivity, consciousness, self-narrative and memory. Feminism, especially under the impact of Foucault's post-structuralist philosophy (Diamond and Quinby 1988), is not about restoring another dominant memory but rather about installing a counter-memory, or an embedded and embodied genealogy. Accordingly, I see feminist philosophy as the activity aimed at articulating the questions of individual gendered identity with issues related to political subjectivity, the production of knowledge, diversity, alternative representations of subjectivity and epistemological legitimation (Braidotti 2002).

The politics of locations is an affirmative approach to the issue of subjectivity in so far as it looks at the workings of power in terms of the complexity and multiplicity of the relations that structure it. In order to achieve this, feminist philosophy has, from the start, rejected the dualistic modes of thought (Lloyd 1984; Irigaray 1985; Cixous and Clément 1986). Instead of thinking in oppositional terms, it stresses the simultaneity of potentially contradictory axes of oppression. This emphasis on diversity among women, coupled with the practice of accountability for one's locations as a critique of power differentials, leads to the necessity of creating alternative forms of theoretical representation. Hence the importance of what I call 'figurations' of alternative feminist subjectivity, like the womanist or the lesbian or the cyborg or the inappropriate(d) other or the nomadic feminist or other possibilities. They differ from classical 'metaphors' precisely in calling into play a sense of accountability for one's locations. They express materially embedded cartographies and as such are self-reflexive and not parasitic upon a process of metaphorization of 'others'. Moreover, self-reflexivity is not an individual activity but an interactive process which relies upon a social network of exchanges. The figurations that emerge from this process act as the spotlight that illuminates aspects of one's practice which were blind spots before. By extension, new figurations of the subject (nomadic, cyborg, black and so on) function like conceptual *personae*.

Feminist theory has worked very hard in the past twenty years to build on these foundations and to formulate its philosophical tradition. In the following sections in this chapter, I will analyse some dominant frameworks for feminist philosophies, following Harding's threefold classification of different feminist epistemologies (Harding 1986, 1991). Let it be clearly understood from the start, however, that these three trends are neither dialectically linked, nor are they hierarchically rated. This means that they are not mutually exclusive: rather, they represent approaches, moments or positions which can coexist, even within the same individual thinkers. The main purpose of drawing categorical distinctions between them, therefore, is to elucidate each category and explore its implications.

Feminist Empiricism

This approach, be it quantitative or qualitative, pays its dues to social constructivism and it assumes that the practice of institutional philosophy disproportionately represents men's interests, needs and expectations. It consequently aims at repairing the under-representation of women at all levels of research, teaching, implementation, policy-making and dissemination of data and information. This policy of equal opportunities for women has been officially adopted by all major professional organizations for feminist philosophy, from the European Network of Women Philosophers to the Society for Women in Philosophy, the women's caucus in the Society for Phenomenology and Existentialist Philosophy and to specific branches of the International Philosophical Association. This empirical or equity-minded approach to philosophy sides resolutely with scientific rationality and objectivity, without questioning any of its tenets, including the distinction knower/known. In fact, it takes these principles of rationality and objectivity so seriously that it applies them to the analysis of the practice of philosophy itself. It argues, therefore, that gender bias and discrimination against women is a failure of scientific rationality. In other words, gender biased or downright sexist scientific practices make for bad science and, thus, they constitute a fault in the proper, objective use of scientific objectivity (Lloyd 1984; Harding 1986). The masculinist bias is, from this perspective, a form of irrationality, an error of judgement that needs to be eliminated in order to produce a type of scientific practice that would be truly worthy of the ideals of objectivity and rationality. Proper scientific objectivity can and must be restored by fighting male domination of the use of reason.

I see two problems with this approach. First, it tends to remain restricted to repair work, that is to say in mending the gender gap in philosophy. This is undeniably important considering the persistence of factors of inequality and of discrimination against women. However, in the long term an equity-minded approach runs into structural difficulties. More complex strategies and frameworks of analysis are needed in order to tackle the continuing issue of male domination of philosophical knowledge. Issues of power and identity need to be raised and a challenge needs to be mounted against the conceptual framework of what we have learnt to recognize as 'scientific objectivity'. Secondly, most equity-minded projects tend to essentialize the category of 'women', flattening out the wide and widening range of differences among women. Diversity is underplayed in the name of an overarching, allegedly universal principle of equity of equality, which often begs the very question it asks, namely: 'equal to whom?' (Irigaray 1985).

Standpoint Feminist Theory

The largest area of feminist philosophical reflection is the 'standpoint feminism' school. This is an attempt to combine the politics of location with a more scientific methodology. Harding's 'standpoint feminism' (1986) argues that women's experience provides a good starting-point for the elaboration of new paradigms of knowledge. Although feminists like Nancy Hartsock (1983) kept this theory closely related to the Marxist idea that 'the oppressed know better', most did not. Evelyn Fox Keller (1985), for instance, relies on the object-relation theory of psychoanalysis in order to demonstrate how power differences work in the production of Western philosophical assumptions about rationality and the universality of reason. Keller raises issues of identity and identity-formation and singles them out as crucial to the whole discussion on feminism and science. Object-relation theory is a very influential school of psychoanalysis which emerged from the Anglo-American tradition and, thus, differs considerably from the

French Lacanian school. It emphasizes both the contextual factors and the social framework and their impact upon the formation of the subject and the process of socialization. Less preoccupied with symbolic and imaginary structures than on concrete social relations, this psychoanalytic tradition, inspired mostly by Winnicott's work, stresses inter-subjectivity and the importance of transitional spaces. Because of this emphasis on interpersonal exchanges, object-relation psychoanalytic theory allows for empirical analyses of patterns of domination and exclusion (Benjamin 1988), as well as for a critique of their privileged bond with masculinity and also for feminist resistance to them.

In a more sociological version, this school of thought finds in Nancy Chodorow's theory of parenting a concrete strategy by which men's role in child-rearing is proposed as the antidote to the bond that patriarchal societies encourage between masculinity and violence. Chodorow (1978) and other object-relation theorists have challenged the masculine bias of science not merely as an accidental or a statistical instance but rather as a structural element in scientific practice. In other words, science is masculine not only because it is empirically dominated by men but because it also implies a male subject and object of science at each and every step of the making of science. The masculine bias that is built into the practice of science reflects the codes of behaviour that are operational in society as a whole. Here, psychoanalytic studies of the psycho-sexual development of individuals cast an important light on the ways in which masculinity comes to be identified with autonomy and femininity with dependence (Benjamin 1988). In turn, this encourages men's access to the use of rationality, the well-defined rules and protocols of scientific objectivity and an inquisitive spirit that results in experimentation. In the female, insecurities and lack of assertiveness are implemented instead.

Difference-minded or standpoint feminism covers a variety of methods which have in common a critique of empirically minded gender equity. The grounds on which 'difference' is defended as a positive value, and not merely as a signifier of inferiority or oppression, vary greatly. While most feminist philosophers tend to be sceptical of specific female or feminine ways of knowing (Code 1991), most emphasize the potential represented by the yet-untapped resources of women's cognitive, intellectual and other experiences. In particular, this gender approach stresses the positive contribution that women and other socially marginal groups can make to the production of scientific knowledge. It assumes that positions of social marginality are ideal sources of knowledge in so far as they do not defend any vested interests and thus end up being more objective and more impartial. Women's ethical powers and sense of moral responsibility, including a wilful rejection of competitiveness and aggression, have also been quoted as a positive source of difference (Gilligan 1982).

In terms of its relationship to the discipline of philosophy, this approach is far more critical than the previous, empiricist one. Scientific objectivity is challenged from without and a more radical critique is offered of the ways in which rationality and objectivity are implemented as a human, a social and a scientific ideal. The assumption behind this critique is that women's socially induced 'difference' is, in fact, a capital, a human and scientific resource that needs to be infused into what our culture has codified as science. The aim here is the enlargement of the notions of rationality and objectivity, in order to make them less discriminatory and more inclusive. A very important element in this approach is the critique of power relations and the relationships of domination and exclusion which operate within the actual practice of philosophy. We are a long way in this view from the unquestioned acceptance of scientific concepts of the empirical tradition. Moreover, by emphasizing the importance of social and cultural mediations, feminist standpoint approaches also stress the degree to which the positionality of the individual thinkers – in terms of gender, class, age, race, religion – affects the kind of projects s/he is likely to engage in. This is not to be confused with a relativistic position but rather with a systematic attention to power relations. A concrete example of feminist standpoint strategies is the re-reading of the philosophical canon by feminist philosophers. This entails a lively dialogue with the history of philosophy and was initiated by Genevieve Lloyd in the 1980s and pursued today in a full-scale attack on the exclusiveness and male domination of the history of philosophy. As Alcoff (2000) points out, Nancy Tuana's editorial series for Pennsylvania State University Press on the philosophical canon is exemplary of this trend.

Feminist Postmodernism

The critique of the essentialism implicit in standpoint gender theory is the starting-point for the more deconstructive approach. Whether it is based on a postmodernist, post-structuralist, post-colonial or, more recently, post-feminist approach, this gender method fundamentally challenges the possibility of speaking in one unified voice about women. The focus is entirely on issues of diversity and differences among women. By crossing questions of gender with a critique of the eurocentric bias in science, this approach questions the idea that science and scientific knowledge can be truly universal (Spivak 1987). Instead, feminist postmodernism tends to see such knowledge as an expression of Western culture and of its drive to mastery. Whereas empirical philosophies efface differences and standpoint feminism enhances them, a postmodernist approach takes off from them in order to transform them into stepping-stones towards cross-border or transversal alliances. As a strategy, this approach tends, therefore, to emphasize differences among women, in terms of class, race and ethnicity, sexual orientation but also of age, thus targeting especially the needs and aspirations of the next generations.

Neither relativistic nor a form of sceptical suspension of belief in values, deconstruction is the simultaneous recognition of the ubiquity of power and hence its non-linear structure, as well as the necessity of resistance in an equally non-linear manner. In a postmodernist framework, philosophical thought is taken not only as an attempt to explore and analyse but also as a way to control and normalize. Scientific discourse is embedded in a network of power relations aimed at disciplining nature, its resources and the many 'others' that are different from an implicit norm of scientific subjectivity. This norm equates science with masculinity and both with white, eurocentric premises. The recognition of the normativity of science and of the partiality of scientific statements as well as their necessary contingency has nothing to do with relativism. Rather, it has to do with a critique of falsely universal pretensions and with the desire to pluralize the options, paradigms and practices within Western reason, in keeping with the basic tenets of deconstructionism (Holland 1997).

In what I consider to be a radical critique of dualistic thinking, postmodernist approaches emphasize the extent to which power is a process of formation of pejorative 'others'. Here 'difference' plays a constitutive, if negative, role. 'Difference' has been colonized by power relations that reduce it to inferiority; further, it has resulted in passing off differences as 'natural', which has made entire categories of beings into devalued and therefore disposable others. Discourse, as Michel Foucault argues in *Discipline and Punish* (1977), is about the political currency that is attributed to certain meanings, or systems of meaning, in such a way as to invest them with scientific legitimacy: there is nothing neutral or given about it. Thus, a deconstructivist approach to the analysis of power and discourse highlights the links that exist between scientific truth and discursive currency or power relations. As

203

such, it primarily aims at dislodging the belief in the 'natural' foundations of socially coded and enforced 'differences' and of the systems of value and representation that they support.

Secondly, a politicized deconstructive method emphasizes the need to historicize the analysis of the creation of scientific concepts as normative formations and, thus, it allows us to take on the historicity of the very concepts that we are investigating. In a feminist frame, this emphasis on historicity means that the scholar needs some humility before the eternal repetitions of history and the great importance of language. We need to learn that there is no escape from the multilayered structure of our own encoded history and language. The political implications are even more striking. They suggest that there is no readily accessible uncontaminated or 'authentic' voice of the oppressed, be it women or blacks or people of colour. This turns, first, into an attack on the essentialism of those who claim fixed identities of the deterministic kind. It also undercuts, however, any claim to 'purity' as the basis for epistemological or political alternatives. Claims to 'purity' are always suspect because they assume subject positions that would be unmediated by language and representation.

Politically, therefore, feminist postmodernist philosophies are opposed to 'identity politics' and to the counter-affirmation of oppositional identities because they end up reasserting the very dualisms they are trying to undo. Simultaneously, they also stress the positivity of difference within a theoretical platform for a politics of diversity in so far as they make a point of carefully avoiding and even undermining any attempt at re-essentializing 'gender', 'race' and 'ethnicity' as natural given 'data'. Feminist postmodernist philosophies are committed both to a radical politics of resistance and to the critique of the simultaneity of potentially contradictory social and textual effects. This simultaneity is not to be confused with easy parallels or arguments by analogy. That gender, race, class and sexual choice may be equally effective power variables does not amount to flattening out any differences between them.

I could sum up post-deconstructivist strategies by saying that all deconstructions are equal but some are more equal than others. Whereas the deconstruction of masculinity and whiteness is an end in itself, the non-essentialistic reconstruction of black perspectives, as well as the feminist reconstruction of multiple ways of being women, also have new values to offer. In other words, some notions need to be deconstructed so as to be laid to rest once and for all: masculinity; whiteness; heterosexism; classism; ageism. Others need to be deconstructed only as a prelude to offering positive new values and effective ways of asserting political presence of newly empowered subjects: feminism; diversity; multiculturalism; environmentalism. We need to fight passionately for the simultaneous assertion of positive differences by, for and among women, while resisting essentialization and claims to authenticity.

The Importance of Psychoanalysis and Post-structuralism

Psychoanalysis is crucial in theorizing and representing a non-unitary vision of the subject. I want to keep clearly in view the enfleshed, sexed and contradictory nature of the human subject, where fantasies, desires and the pursuit of pleasure play as important and constructive a role as rational judgement and standard political action. I would like to try to reconnect the wilful agency required of politics with the respect that is due, both theoretically and ethically, to the affective, libidinal and therefore contradictory structures of the subject. Sexuality is also central to this way of thinking about the subject.

In her important critique of the sex/gender distinction, Moira Gatens (1996) stresses the extent to which gender theory tacitly assumes a passive body onto which special codes are imprinted. The social-psychology-inspired gender model is diametrically opposed to the insights of psychoanalysis. The points of divergence concern, first, the structure of human embodiment: passive for gender theory, dynamic and interactive for post-structuralist theory. A second very important point concerns the notion of sexuality and of its role in the constitution of subjectivity which is of great importance for post-structuralism, not so for social psychological gender theories (Chanter 1995).

Although the body has been, in fact, a permanent feature of radical feminism from the start and has already undergone several brilliant redefinitions, the feminist theorists of sexual difference put a new *kind* of emphasis on the embodied female subject. They de-essentialized the body, that is to say they refused to reduce it to either raw nature (one is born a woman) or to mere social construction (one becomes a woman). Instead, they situated the body at the intersection of nature and culture, in a zone of high turbulence of power (de Lauretis 1987). By emphasizing the embodied structure of female subjectivity, these feminists politicized the whole issue. Moreover, by setting the ques-

205

tions of political subjectivity in the framework of a critique of phallo-logocentrism, they aimed at the empowerment of women in the deep structures of subjectivity. Embodiment provided a common but highly complex ground on which to postulate the feminist project. In a feminist postmodernist perspective, the body is an interface, a threshold, a field of intersecting material and symbolic forces. The body is a surface where multiple codes (race, sex, class, age and so on) are inscribed; it is a cultural construction that capitalizes on energies of a heterogeneous, discontinuous and unconscious nature.

In other words, the body, which for Beauvoir was one's primary 'situation' in reality, is now seen as a situated self, as an embodied positioning of the self. Although the terminology may appear similar, the conceptual and political differences are considerable. In spite of her phenomenological roots, Beauvoir upholds a rather Cartesian attitude towards the embodied structure of subjectivity. This means that she tends to reduce the body to the facticity of existence, which is to say its material roots; these are thought of as inevitable but are also inevitably opposed to the subject's capacity for thinking. The mind–body dualism in Beauvoir reduces the embodied self to the level of a material site in opposition to the subject's intentionality. Feminist post-structuralist philosophers critique this dualistic opposition, as they do all binary systems, but in addition they reinvest the body and the embodied roots of subjectivity with a more pervasive sense of what a body can actually do and of how it incorporates modes of thinking and knowing which extend beyond dualistic oppositions to the mind. This renewed sense of complexity aims to stimulate anew a revision and redefinition of contemporary subjectivity.

For Irigaray (1985) the body, and especially sexuality, is clearly perceived as the site of power struggles and contradictions and, consequently, it is viewed critically. But it is also addressed and re-visited precisely because of its crucial importance as a site of constitution of the subject. In other words, the signifier 'woman' is both the concept around which feminists have gathered in their recognition of a general condition and also the concept that needs to be analysed critically and eventually deconstructed. This is, furthermore, an historically situated statement: it is a suitable description of the condition of women in postmodern late capitalism. In my reading of post-structuralist philosophies of difference from Foucault to Irigaray and Deleuze (Braidotti 2002), I emphasize the material, sexualized structure of the subject. This sexual fibre is intrinsically and multiply connected to social and political relations; thus, it is anything but an individualistic entity.

Sexuality as a social and symbolic, material and semiotic institution is singled out as the primary location of power in a complex manner which encompasses both macro- and micro-relations. Sex is the social and morphological assignation of identity and suitable form of erotic agency to subjects that are socialized/sexualized in the polarized dualistic model of masculine/feminine implemented in our culture. Far from marginalizing sexuality, in this feminist conceptual framework it is a central point of reference which acts as the matrix for power relations in the broad but also most intimate sense of the term.

In American feminist philosophy through the 1990s, the sex/gender dichotomy swung towards the pole of gender with a vengeance, embracing it either as the preface to liberal individual 'rights' or in terms of social constructivist 'change'. In both cases, gender occupies the centre of the political spectrum and establishes the sex/gender dichotomy as a crucial term of reference, to the detriment of issues of sexuality and of sexual difference. It was left to the gay and lesbian and queer campaigners to try to re-write sexuality into the feminist agenda. In this framework, homosexuality is almost always synonymous with transgression or subversion. The tendency is also to critique heterosexuality as the dominant matrix of power and to target specifically the maternal roots of female sexuality for critique. Judith Butler (1990, 1993), following on from the work of Gayle Rubin (1975) and Monique Wittig (1992), makes an important intervention, pointing out that the distinction sex/gender is, in fact, untenable. If anything, argues Butler, it is the always-already sexualized matter that constructs the possibility of this dichotomy in the first place. Butler then proceeds to propose her own theory of performativity as a form of affirmative deconstruction of all identities, even those they taught us to despise.

Beyond Postmodernism: The Return of the Body

From the mid-1990s, a new brand of materialism emerges in feminist philosophies, following on from the postmodernist phase. It addresses both issues of technological change and the subsequent structural inequalities, and also issues of ethnicity, race, national and religious identity in the age of globalization. The work on the politics of location offered by post-colonial and anti-racist feminist thinkers like Gayatri Spivak (1987), Grewal and Kaplan (1994) and many others, helps us illuminate the present. The paradoxes, power dissymmetries and fragmentations of the present historical context require that we shift the political debates from the issue of differences between cultures, to differences *within* the same culture. In other words, one of the features of our present historical condition is the shifting grounds on which periphery and centre confront each other, with a new level of complexity which defies dualistic or oppositional thinking.

Black, post-colonial and feminist critics have rightfully *not* spared criticism of the paradoxes as well as the rather perverse division of labour that has emerged in the age of globalization. According to this paradox, it is the thinkers who are located at the *centre* of past or present empires who are actively deconstructing the power of the centre and, thus, contributing to the discursive proliferation and consumption of former 'negative' others. Those same others, however, especially in post-colonial, but also in post-fascist and post-communist societies, are more keen to reassert their identity, rather than to deconstruct it. The irony of this situation is not lost on any of the interlocutors. We can think, for instance, of the feminist philosophers saying: 'how can we undo a subjectivity we have not even historically been entitled to *yet*?' Or we consider the black and post-colonial subjects who argue that it is now their historical turn to be self-assertive and thus reject postmodernism as a discourse of crisis. And if the white, masculine, ethnocentric subject wants to 'deconstruct' himself and enter a terminal crisis, then – so be it! The point remains that 'difference' emerges as a central – albeit contested and paradoxical – notion and this means that a confrontation with it is historically inevitable as we – postmodern subjects – are historically condemned to our history. Accounting for these differences through adequate cartographies consequently remarks a crucial priority.

A significant example of the often paradoxical affinity between feminist theory and philosophical nomadology is Donna Haraway's redefinition of materialism (1988) which redesigns the epistemological grounds of feminist theory after postmodernism. She redefines the idea of politics of location in the late 1980s which will remain influential throughout the 1990s. Haraway's argument is that, in the age of globalization, under the impact of technology, there is no unmediated relationship to experience. Our social life is marked by a set of technological mediations. This calls on us to readjust our schemes of thought to a social reality which is pervaded by structural injustices engendered by late post-industrial societies the world over. In this line of thinking the practice of theoretical reason and, hence, of the philosophy of science is not seen as narrowly rationalistic but rather allows for a broadened definition of the term, to include the play of the unconscious, dreams and the imagination in the production of scientific discourse. Following Foucault (1977), Haraway draws our attention to the construction and manipulation of docile, knowable bodies in our present social system.

This view was elaborated further in Haraway's 'A Cyborg Manifesto' (1991), which is one of the most quoted and influential feminist figurations for an alternative view of subjectivity. I read the figuration of the cyborg along three distinct, though interrelated axes: as an analytical, a normative and a utopian category. On the analytical level, it assists in framing and organizing a politically invested cartography of present-day social and cognitive relations. As a normative value, it points towards more adequate and precise standards of evaluation and judgement of the social processes currently under way. Finally, as a utopian manifesto, endowed with a remarkable visionary charge, it draws virtual and possible scenarios for the advancement of the project of reconstructing subjectivity in the age of advanced technology. Haraway herself describes the hybrid figuration of the cyborg as a mix of political fiction, of mythology and of lived experience – especially women's – at the end of the twentieth century.

As a hybrid, or body-machine, the cyborg is a connection-making entity; it is a figure of interrelationality, receptivity and global communication that deliberately blurs categorical distinctions (human/machine; nature/culture; male/female; oedipal/non-oedipal). It allows Haraway to think specificity without falling into relativism. The cyborg is Haraway's representation of a generic feminist human-ity. By redefining it radically, it answers the question of how feminists might reconcile the radical historical specificity of women with the insistence on constructing new values that can benefit humanity as a whole. Moreover, the body in the cyborg model is neither physical nor mechanical – nor is it only textual. As a counter-paradigm for the inter-action between the inner and the external reality, it offers a reading not only of the body, nor only of machines but also of what goes on between them. As a new powerful replacement of the mind–body debate, the cyborg is a post-metaphysical construct.

In my reading, the figuration of the cyborg reminds us that meta-physics is not an abstract construction but, rather, a political ontology. The classical dualism body–soul is not simply a gesture of separation and of hierarchical coding; it is also a theory about their interaction, about how they hang together. It suggests how we should go about rethinking the unity of the human being. Balsamo (1996), in her reading of Haraway, stresses two crucial aspects of the cyborg; namely, that it corrects the discursive body with the materially constructed body. Secondly, she indicates that it bears a privileged bond to the female body. Woman as the 'other of the same' is in fact the primary artefact, produced through a whole social interaction that is both constructed by and is the expression of the various 'technologies of gender' that are currently operational (de Lauretis 1987).

Haraway is a non-anthropocentric philosopher with a strong affinity to eco-feminism: she reconceptualizes the process of knowledge starting from a machine-based or an animal-centred or an earth-grounded perspective. The cyborg theories emphasize that multiplicity need not lead necessarily to relativism. Haraway argues for a multifaceted foundational theory, for an anti-relativistic acceptance of differences, so as to seek for connections and articulations in a non-gender-centred and non-ethnocentric perspective.

Towards the Posthuman?

Interest in Darwin and evolutionary theory has grown considerably as a result of the renewal of interest in the body within feminist philosophy, on the one hand, and the rise of feminist studies of science and technology, on the other. This intensifies the crisis of philosophical humanism that post-structuralists had already celebrated in their interest in Freud, Marx, Nietzsche and Darwin. The point of their radical critique is both humanism and anthropocentrism; both have to do with the role and function of reason and the implicit assumptions it contains not only about subjectivity but also about the human as such. Traditionally, the self-reflexive control of life is reserved for the humans, whereas the mere unfolding of biological sequences is for the non-humans. The former is holy (*bios*), the latter quite gritty (*zoe*). That they intersect in the human body turns the physical self into a contested space, that is, a political arena. The mind–body dualism has historically functioned as a shortcut through the complexities of this in-between contested zone. Artists have crowded into this in-between area, offering a number of interconnections. And so have feminist philosophers who are engaged in rethinking feminist subjectivity in a dialogue with contemporary biology, while disagreeing with the neo-determinism of social biologists and evolutionary psychologists. Feminists attempt to disengage biology from the structural functionalism of DNA-driven linearity and to veer it instead towards more creative patters of development (Halberstam and Livingston 1995).

Social accountability is also high on the agenda. Elizabeth Grosz has stressed the importance for feminists to rethink the biological structure of the human. This call for a return to the body reiterates the rejection of social constructivism which, as I noted earlier, is crucial to feminist theory in the third millennium (Grosz 1994). In other research fields, such as science studies, however, where attention for and a critical engagement with evolutionary theories has always been central to the agenda, a more sceptical note is being struck. Thus, in their recent and quite masterful critique of evolutionary theories, Hilary and Steven Rose (2000) denounce their profound misogyny and their complicity with imperial and colonialist projects of white, eurocentric pseudo-science. They also track down the increasing interdependence of contemporary biological research and commercial as well as industrial concerns which are far from politically neutral.

The need for a new ethical project that would integrate a renewed interest in corporeality or bodily materialism with a serious critique of the limitations of the linguistic turn within postmodernism has been voiced by several feminist philosophers. Bio-ethics as an area has grown in importance of late (Diprose 1994); some humanistic philosophers like Martha Nussbaum (1986) point to the need for a return to Aristotelian principles of moral virtue; others, like Benhabib (1992), argue for the unavoidable confrontation with Kantian morality. In a more creative vein, Gatens and Lloyd (1999) re-visit Spinozist ethics with Gilles Deleuze so as to provide a robust new ethical standpoint. Noteworthy in this context is the interest in the philosophical work of Gilles Deleuze (Buchanan and Colebrook 2000) and in its applications to feminist philosophy (Braidotti 2002).

Conclusion

It is important to emphasize that, because of the great variety and high quality of the work accomplished over the past thirty years, feminist philosophy has moved beyond the premises that mark its beginnings. These are respectively a concern with mere criticism of the established canon, on the one hand, and, on the other, an exaggerated fascination with the 'philosopher queens' whose thought and personalities have marked the feminist movement with particular intensity. The rich variety offered by the field today shows that critique has been replaced by creative alternatives and the invention of new approaches and theoretical tools. As a result, the seduction of philosophical theory has been reduced accordingly and subjected to rigorous scrutiny. I think that both non-closure and the rejection of master figures and master theories have been accepted as ruling principles in the practice of feminist philosophies. This also implies going beyond the different 'isms' of our respective traditions of thought, to accept diversity but also the increasingly high degrees of specialization and the distinctive conceptual style of each tradition. I would locate in this approach the making of a distinctive feminist philosophical culture, which has moved from critique to affirmation, from negative readings to positive re-invention of the discipline, becoming both more complex and more focused in the process.

I think it remains of the greatest importance, now that the field of feminist philosophy is so well organized and methodologically sound, to keep on interrogating the criteria and the norms by which we organize the many micro-narratives that rule our thinking and generate our research. Resisting the temptation of teleological closure, self-transparency and hegemony, I would like to stress the importance of continuing to work on the very systems of indexation, the categories by which we, as feminist philosophers, organize our own work. The politics of location as an objective, accountable methodology that accepts partiality while avoiding relativism can be of the greatest assistance in this process. We need to interrogate the very ways in which the new feminist philosophical canon is being formed and transformed, while we passionately pursue this aim.

References and Further Reading

Alcoff, L. (2000) Philosophy matters: a review of recent work in feminist philosophy. *Signs*, 25 (3): 841–82.

Andermahr, S., Lovell, T. and Wolkowitz, C. (1997) *A Concise Glossary of Feminist Theory*. London: Arnold.

Balsamo, A. (1996) *Technologies of the Gendered Body*. Durham, NC: Duke University Press.

Beauvoir, S. de (1953) *The Second Sex*. London: Picador.

Benhabib, S. (1992) *The Situated Self*. Cambridge: Polity Press.

— and Cornell, D. (eds) (1987) *Feminism as Critique*. Cambridge: Polity Press.

Benjamin, J. (1988) *The Bonds of Love*. New York: Pantheon Books.

Braidotti, R. (1994) *Nomadic Subjects: Embodiment and Sexual Difference in Contemporary Feminist Theory*. New York: Columbia University Press.

— (2002) *Metamorphoses: Towards a Materialist Theory of Becoming*. Cambridge: Polity Press.

Buchanan, I. and Colebrook, C. (eds) (2000) *Deleuze and Feminist Theory*. Edinburgh: Edinburgh University Press.

Butler, J. (1990) *Gender Trouble: Feminism and the Subversion of Identity*. New York: Routledge.

— (1993) *Bodies that Matter: On the Discursive Limits of 'Sex'*. New York: Routledge.

Chanter, T. (1995) *Ethics of Eros: Irigaray's Re-writing of the Philosophers*. New York: Routledge.

Chodorow, N. (1978) *The Reproduction of Mothering: Psychoanalysis and the Sociology of Gender*. Berkeley, CA: University of California Press.

Cixous, H. and Clément, C. (1986) *The Newly Born Woman*. Minneapolis, MN: University of Minnesota Press.

Code, L. (1991) *What Can She Know? Feminist Theory and the Construction of Knowledge*. Ithaca, NY: Cornell University Press.

Colebrook, C. (2000) From radical representations to corporeal becomings: the feminist philosophy of Lloyd, Grosz and Gatens. *Hypatia*, 15: 76–93.

Diamond, I. and Quinby, L. (eds) (1988) *Foucault and Feminism*. Boston, MA: Northeastern University Press.

Diprose, R. (1994) *The Bodies of Women*. London: Routledge.

Eagleton, M. (1996) *Working with Feminist Criticism*. Oxford: Blackwell.

Foucault, M. (1977) *Discipline and Punish: The Birth of the Prison*, trans. A. Sheridan. London: Allen Lane.

Fraser, N. (1989) *Unruly Practices: Power, Discourse, and Gender in Contemporary Social Theory*. Minneapolis, MN: University of Minnesota Press.

Gatens, M. (1996) *Imaginary Bodies: Ethics, Power and Corporeality*. New York: Routledge.

— and Lloyd, G. (1999) *Collective Imaginings*. New York: Routledge.

Gilligan, C. (1982) *In a Different Voice: Women's Conceptions of the Self and Morality*. Cambridge, MA: Harvard University Press.

Grewal, I. and Kaplan, C. (1994) *Scattered Hegemonies: Postmodernity and Transnational Feminist Practices*. Minneapolis, MN: University of Minnesota Press.

Grosz, E. (1994) *Volatile Bodies: Towards a Corporeal Feminism*. Bloomington, IN: Indiana University Press.

Halberstam, J. and Livingston, I. (1995) *Posthuman Bodies*. Bloomington, IN: Indiana University Press.

Haraway, D. (1988) Situated knowledges: the science question in feminism as a site of discourse on the privilege of partial perspective. *Feminist Studies*, 14 (3): 575–99.

— (1991) A cyborg manifesto: science, technology and socialist feminism in the late twentieth century. In *Simians, Cyborgs, and Women: The Reinvention of Nature*, pp. 149–81. London: Free Association Press.

Harding, S. (1986) *The Science Question in Feminism*. London: Open University Press.

— (1991) *Whose Science? Whose Knowledge?* London: Open University Press.

Hartsock, N. (1983) The feminist standpoint: developing the ground for a specifically feminist historical materialism. In S. Harding and M. B. Hintikka (eds), *Discovering Reality*, pp. 283–310. Dordrecht: Reidel.

Holland, N. J. (1997) *Feminist Interpretations of Jacques Derrida*. University Park, PA: Pennsylvania State University Press.

Irigaray, L. (1985) *The Speculum of the Other Woman*. Ithaca, NY: Cornell University Press.

Jaggar, A. and Young, I. Marion (eds) (1998) *A Companion to Feminist Philosophy*. Malden, MA and Oxford: Blackwell.

Keller, E. F. (1985) *Reflections on Gender and Science*. New Haven, CT: Yale University Press.

de Lauretis, T. (1987) *Technologies of Gender: Essays on Theory, Film, and Fiction*. Bloomington, IN: Indiana University Press.

Lloyd, G. (1984) *The Man of Reason*. London: Methuen.

Nagl-Docekal, H. and Klinger, C. (eds) (2000) *Continental Philosophy in Feminist Perspective: Re-reading the Canon in English*. Pennsylvania, PA: Pennsylvania State University Press.

Nussbaum, M. (1986) *The Fragility of Goodness*. Cambridge: Cambridge University Press.

Rich, A. (1985) *Blood, Bread and Poetry: Selected Prose, 1979–1985*. New York: Norton.

Rose, H. and Rose, S. (2000) *Alas, Poor Darwin: Arguments against Evolutionary Psychology*. London: Jonathan Cape.

Rubin, G. (1975) The traffic in women: notes towards a political economy of sex. In R. Reiter (ed.), *Towards an Anthropology of Women*, pp. 157–210. New York: Monthly Review Press.

Spivak, G. Chakravorty (1987) *In Other Worlds: Essays in Cultural Politics*. New York: Routledge.

Tronto, J. (1993) *Moral Boundaries: A Political Argument for an Ethic of Care*. New York: Routledge.

Wittig, M. (1992) *The Straight Mind and Other Essays*. Hemel Hempstead: Harvester Wheatsheaf.

11

Cyberculture

Jenny Wolmark

Over the past decade an extraordinarily wide-ranging field of related studies has developed which focuses on cybernetics and information technology. This chapter is concerned with the relationship between feminist theory and the emerging fields of enquiry which come under the broad heading of cyberculture. All these fields are concerned with the social and cultural impact of information technology and with the ways in which the barriers between 'real' and 'virtual' space are being broken down. Indeed, the conceptual, electronic environment of cyberspace, initially described as a 'consensual hallucination' in the fiction of science-fiction writer William Gibson, is now taken for granted, so much so that, as Michael Heim suggests, cyberspace has become 'a tool for examining our very sense of reality' (1991: 59).

In order to address what she refers to as 'scary new networks' being set in place by the increasing domination of information technologies, Donna Haraway invokes the term 'informatics' (1990: 203) to describe the inextricably linked cultural, linguistic, social, sexual and biological connections and networks that derive from these technologies. New technologies have also generated an abundance of utopian and dystopian fantasies, many of which are reiterated in cyberculture, but as Constance Penley and Andrew Ross argue, such fantasies are an expression of 'real popular needs and desires' as well as being a 'powerful and persuasive means of social agency' (1991: xiii). The pervasive nature of these fantasies is emphasized by Judith Squires, who rightly suggests that 'the cybernetic has gripped our imaginations. It

increasingly structures our fantasies, phobias and political aspirations'
(1996: 194).

Although the main emphasis of the chapter will be on cyberculture,
there is an important connection to be made with feminist accounts
of science and technology. Cyberfeminism in particular is shaped by
existing debates about the relationship of gender to both science and
technology, and information technology has given a particular inflection to these debates. The new electronic spaces and places of
information technology provide an unparalleled opportunity both to
explore the interaction between human and machine, body and technology, and to challenge existing definitions of gendered identity and
the human.

A useful overview of debates focusing on the gendered nature of
science and technology is presented in *Inventing Women: Science, Technology and Gender* (1992). The editors of the collection of essays, Gill
Kirkup and Laurie Smith Keller, sum up the main issues in the
following way:

> Science, mostly done by men, seeks to define women in particular ways;
> not surprisingly, these definitions are often selective in the 'facts' they
> use and support cultural notions of male superiority and dominance/
> female inferiority and submission. Women, of whatever class, race, caste,
> and in whatever part of the world, are deeply affected by technology,
> yet they are often the last to benefit, if at all. (1992: 2)

While this is clearly a generalized view, it encapsulates the argument
made by feminist theorists of science and technology that not only is
knowledge socially constructed but also that gender is crucial to that
construction. Evelyn Fox Keller (1992) has suggested that the relationship between gender and science reveals 'the deep interpenetration between our cultural construction of gender and our naming of
science'. Further, she argues that contemporary science 'is constituted
around a set of exclusionary oppositions, in which that which is named
feminine is excluded, and that which is excluded – be it feeling, subjectivity or nature – is named female' (1992: 47). Feminist critiques of
science take issue with the claims of science to be an objective, and
thus neutral, account of the truths of the physical world, and argue
that all scientific knowledge is subject to wider social and political considerations and practices. Informed by what Mary Maynard calls 'an
alliance of the sociology of knowledge with feminist epistemology'
(1997: 5), feminist critiques of the gendered nature of scientific knowl-

edge seek to take account of the way in which that knowledge both produces and is produced by existing relations of power. In a similar vein, Judy Wajcman argues in her feminist analysis of technology that, as with science, 'the very language of technology, its symbolism, is masculine. It is not simply a question of acquiring skills, because these skills are embedded in a culture of masculinity that is largely coterminous with the culture of technology' (1991: 19).

In the context of this gender bias and inequality in both science and technology, it is understandable that arguments have been put forward for the development of a woman-centred science and technology. The difficulty with such arguments is that they must inevitably rely on essentialist definitions of masculinity and femininity, in particular the notion that, since women are closer to nature than men, they would therefore develop less exploitative science and technology. There is no guarantee of this, however, for as one of the central female characters in Pat Cadigan's cyberpunk novel *Synners* says: 'Think on this one. All *appropriate technology* hurt somebody. A whole lot of somebodies. Nuclear fission, fusion, the fucking Ford assembly line, the fucking airplane. *Fire*, for Christ's sake. Every technology has its original sin' (1991: 435). In an essentialist approach, definitions of nature and gender are regarded as being fixed and unchanging rather than socially and culturally constructed, with the result that existing gender relations are left intact. By linking women and nature in this way, femininity is associated with the irrational and unscientific: women can be thought of as a resource which, like nature, is suitable for and subject to exploitation by the masculine forces of rationality, civilization and progress. Thus, both science and technology can continue to be defined as predominantly masculine activities that are inextricably associated with notions of progress, while femininity is confined to the sphere of the irrational. Although men and women are undoubtedly positioned differently in relation to the processes and practices of science and technology, a less essentialist view would recognize that not only are such processes and practices gendered but also that they are instrumental in the construction of gendered subjectivity.

Analyses of the impact of science and technology on the lives of women at both micro- and macro-levels indicate that the boundaries between science and technology have been significantly eroded in recent years. The limited definitions put forward by Laurie Smith Keller of science as being 'about discovering and explaining' and technology as being about 'designing and making' (1992: 25) have been superseded by an awareness that both science and technology are related sets of knowledges and gendered practices. As a marker of this shift of emphasis, the portmanteau term 'technoscience' is frequently used in order to demonstrate both the proximity and the indivisibility of the two fields of knowledge and sets of practices, as well as indicating that they are inextricably linked to other forms of social and cultural knowledge. As used by Donna Haraway, the term signifies the 'implosion of science and technology into each other in the past two hundred years around the world'. According to Haraway, technoscience is inseparable from the complex social and cultural structures within which it occurs and by which it is shaped, so that it should be regarded as 'a form of life, a practice, a culture, a generative matrix' (1997: 50). This way of looking at science and technology, or technoscience, can move the debate into new and interesting territory, away from the binaries of technophilia and technophobia that have occasionally characterized the feminist engagement with science and technology. By viewing technoscience as a cultural practice, its seeming isolation from other cultural practices is undermined and, crucially, it allows analysis of the gendered nature of those practices to be undertaken.

Cyberculture, Cybertheory and Cyberspace

Contemporary technoscience, at least in the popular imagination, is dominated by information technology and cybernetics. Post-war developments in these fields have been rapid. As Mark Dery describes them: 'We are moving, at dizzying speed, from a reassuringly solid age of hardware into a disconcertingly wraithlike age of software, in which circuitry too small to see and code too complex to fully comprehend controls more and more of the world around us' (1996: 4). Information technology increasingly dominates social, cultural, political and economic interactions on a global scale and its applications and manifestations have had a profound impact on notions of space and time as well as definitions of self and other, human and machine. As the concept of time as linear progression has eroded, the postmodern cultural environment has been described not only as having lost a sense of history but also as manifesting a feeling that the future has imploded into an increasingly science-fictional present. There has, however, been a subsequent shift in this view of the cultural conditions of postmodernity, as information and bio-technologies have enabled a revision of the relation between the real and the virtual, the human and

218

the artificial, the self and the other. As the interface between the body and technology is redefined, the discourses of the body are opened up for interrogation and the question of what it means to be human becomes more urgent. Debates around these issues have increased over the past decade and the impact on embodiment of the destabilization of boundaries has resulted in the emergence of a set of critical concerns that is increasingly defined as cybertheory.

Cybertheory has emerged from debates in postmodern theory about the collapse of boundaries and fixed categories of meaning and it has been theorized most notably from within the humanities. However, as the emergence of technoscience indicates, the questioning of the 'grand narratives' of the Enlightenment has generated a series of overlapping agendas between disciplines. Cybertheory has, then, emerged from the interaction of a diverse range of theoretical and critical discourses and it is presently struggling for clearer definition as a critical field. The numerous edited collections and anthologies, such as *The Cybercultures Reader* (Bell and Kennedy 2000), that have appeared in the past decade are evidence of this struggle, and they also illustrate the kind of critical thinking that actively demolishes previously accepted academic categories and hierarchies. Although not a unified field of enquiry, cybertheory demonstrates a general concern with the interface between the body and technology and with elaborating forms of identity in which difference and otherness can be defined in nonexclusionary terms.

Although cyberculture and cybertheory are sometimes used as if they were interchangeable terms, there are distinctions to be made between them. Cyberculture is a term that is broad enough to include the kind of celebratory journalism found in magazines such as *Mondo 2000* and *Wired*, as well as academic discourses on virtual communities and identities. In one attempt to differentiate between the different approaches contained within cyberculture, David Silver has defined them as 'popular cyberculture', 'cyberculture studies' and 'critical cyberculture studies' (2000: 19). These terms reflect both the heterogeneity of cyberculture and its distance from those traditional academic discourses within which discipline boundaries remain largely intact. There would seem to be some advantages in this approach for feminist theory, since it allows for the possibility that an oppositional and different gender dynamic can be constructed in relation to the analysis of, and engagement with, new technologies. However, the weakness of this approach is that it fails to address the way in which cyberculture uncritically celebrates and re-enacts a Cartesian separation of mind from body. Mark Dery describes this striking concern with discorporation as 'body loathing' and claims that it 'rises to a crescendo in cyberculture' (1996: 236). Feminist computer scientist Alison Adam describes cyberculture in its popular form as a 'masculine youth culture which once again promises an escape from the body' (1998: 8). She notes the influence that the science-fiction genre of cyberpunk has had on cyberculture, not least in its emphasis on the desire to transcend the mere 'meat' of the body. As she suggests, this form of cyberculture would seem to have few attractions for feminists. Judith Squires describes cyberculture as 'a particularly masculine exploration of the new-found continuity between mind and machine, of particular import to the masculine notion of the self which had defined itself in terms of the mind as distinct from the materiality of both body and machine' (1996: 198). For these reasons, it is not surprising that, thus far, feminists have expressed some scepticism towards the masculinist and universalizing tendencies in cyberculture in which gendered bodies persist.

Electronically constituted virtual environments are a significant feature of postmodernity, and cyberspace has become a potent metaphor for the temporal and spatial dislocations that mark the contemporary postmodern social and cultural environment. Cultural anxieties about the destabilizing effects of information technology and cybernetic systems have been articulated at the level of popular culture as well as in academic discourse. As a genre that is closely associated with temporal and spatial dislocation, science fiction has provided peculiarly apposite metaphors through which these anxieties can be articulated. Indeed, as Teresa de Lauretis has suggested: 'In tracing cognitive paths through the physical and material reality of the contemporary technological landscape and designing new maps of social reality, SF is perhaps the most innovative fictional mode of our historical creativity' (1980: 169). Representation of the malign influence of cybernetics can be found in high-grossing science-fiction films such as the *Terminator* films (1984, 1991) or *The Matrix* (1999), and it is an unspoken irony that the visually arresting special effects in these and other science-fiction films rely on computer-generated imagery. These films share a largely unquestioned assumption that the blurring of the boundaries between human and machine is likely to result in the usurpation of the human by the machine. The complexity of living in computer-mediated and information-saturated environments is explored in William Gibson's hugely influential cyberpunk trilogy *Neuromancer* (1984), *Count Zero* (1986) and *Mona Lisa Overdrive* (1988).

Although the term 'cyberspace' was originally coined by Gibson to describe the artificial spatial and temporal environment of electronic information, the connotations of cyberspace have expanded far beyond those associated with fictional worlds. It is used to refer equally to both virtual reality and to the Internet, and has become part of the ever-widening discourse which celebrates what Claudia Springer has called 'the pleasure of the interface' (1991).

Competing definitions of cyberspace attest to the fact that, while the virtual environment of cyberspace has undoubtedly become a recognizable social and cultural space, it has not become fully assimilated in cultural terms. This is partly to do with ambivalent responses to the increasing dominance of new technologies, which have been both demonized and hailed as instruments of liberation. Margaret Morse suggests that the virtual environment of cyberspace undermines familiar cultural definitions of reality to produce a 'dematerialized, and for that reason ontologically uncertain mode of presence' (1998: 24). Such ontological uncertainty allows cyberspace to be conceived of either in utopian or in dystopian terms. A utopian view of the transcendent possibilities of cyberspace is offered by Michael Benedikt, who claims that cyberspace is:

> another life-world, a parallel universe, offering the intoxicating prospect of actually fulfilling – with a technology very nearly achieved – a dream thousands of years old: the dream of transcending the physical world, fully alive, at will, to dwell in some Beyond – to be empowered or enlightened there, alone or with others, and to return. (1991: 131)

Similarly, utopian claims that cyberspace can provide a replacement sense of community for the one that has been lost in real life have been made, most notably by Howard Rheingold (1994). He suggests that the electronic environment of cyberspace can facilitate the revitalization of a sense of community by generating new, electronic public spaces. There are other, more critical accounts of cyberspace, however, in which the identification of cyberspace as a transcendent and utopian environment is not endorsed. As Michael Heim points out, although we may enjoy a relationship with technology that is both erotic and symbiotic, there is a distinct possibility that 'the machine interface may amplify an amoral indifference to human relationships' (1991: 76). Although criticisms are made of the way in which existing power structures are reproduced in cyberspace, all too often the gendered nature of those power structures is left untheorized.

221

In contrast, feminist theorists such as Nicola Nixon (1992) and Zoë
Sofia (1999) argue that the relations of power in cyberspace are produced and reproduced precisely because cyberspace is conceptualized
as a feminized space. For Sofia, the masculinization of technoscience
stems from the framework of corporate and military control within
which it is situated. In such a framework, women and computers can
be thought of as having a structural equivalence in the sense that both
are subject to use by others who exert control over them. Thus, cyberspace can be thought of as feminized space that is both passive and
maternal, subject to manipulation and technological penetration by
the figure of the hacker, who remains predominately a male figure.
The definition of the matrix as feminized space is also developed by
Nicola Nixon in her discussion of cyberpunk. She argues that cyberpunk texts depict cyberspace as a space that is fatally compromised by
computer viruses and thus becomes 'a form of scary feminised soft-
ware' (1992: 231). It is this feminized Other against which the masculinity of the console cowboys is defined; their task is to penetrate a
potentially emasculating feminine matrix or die. As Nixon (1992: 228)
succinctly states: 'If the cowboy heroes fail to perform brilliantly, they
will be "flatlined" or have their jacks melted off, whichever is worse.'
The arguments put forward by both Nixon and Sofia suggest that,
despite claims that cyberspace can be a means of transcending the
body, the feminization of cyberspace strongly reiterates normative
gender identities, while continuing to privilege masculine control over
the technology.

These widely divergent views of cyberspace indicate that, while it
may be a virtual or non-space, nevertheless it has both a geography
and a complex set of social relations, implicit in which is the gendered
nature of the social relations of the technology itself. As Jennifer Terry
and Melodie Calvert remind us, technologies are organized systems
that 'shape our lives, structuring not just what we do and how we do
it, but even fashioning our vision of social relations and what it means
to be human' (1997: 5). From this perspective, the notion of the virtual
has profound implications for the materiality of the body and definitions of embodiment. Cyberspace has subsumed virtuality within its
parameters and, in so doing, the debate about the virtual nature of
gender has become part of the debate about definitions of gendered
identity in cyberspace and the question of whether or not cyberspace
itself can be coded as masculine or feminine. Margaret Morse (1998:
179) argues that 'virtualities are inevitably linked to materiality and
physical space, be they in terms of the body or the technological appa-

ratuses that generate virtual images or the geographical localities over which they are mapped.' Thus the metaphoric realms of cyberspace are unavoidably and intimately connected to the social relations of technology in the material world, despite celebratory claims to the contrary. It is possible, of course, to see the complex relationship between material and virtual existence in a highly reductive way, as Tim Jordan (1999) does, by presenting it as an opposition between utopian and dystopian views of cyberspace that can be resolved by the 'awed realisation that everything is controlled by information codes that can be manipulated, transmitted and recombined through cyberspace' (1999: 205). A less 'awed' view of the primacy of information is presented by Katherine Hayles, who argues against acceptance of either 'the disembodiment of information' or the notion that 'we are *essentially* informational patterns' (1999: 22). Indeed, Hayles suggests that humans 'have something to lose if they are regarded solely as informational patterns' (1999: 29).

Cyberfeminism

Although feminist theory has engaged with postmodern theory in specific ways, it has at the same time remained distinct from it. The destabilization of the unitary subject in postmodern theory has resulted in an emphasis on multiplicity and diversity, and the shifting categories of space and time raise questions about the boundaries between self and other, nature and culture. While feminist theory shares with postmodern theory a concern to redefine notions of subjectivity, identity and difference, many feminists have been highly critical of the way in which postmodernist theory has reconfigured the decentred subject as white and male, while the female subject is dissolved into a multiplicity of other differences. Gender has not been privileged in postmodern theory in the same way that it has in feminist theory and, as a consequence, it is difficult to describe feminist theorists as postmodernist in any general sense.

A similarly critical relationship is developing between cybertheory and feminist theory. Postmodern theory can be situated in the context of the radical changes in social, economic and political structures brought about by the intensification and globalization of capital. Cybertheory shares this general context but its specific concern is the transformational qualities of information technologies and the interface between the human and the machine. The redefinition of the

223

human through a merging with technology can result in an uncritical celebration of technology – sometimes referred to as 'cyberdrool' – that studiously ignores the relations of power that structure the technologies. As indicated earlier, journals such as *Wired* and *Mondo 2000* express an uncritical celebration of the technology which reinscribes existing inequalities in social and cultural relations. Feminist critics have taken both journals to task. In her critique of *Mondo 2000*, Vivian Sobchak (1994) points out that, despite its seemingly utopian agenda, the journal persistently fails to relate the issue of access to the technologies to socioeconomic factors, or race or gender. Thus, *Mondo 2000* resolutely ignores the positioning of the new technologies within enormous state and corporate structures that inevitably have different sets of criteria for their development, many of which may be entirely antithetical to the interests of individuals. Significantly, working practices at the journals themselves do not appear to operate equally in the interests of those individuals who are either writers for, or readers of, the journal. Research conducted by Paulina Borsook (1996), a one-time journalist with *Wired,* reveals that, in 1995, as little as 15 percent of articles in *Wired* featured women as the main subject, and an even smaller percentage of the front covers of the magazine featured women. Similarly, perhaps 15 percent of authors writing for *Wired* were women. Borsook suggests that not only do few of the views printed in *Wired* come from female writers but also that the dominance of male writers invariably results in the exclusion of issues that are of concern to women. *Mondo 2000* and *Wired* are journals that have positioned themselves at the forefront of both cyberculture and cybertheory but, as Sobchak and Borsook argue, they nevertheless reveal a fundamental unwillingness to recognize the transformational effects of technology on the interface between human and machine in terms of gender.

The distinctiveness of the feminist engagement with cybertheory, in which gender remains central to the critical approach adopted towards analysis of communication and biotechnologies, is signalled in the term 'cyberfeminism'. This is a broad and inclusive term, and cyberfeminists can be defined not only as those who theorize from various feminist perspectives about the new electronic technologies but also those who are active on the Net in some way, as writers, artists or hackers. While there is considerable creative interaction between these groups, there is no particular agreement about what constitutes cyberfeminism. In a round-table web-based discussion chaired by Jennifer Ley and entitled 'Women and Technology: Beyond the Binary'

(1999–2000), Katherine Hayles suggests that cyberfeminism means 'feminism practiced in electronic environments, particularly on the Internet and on the Web'. Linda Carroli's view in the same discussion is that it 'conjures a hybridity or contingency that I am comfortable with – more so than a feminism that says women are victims – because power is implicit or fragmented'. Cyberfeminism is given a useful context within contemporary post-humanism by Cornelia Sollfrank (2001) and Yvonne Volkart of Old Boys Network, who argue that the capacity of cyberfeminism to be open to diversity allows it to be both a utopian ideal and a strategic construction. They point out that cyberfeminism is crucial in a period in which key notions such as subjectivity, identity, sex/gender, representation, and agency are in the process of being redefined, not least because of the impact of virtualization. For Sollfrank and Volkart, cyberfeminism is resolutely political and is thus opposed to essentialist assumptions that cyberspace is an inherently supportive environment for female resistance.

In this reference to a form of cyber-essentialism, it is clear that debates within both feminist and postmodern theory have, not surprisingly, been transferred to the virtual realms of cyberspace. Faith Wilding and the Critical Art Ensemble (1998) explore some of the ramifications of this transfer in their article 'Notes on the Political Condition of Cyberfeminism', in which cyberfeminism is described as a 'promising new wave of (post)feminist thinking and practice'. Locating it within the overall development of feminist theory, the authors argue that, although there is a 'distinct cyberfeminist Netpresence that is fresh, brash, smart, and iconoclastic of many of the tenets of classical feminism', the need to critique the gendered nature of cyberspace means that 'key feminist issues such as feminine subjectivity, separatism and boundary maintenance, and territorial identification are bound to arise again, even if they seem dead in other feminist territories.' Other writers argue that feminist concerns will be subsumed into the new virtual environment of cyberspace, thus becoming increasingly irrelevant. Sadie Plant takes this view, and chooses to describe cyberfeminism as having 'neither theory nor practice, no goals and no principles'. It is, she concludes, 'simply the acknowledgement that patriarchy is doomed' (1993: 13).

Plant has been a key figure in the popularizing of the connection between women and cyberspace, although her approach is not without its critics. She characterizes the relationship between women and technology as one that is 'sedimented in patriarchal myth: machines were female because they were mere things on which men worked' (1993: 13). Thus, the relationship between women and machines can be considered to have been the same as that between women and nature, in that both are without agency and thus subject to the will of men in the interests of history. Drawing on the work of Luce Irigaray, Plant refers here to the kind of history that is made as man struggles to escape from what he perceives to be his subordination to nature and to biology: the flight from the material and the maternal turns into the drive for dominance and the dream of transcendence. As Plant points out, even though women have never been the subjects of history, nevertheless they have woven themselves into its fabric through mimicry and simulation: woman 'learns how to imitate; she learns simulation' (1995: 59). Plant uses the notion of weaving to suggest that there is a convergence between women and cybernetic systems; thus, weaving is seen as being quintessentially women's work, while the model of the Jacquard loom was used by Ada Lovelace and Charles Babbage to devise an 'Analytical Engine', a fledgling cybernetic system. The computer, then, is a 'simulation of weaving: threads of ones and zeros riding the carpets and simulating silk screens in the perpetual motions of cyberspace' (Plant 1995: 63). Plant argues, somewhat controversially, that cyberfeminism does not require for women 'a subjectivity, an identity or even a sexuality of her own: there is no subject position and no identity on the other side of the screens' (1995: 63). She calls for an 'irresponsible feminism – which may not be a feminism at all' (1996: 182) and which understands that it is part of an 'emergent process for which identity is not the goal but the enemy' (1996: 183). Cyberfeminism is thus defined as 'a dispersed, distributed emergence composed of links between women, women and computers, computers and communication links, connections and connectionist nets' (1996: 182). For Plant, the technology is feminized through the metaphor of weaving, and digitalization-as-weaving allows woman's desire 'to flow in the dense tapestries and complex depth of the computer image' (1993: 14). Further, since the 'cyberfeminist infection' of technology leads to the 'return of the repressed, the return of the feminine', women's use of technology can be turned against patriarchy itself (1993: 14).

Sadie Plant's version of cyberfeminism produces a thought-provoking but highly rhetorical account of the transformative possibilities of technoscience. It is couched in such general terms that it cannot adequately address existing inequalities within the networks of power in technoscience which continue to affect women adversely. In addition, the way in which Plant imbues the technology itself with the feminine has led to criticisms of essentialism. Alison Adam (1998) has pointed out the significant loss of the political project that has animated the work of writers such as Donna Haraway, who argues that complex and multifaceted agency is crucial in transforming relations of power. Adam rightly suggests that Plant is in danger of becoming 'overwhelmed by the mystical qualities of these systems which organize themselves outside our control' (1998: 176). From a similarly critical position, Judith Squires also takes issue with Plant's 'distinctly apolitical' (1996: 209) version of cyberfeminism, which relies on the fiction of the 'essential, though disembodied, woman' (1996: 210). More generally, Squires argues that, 'whilst cyberfeminism might offer a vision of fabulous, flexible, feminist futures, it has as yet largely failed to do so' (1996: 209), primarily because it has adopted an uncritical view of the human–machine interface in which the complex relations between embodied identity and technology are ignored.

There are, then, some aspects of cyberfeminism which suggest that it shares with cyberculture an emphasis on transcendence and escape from the body. However, as Squires insists, cyberfeminism can also be seen as 'a metaphor for addressing the inter-relation between technology and the body, not as a means of using the former to transcend the latter' (1996: 195). This is the position adopted by Zoë Sofia (1999), who stresses the ambiguity of the pleasures of the interface, rather than simply endorsing its utopian possibilities. She suggests that there are productive ways in which women can engage with the technology while being fully aware that the female body appears to have limited purchase on cyberspace. Sofia argues that the particular seductions of virtual bodies and spaces that are offered in cyberspace can be tempered by an ironic awareness of the power structures within which the technologies are embedded.

Cyberbodies and Virtual Genders

The interface between the body and technology inevitably begins to address the question of whether or not the interpenetration of information and flesh will resolve itself in the obsolescence of the body. Speculation that it may be possible, in a not too distant future, to download consciousness as data onto disk not only questions the relevance of embodiment, it also reiterates the Cartesian dualism of mind and body. In those discourses of cyberspace in which the body is reconstructed as information, the body can be transcended and the unitary

227

subject, specifically coded as masculine, can be left intact. These gendered fantasies of disembodiment reproduce the familiar binaries of male/female, human/machine, self/other and fail to recognize that subjectivity itself is a cultural construction, as feminist critics have long argued. Indeed, as Anne Balsamo (1996) points out in her discussion of the 'technologies of the gendered body', the cultural construction of the techno-body itself allows normative gender identity to be reinscribed, despite much vaunted promises to the contrary. Furthermore, fantasies centred on the technological transformation of bodies underestimate the complexity of the relationship between bodies and technology, in which technology itself must also be thought of as intervening in the construction of gendered subjects. All of this supports the contention that both bodies and subjectivities are inescapably embodied. It is self-evident that we require a corporeal presence to enter cyberspace in the sense that we sit in front of a computer and manipulate a keyboard, just as human programmers have created the virtual environment itself. The relationship of the virtual body to the corporeal body is, then, of some importance for cyber-feminism, and as Allucquère Rosanne Stone has argued: 'No matter how virtual the subject may become, there is always a body attached' (1991: 111).

A concern with the body and embodiment is central to feminist theory and the relationship between embodiment and virtuality therefore raises complex issues for feminist theory in these postmodern, indeed, post-human times. The notion of the virtual body raises interesting possibilities for the redefinition of subjects and identities for which feminist theorists call. The reconceptualization of the subject is predicated on the complex interactions that take place between the body and technology, rather than on the fantasy that the body itself can be transcended or that it is distinct from technology. The figure of the cyborg invoked by Haraway emerges from such interactions to call into question the binarisms that structure Western thought. In 'A Manifesto for Cyborgs', Haraway (1990: 220) argues that cyborgs are contradictory boundary creatures who 'make very problematic the statuses of man or woman, human, artefact, member of a race, individual identity, or body'. They can be thought of as 'promising and dangerous monsters who help redefine the pleasures and politics of embodiment and feminist writing' (1990: 221). While the cyborg metaphor has been criticized for its tendency towards universality, it nevertheless makes evident a commitment to embodied existence and experience, as well as a resistance to sameness and a recognition of difference. The figure of the cyborg makes it possible to move reflexively between virtuality and embodiment, since it is constituted as a fragmented, fluid and multiple, rather than unitary, self. In the sense that they refuse essentialism, then, cyborg bodies can be thought of as virtual bodies.

As the active involvement of women in these new technologies has increased, so have theoretical accounts of the gendered nature of inter-actions in the information environment. This has provided an impor-tant counter-balance to the somewhat valedictory approaches taken towards information technology and the virtual environment of cyber-space. Critics of cyberculture and of the more utopian manifestations of cyberfeminism have focused on the difficulties of dealing with notions of embodiment in the virtual realm and on the construction of gendered bodies in cyberspace. Debate tends to centre on whether virtual reality can be a site for the construction of alternative identi-ties or whether cyberspace simply reproduces existing cultural con-ventions and identities. This is not an easy debate to resolve, especially since life online currently remains the privilege of a relatively small, if increasing, number of people. Although the number of women online is also increasing, they remain in a minority both in the public spaces of cyberspace such as discussion groups and also in soft-ware engineering and computer science generally. This has provoked differing views about the way in which women are able to access the Net, with critics such as Dale Spender (1995) and Zoë Sofia (1999) arguing that the inequalities inherent in the educational system are predisposed to exclude the widespread participation of young women in computer studies. Susan Herring's study (1996) of the way in which men and women engage in computer-mediated communication reveals that both genders actively participate in electronic mailing lists and that there are interesting gender differences in the way in which they interact and exchange information online. Overall, however, Herring concludes that not only are existing cultural stereotypes of masculinity and femininity reproduced in online exchanges, but they also affect the way in which users behave online. It is not surprising, she argues, that 'women are more reluctant to go online, less confi-dent of their abilities when they do so, less participatory in online group discussions, and less represented among computer network policy makers and designers than men' (Herring 1996: 105).

Even if culturally constructed conventions of gender do not disap-pear in cyberspace and gendered communication remains a funda-mental part of virtual life, nevertheless the dissolution of the link between the physical body and identity provides an opportunity for the conventions underlying the construction of both gender and sexuality to be subverted. Cyberspace offers opportunities to experiment with the performance of gender identity, and in her account of 'life on the screen' Sherry Turkle suggests that 'virtual cross-dressing' provides an 'opportunity to explore conflicts raised by one's biological gender' (1995: 213) and claims that participants gain a greater understanding of the profound impact of gender on human relations as a result of their own online experiences of swapping gender. Similarly, in her discussion of the pleasures of text-based, interactive sex in MUDs, Shannon McRae (1996) argues that existing definitions of sex, gender and sexuality are challenged by the opportunity for experimentation provided in MUDs. For McRae, the virtual enactment of gender undermines the supposedly immutable nature of gender categories and the eroticization of the technology adds to corporeal pleasure. Mutating gender identities and hybrid bodies which destabilize the hegemonic discourses of both gender and sexuality have also been explored in the interactive multimedia work of VNS Matrix. This group of feminist cyberartists declare that they are concerned to 'explore the construction of social space, identity and sexuality in cyberspace' (Schaffer 1999: 153). In her account of their work, Kay Schaffer argues that VNS Matrix are part of a general move towards the positive use of the Internet for the exploration of 'new alliances, new subjectivities, and new possibilities for power relations, for desire, and for "perverse" bodily pleasures' (1999: 166). Thus, the creation of multiple and fragmented identities in cyberspace and new social spaces within which to interact is generally regarded as one of the most liberating aspects of virtual life. There is, therefore, a strong case to be argued that virtual reality provides an imaginative space in which the norms and expectations of conventional gender identity can be undermined, thus enabling gender identity to be reconceptualized.

The question of embodiment and the construction of gender identity have been made more complex as a result of the unfixing of gender identity in cyberspace. As Turkle argues, the Internet encourages us to think of ourselves as 'fluid, emergent, decentralized, multiplicitous, flexible, and ever in process' (1995: 263–4). From this point of view, cyberspace has become more than a metaphor or a technology: it has become a means of rethinking both social interaction and gender identity. Allucquère Rosanne Stone (1995) has argued that in cyberspace the technological and the social have been realigned to become a new technosocial space in which multiplicity has become part of a new and unruly social identity that exceeds the constraints of 'the bounded individual as the standard social unit and validated social actant' (1995: 43). Stone has made clear in earlier work also (1991) that this does not entail a denial of the body; rather, a reconfigured embodiment takes account of both the dissolution of the unitary subject and the performative nature of gender. Instead of being constrained by the normative and regulatory power of gender relations, virtual identities have the capacity to reinscribe cultural narratives of gender in ways that challenge existing definitions.

This is, however, less easy to achieve than may seem possible from some of the more utopian accounts of virtual life, and the dissonance between virtual and real life is revealed in several, by now well-known, accounts of online gender swapping, sexual harassment and virtual rape. Stone recounts the case of 'Julie', a disabled older woman who appears to have had a powerful and enabling effect on the many women who interacted with her in cyberspace. Eventually, 'Julie' was revealed to be a man, the disclosure provoking accusations of betrayal by the many online friends of the erstwhile 'Julie'. The uncoupling of the physical body from gender identity proved impossible to enact in this case, revealing the persistent presence of 'the war of desire and technology' as Stone has expressed it (1995: 75). The desire to attribute 'real' gender characteristics to the virtual persona of 'Julie' is shown to be in conflict with the ability of technology to intervene in the construction of gender through the generation of multiple identities, both 'real' and simulated. The expectation that gender identity in cyberspace will mirror that in 'real life' enshrines the notion that gender is 'natural' and ignores the potential for the blurring of gender differences that becomes apparent when individuals are able to choose which gender they wish to perform.

The occurrence of online textual harassment indicates another facet of the disjuncture between desire and technology. An extreme example of such harassment is described by Julian Dibbell (1994) in his account of a MUD-rape in LambdaMOO, an incident that has generated much continuing debate, not least regarding the use of the term 'rape' to describe a non-physical violation. These examples suggest that the social and cultural values and expectations of real life persist in cyberspace, despite the promise of a more gender-neutral existence offered by virtual reality. The difficulties of dealing with online harassment of women are not made any easier by sensationalized media accounts. Indeed, media articles about the sexual harassment of women on the 'electronic frontier' have clearly had a tendency to reproduce the stereotype of the woman as helpless victim in a lawless environment in need of protection from chivalrous males. The deeply ingrained nature of these stereotypes is evident in the frequent reprise of the frontier mythology of the American West in journalistic accounts of cyberspace. In her critique of such accounts, Laura Miller (1995) argues that media representation of cyberspace as a highly gendered environment that is inimical to women reveals, not the reality of life online, but the culturally constructed nature of gender. The crucial issue remains that of finding ways of making women feel that cyberspace is an environment that they can inhabit without feeling threatened.

The formation of women-only networks and online support groups that are specifically for women is in part a response to online harassment but it is also an indication that women are an increasingly powerful presence in cyberspace. Cyberspace is clearly a contradictory space in which the fluidity of gender identity has both positive and negative connotations. For many users, it opens up a space of play and experimentation in which the gender conventions are destabilized. The creation of cyberqueer spaces on the Internet demonstrates that the Net can be used to create virtual communities that challenge the dominance of heterosexism and provide a virtual environment in which queer identity can be both defined and transformed. Nevertheless, critics of the utopian rhetoric of disembodiment and liberation point out that it remains a space in which the normative function of gender ideology is reinforced through the persistent use of gender stereotypes, even in role-play situations encountered in MUDs. As Nina Wakeford (1999) has argued, even where the continuing dominance of the practices of white masculinity is challenged – through the subversive games of VNS Matrix or through private lists, for example – this challenge tends to remain confined to specific online spaces rather than being taken up in any general way. Her analysis of the complex way in which gender relations are enacted through real bodies in the physical environment of an Internet café is a corrective to the notion that the gendered body can be transcended in cyberspace. The connection between embodiment and technology is central to any understanding of the way in which both gender and subjectivity are produced. The evolving relationship between humans and machines suggests that some form of post-human embodiment may generate a radically different discourse about the body, the investigation of which may give cyberfeminism the critical edge that it currently appears to lack.

References and Further Reading

Adam, A. (1998) *Artificial Knowing: Gender and the Thinking Machine*. London: Routledge.

Balsamo, A. (1996) *Technologies of the Gendered Body: Reading Cyborg Women*. Durham, NC: Duke University Press.

Bell, D. and Kennedy, B. (eds) (2000) *The Cybercultures Reader*. New York: Routledge.

Benedikt, M. (1991) Cyberspace: some proposals. In M. Benedikt (ed.), *Cyberspace: First Steps*, pp. 119–224. Cambridge, MA: MIT Press.

Borsook, P. (1996) The memoirs of a token: an ageing Berkeley feminist examines *Wired*. In L. Cherny and E. R. Wiese (eds), *Wired Women: Gender and New Realities in Cyberspace*, pp. 24–41. Seattle, WA: Seal Press.

Cadigan, P. (1991) *Synners*. New York: Bantam Press.

Dery, M. (1996) *Escape Velocity: Cyberculture at the End of the Century*. London: Hodder and Stoughton.

Dibbell, J. (1994) A rape in cyberspace; or, how an evil clown, a Haitian trickster spirit, two wizards, and a cast of dozens turned a database into a society. In M. Dery (ed.), *Flame Wars: The Discourse of Cyberculture*, pp. 237–61. Durham, NC: Duke University Press.

Haraway, D. (1990) A manifesto for cyborgs: science, technology, and socialist feminism in the 1980s. In L. Nicholson (ed.), *Feminism/Postmodernism*, pp. 190–233. New York: Routledge.

— (1997) *Modest_Witness@Second_Millennium: FemaleMan©_Meets_OncoMouse™*. New York: Routledge.

Hayles, K. (1999) *How We Became Posthuman: Virtual Bodies in Cybernetics, Literature, and Informatics*. Chicago: University of Chicago Press.

Heim, M. (1991) The erotic ontology of cyberspace. In M. Benedikt (ed.), *Cyberspace: First Steps*, pp. 59–80. Cambridge: MA: MIT Press.

Herring, S. (ed.) (1996) *Computer-mediated Communication: Linguistic, Social and Cross-cultural Perspectives*. Amsterdam and Philadelphia: John Benjamins.

Jordan, T. (1999) *Cyberpower: The Culture and Politics of the Internet*. London: Routledge.

Keller, E. F. (1992) How gender matters, or, why it's so hard for us to count past two. In G. Kirkup and L. S. Keller (eds), *Inventing Women: Science, Technology and Gender*, pp. 42–56. Cambridge: Polity Press and The Open University.

Keller, L. S. (1992) Discovering and doing: science and technology, an introduction. In G. Kirkup and L. S. Keller (eds), *Inventing Women: Science, Technology and Gender*, pp. 12–32. Cambridge: Polity Press and The Open University.

Kirkup, G. and Keller, L. S. (eds) (1992) *Inventing Women: Science, Technology and Gender*. Cambridge: Polity Press and The Open University.

—, et al. (eds) (2000) *The Gendered Cyborg: A Reader*. London: Routledge.

de Lauretis, T. (1980) Signs of Wa/onder. In T. de Lauretis et al. (eds), *The Technological Imagination*, pp. 159–74. Madison: Coda Press.

Ley, J. (ed.) (1999–2000) *Women and Technology: Beyond the Binary. Riding the Meridian*, 2 (1) (http://www.heelstone.com).

McRae, S. (1996) Coming apart at the seams: sex, text and the virtual body. In L. Cherny and E. R. Wiese (eds), *Wired Women: Gender and New Realities in Cyberspace*, pp. 242–63. Seattle, WA: Seal Press.

Maynard, M. (ed.) (1997) Revolutionizing the subject: women's studies and the sciences. In M. Maynard (ed.), *Science and the Construction of Women*, pp. 1–14. London: University College London Press.

Miller, L. (1995) Women and children first: gender and the settling of the electronic frontier. In J. Brook and I. Boal (eds), *Resisting the Virtual Life: The Culture and Politics of Information*, pp. 49–57. San Francisco, CA: City Lights.

Morse, M. (1998) *Virtualities: Television, Media Art and Cyberculture*. Bloomington, IN: Indiana University Press.

Nixon, N. (1992) Cyberpunk: preparing the ground for revolution or keeping the boys satisfied? *Science Fiction Studies*, 19: 219–35.

Penley, C. and Ross, A. (eds) (1991) *Technoculture*. Minneapolis, MN: University of Minnesota Press.

Plant, S. (1993) Beyond the screens: film, cyberpunk and cyberfeminism. *Variant*, 14: 13–17.

— (1995) The future looms: weaving women and cybernetics. In M. Featherstone and R. Burrows (eds), *Cyberspace, Cyberpunk, Cyberbodies: Cultures of Technological Embodiment*, pp. 45–64. London: Sage.

— (1996) On the matrix: cyberfeminist simulations. In R. Shields (ed.), *Cultures of Internet: Virtual Spaces, Real Histories, Living Bodies*, pp. 170–83. London: Sage.

Rheingold, H. (1994) *The Virtual Community: Finding Connection in a Computerised World*. London: Secker and Warburg.

Schaffer, K. (1999) The game girls of VNS Matrix: challenging gendered identities in cyberspace. In M. A. O'Farrell and L. Vallone (eds), *Virtual Gender: Fantasies of Subjectivity and Embodiment*, pp. 147–68. Michigan: University of Michigan Press.

Silver, D. (2000) Looking backwards, looking forwards: cyberculture studies 1990–2000. In D. Gauntlett (ed.), *2000: Web. Studies: Rewiring Media Studies for the Digital Age*, pp. 19–30. London: Arnold.

Sobchak, V. (1994) New age mutant ninja hackers: reading *Mondo 2000*. In M. Dery (ed.), *Flame Wars: The Discourse of Cyberculture*, pp. 11–28. Durham, NC: Duke University Press.

Sofia, Z. (1999) Virtual corporeality: a feminist view. In J. Wolmark (ed.), *Cybersexualities: A Reader on Feminist Theory, Cyborgs and Cyberspace*, pp. 55–68. Edinburgh: Edinburgh University Press.

Sollfrank, C. (2001) *Next Cyberfeminist International*. Hamburg: Old Boys Network.

Spender, D. (1995) *Nattering on the Net: Women, Power and Cyberspace.* Melbourne: Spinifex.

Springer, C. (1991) The pleasure of the interface. *Screen,* 32 (3): 303–23.

Squires, J. (1996) Fabulous feminist futures and the lure of cyberculture. In J. Dovey (ed.), *Fractal Dreams: New Media in Social Context,* pp. 194–216. London: Lawrence and Wishart.

Stone, A. R. (1991) Will the real body please stand up? Boundary stories about virtual cultures. In M. Benedikt (ed.), *Cyberspace: First Steps,* pp. 81–118. Cambridge, MA: MIT Press.

— (1995) *The War of Desire and Technology at the Close of the Machine Age.* Cambridge, MA: MIT Press.

Terry, J. and Calvert, M. (1997) *Processed Lives: Gender and Technology in Everyday Life.* New York: Routledge.

Turkle, S. (1984) *The Second Self: Computers and the Human Spirit.* London: Granada.

— (1995) *Life on the Screen: Identity in the Age of the Internet.* New York: Simon and Schuster.

Wajcman, J. (1991) *Feminism Confronts Technology.* Cambridge: Polity Press.

Wakeford, N. (1999) Gender and the landscapes of computing in an Internet café. In M. Crang et al. (eds), *Virtual Geographies,* pp. 178–201. New York: Routledge.

Wilding, F. and the Critical Art Ensemble (1998) Notes on the political condition of cyberfeminism. *Art Journal,* 57 (2): 46–59. This article is also widely available online.

12

Feminist Futures

Sara Ahmed

How can we think about the future of feminism? The question of 'feminist futures' cannot be asked without reference to the pasts and presents of different feminisms. Already, from reading this book, you will have a sense of the differences between feminisms and the different ways in which feminists have intervened in 'the world' as it is constituted by ways of thinking and knowing (epistemology), ways of being and inhabitance (ontology), forms of representation (culture, aesthetics and language) and ways of doing (politics, ethics and work). There is no singular feminist subject that we can address when we ask the question of the future of feminism, nor is there one way of thinking about the relationship between feminism and the world that feminism both inhabits and seeks to transform.

Yet we must ask the question of the future with the love and care that such a question demands. In some sense, what feminists share is a concern with the future; that is, a desire that the future should not simply be a repetition of the past, given that feminism comes into being as a critique of, and resistance to, the ways in which the world has already taken shape. Perhaps when we think about the question of feminist futures, we need to attend to the legacies of feminist pasts, in order to think through the very question of what it would mean to have a world where feminism, as a politics of transformation, is no longer necessary. It is certainly the case that what structures many feminist interventions is not only a way of thinking about how we can understand what is 'wrong' with the world, but also how what is

wrong might be resisted and changed. In this sense, what characterizes feminist interventions is a presumption of a necessary link
between theory and practice, between ways of understanding what
it is that we seek to transform and forms of action that enable such
transformation.

This presumption that theory is linked to both activism and practice certainly is structuring for feminism but it has also been a source
of dispute. Some feminists have argued that what characterizes more
recent feminist scholarship, especially scholarship informed by post-
structuralism and postmodernism, is the detachment of theory and
knowledge from both practice and feminist activism. For example,
Somer Brodribb (1992: xxiii) argues that postmodern feminist theory
has used 'male theory' as the expense of women's practice. Others
have suggested that the very institutionalization of feminist knowledge
within the academy has led to the loss of a direct link between feminist theory and activism or more passionate forms of politics (Klein
1991). Indeed, although women's studies has its 'roots' in the women's
movement, the difficulty of maintaining the links between knowledge
and action has been a central question in the debates about women's
studies. Sue Lees (1991) has argued that the perceived separation
between women's studies and the women's movement comes from a
failure to recognize that knowledge/education is itself a site of struggle. The relationship between theory and practice is hence understood
to be essential to what makes feminism feminist, as well as being perpetually under threat. So rather than providing a point of commonality between feminisms, the relationship between theory and practice
represents a site of difference, tension and dispute. In other words,
what binds different feminists together is also what divides them.

More generally, feminists have argued that there has been insufficient attention to the changing forms of feminist practice. For example,
Sasha Roseneil argues that feminist theory 'has been better at exposing, naming and analysing the structural oppression of women than it
has been at theorising and tracing the contours of women's agency
and resistance' (1995: 1). In other words, while feminist theory has
provided different ways of understanding what it is that we are seeking
to transform, it has yet actually to theorize the ways in which activist
politics is actually doing that work of transformation. As Gabriele
Griffin (1995: 3) has argued, it is important to document the histories
of feminist activism and to attend to the multiple forms that activism
has taken. We need to reflect on how activist groups also do the work
of feminist theory, rather than assuming that such theory is only pro-

237

duced within the academy (Ahmed 1998: 23–5). Part of our task then might be to broaden our understanding of activism, to involve different ways of doing feminist politics within different institutional and everyday contexts.

In this chapter, I want to provide another way of thinking about the relationship between feminist theory and knowledge and the politics of transformation. Rather than rehearsing arguments about the success or failure of feminist theory to be linked to feminist practice, I want to develop another way of thinking about how the links between theory and practice come to be determined in the first place. My analysis will echo the genealogical approach to feminism offered by Vikki Bell in *Feminist Imagination* (1999). Rather than providing a map of the production of feminist theory, her approach is about 'finding how movements, of real people, of concerns and of concepts, resonate through the motions and emotions of contemporary feminist theory' (1999: 14). My own argument suggests that we need to think about the role of emotion in the forming of feminist alliances and identifications, as emotions work as forms of mediation between knowledge/theory and practice/activism. My argument will be speculative and suggestive, rather than providing a review of current debates. I will provide an alternative way of understanding 'the impulse to feminism', at the same time as I will challenge us to think differently about the relationship between emotion, politics and transformation.

Emotion and Feminism

Why reflect on the role of emotion in the production of feminist theory? Part of my concern is not only to think about how one becomes attached to feminism, but also to consider how feminism is an affect as well as an effect, as an emotional response to the world as such. Clearly, one can reflect on the role of emotions in the politicization of subjects. When I think of my relationship to feminism, I can re-write my coming into being as a feminist subject in terms of different emotions or in terms of how my emotions have involved particular readings of the worlds that I have inhabited: the anger that I felt about how being a girl seemed to be about what you should not do; the pain that I felt as an effect of forms of violence; the love for my mother and for those other women whose capacity for giving has given me life; the joy I felt as I began to make different kinds of connections with others and to realize that the world was alive and could take new shapes and forms; the wonder I felt at the way in which the world came to be organized the way that it is, a wonder that allowed me to be surprised at this organization; and the hope I felt that guides every moment of rejection and refusal and that structures the desire for change with the trembling that comes from an opening up of the future, an opening up of what is possible.

For me, such emotional journeys are bound up with politicization, in a way that brings a subject into a collective and a collective into a subject. But they are bound up with that politicization in a mediated rather than immediate way. It is not that anger at women's oppression 'makes us feminists'; such an anger already involves a reading of the world in a particular way and also involves a reading of the reading. Thus, identifying as a feminist is dependent upon taking that anger as the grounds for a critique of the world, as such. This is important: we may think of emotions as immediate, as what moves us (indeed, the word emotion comes from the Latin *emovere*, which means to move or to move out). But what moves us, and how we are moved, also involve interpretations of sensations and feelings not only in the sense that we interpret what we feel, but also in that what we feel might be dependent on past interpretations that are not necessarily made by us but that come before us. So emotions are mediated, however immediately they seem to impress upon us. Focusing on emotions as mediated rather than immediate also reminds us that knowledge cannot be separated from the bodily world of feeling and sensation. Knowledge is also bound up with what makes us sweat, shudder, tremble, all those feelings that are crucially felt on the bodily surface, the skin surface where we touch and are touched by the world.

But do these attachments to feminism relate to attachments that already exist in the everyday world, including those that are bound up with the reproduction of the very forms of power that feminism comes into being to contest? I am interested in the relationship between feminist attachments and the attachments that are already formed precisely because I am keen to address how feminism becomes a 'movement' that sticks and the relationship between what moves subjects into feminism and what moves them more generally, what makes them feel this way or that in response to a world that is not 'exterior' to the feminist subject.

It is certainly the case that feminist scholars have recently paid more attention to the passionate nature of attachments to forms of subjectivity and subjection. My work supports arguments made by Judith Butler (1997) and Lois McNay (2000), for example, that emotions are crucial to politics, in the sense that subjects must become 'invested' in and attached to the forms of power in order to consent to that power. We need to think about the relationship between everyday attachments and those that are felt and lived through processes of politicization. If emotions are crucial to how subjects become invested in relations of power, then they are also crucial to how subject's become invested in the project of dis-investing from power relations. The implication of such an argument is not that there are 'feminist emotions' or even 'outlaw emotions' that are 'distinguished by their incompatibility with the dominant perceptions and values' (Jaggar 1996: 180) and which are necessary to forms of resistance. Rather, I want to suggest that feminism is not innocent of the attachments it critiques as bound up with the reproduction of power relations. As a result, emotions are crucial to showing us why transformations are so difficult (we remain invested in what we critique and resist), but also how they are possible (our investments move as we move/move away).

Indeed, we can reconsider the relationship between movement and attachment implicit in emotion. As I have already pointed out, the word emotion is linked to movement; emotions are what move us. But emotions are also about attachments, about what connects us to this or that. The relationship between movement and attachment is instructive. What moves us, what makes us feel, is also what holds us in place or gives us a dwelling place. Hence, movement does not cut the body off from the 'where' of its inhabitance but connects bodies to other bodies – indeed, attachment takes place through movement, through being moved by the proximity of others. The relationship between movement and attachment is contingent and this suggests that movement may affect different others differently (Ahmed 2000).

Emotions then are bound up with how we inhabit the world 'with' others. Since emotions are in the phenomenological sense always intentional, that is, they are 'directed' towards an object or other (however imaginary), then emotions are precisely about the intimacy of the 'with', of the relationship between selves, objects and others. I want to argue that intensifications of feeling create the very effect of the distinction between inside and outside or between the individual and the social, which allows the 'with' to be felt in the first place. Take, for instance, the sensation of pain. As Freud argued, it is through the intensity of experiences of pain that we become aware of bodily surfaces, or of the skin as bodily surface (Freud 1964: 26). However, it is not that pain causes the forming of the surface. Such a reading would ontologize pain (and indeed sensation more broadly) as that which 'drives' being itself. Rather, it is through the flow of sensations and feelings that become conscious as pain and pleasure that different surfaces are established. For example, say I stub my toe on the table. The impression of the table is one of negation; it leaves its trace on the surface of my skin and I respond with the appropriate 'ouch' and move away, swearing. It is through such painful encounters between this body and other objects, including other bodies, that 'surfaces' are felt as 'being there' in the first place. To be more precise, the impression of a surface is an effect of such intensifications of feeling. I become aware of my body as having a surface only in the event of feeling discomfort (prickly sensations, cramps), that become transformed into pain through an act of reading and recognition ('it hurts!'), which is also a judgement ('it is bad!'). This transformation of sensations into an 'emotion reading' might also lead to moving my body away from what I feel has caused the pain. That is, the transformation affected by recognizing a sensation as painful (from 'it hurts' to 'it is bad' to 'move away') also involves the re-constitution of bodily space.

Such an argument suggests an intimate relationship between what Judith Butler has called materialization – 'the effect of surface, boundary and fixity' (1993: 9) – and what I would call 'intensification'. It is through the intensification of feeling that bodies and worlds materialize and take shape or that the effect of surface, boundary and fixity is produced. What this argument suggests is that feelings are not about the inside getting out or the outside getting in but that they 'affect' the very distinction of inside and outside in the first place. Clearly, to say that feelings are crucial to the forming of surfaces and borders is also to suggest that what 'makes' those borders also unmakes them. In other words, what separates us from others also connects us to others. This paradox is clear if we think of the skin surface itself not only as that which appears to contain us, but also as that where others impress upon us. This contradictory function of skin begins to make sense if we unlearn the assumption that the skin is simply already there and think of the skin as a surface that is felt only in the event of being 'impressed upon' in the encounters we have with others (Ahmed and Stacey 2001). More generally, surfaces and boundaries (including the surfaces and boundaries of communities, as I will show later) are effects of the impressions of others.

Emotions do not simply come from within (the psyche) or without (society); they affect the very distinction between inside and outside, as well as the very surfacing of entities (including objects, bodies and communities). Despite the seeming immediacy of feelings, emotions are mediated; they are dependent on past associations and readings that effect the very affect. But what has this got to do with feminist attachments? I have already described how I can re-write my own coming into being as a feminist subject in terms of different feelings and emotions. At the same time, I suggested that such emotions were not the 'cause' of my identification with feminism (it is not a question of being driven into feminism as a necessary consequence of feeling a certain way), but were dependent on, and generative of, readings of the world. I will now investigate this relationship between reading and affect by focusing on how the 'mediation' of attachments is dependent on collectivity.

Feminism and Pain

Where else to begin but with pain? – a sensation or bodily feeling that I have already mentioned. There is a long history of thinking about the relationship between feminism and pain, in the sense that women's experiences of violence, injury and discrimination have been crucial to feminist politics (West 1999). Women's testimonies about pain – for example, about their experiences of violence or abuse – have been crucial not only to the formation of feminist subjects (a way of reading pain as a structural rather than incidental violence), but also to feminist collectives, which have mobilized around the injustice of that violence and the political and ethical demand for reparation and redress. We can think about feminist therapy and consciousness-raising groups in the 1970s precisely in terms of the transformation of pain into collectivity and resistance (Burstow 1992). Tauris argues that consciousness-raising groups were important because 'to question legitimate institutions and authorities, most people need to know that they are not alone, crazy or misguided' (1982: 246). Burstow suggests, in her work on radical feminist therapy, that 'the context in which this book is written is the fundamental unhappiness and alienation of women . . . It is that *unnecessary and yet unavoidable, individual yet common, suffering born of patriarchy and other systematic oppression*' (1992: xiii; emphasis in original). Feminist therapy and consciousness-raising groups allowed women to make connections between their lived experiences of pain and frustration in order to read such feelings as implicated in social and power relations. Hence, women's experiences of pain seem crucial to the mobilization of feminism as a response to the injustice of a violence that is structural as well as lived and bodily. But how does pain become a form of attachment to feminism that opens up the possibility of transformation?

Within some recent feminist scholarship there has been some criticism of the emphasis on pain as the condition of membership of a feminist community or, indeed, as the means by which the subjectivity of those who are subordinated is formed. Wendy Brown (1995: 55), for example, argues that there has been a 'fetishisation of the wound' in subaltern politics. Here, subaltern subjects become invested in the wound, such that the wound comes to stand for identity itself. For Brown, the idea that pain is what compels feminism into being is a sign of feminism's failure to 'move away' from the site of subordination or, more specifically, to resist transforming that subordination into an identity claim. I agree that the transformation of the wound into an identity is problematic. For example, we can see how, in Burstow's account of radical feminist therapy described above, pain becomes a means by which women's experience is universalized as an effect of patriarchy, at the same time as it remains individuated at the level of experience. This model is problematic precisely because of its fetishism: the transformation of the wound into an identity cuts the wound off from the complex histories of 'being hurt' or injured, histories which cannot be gathered together under a singular concept such as patriarchy. But our response to this ought not to be to 'forget' the wound: this would simply repeat the forgetting that is already implicated in the fetishization of the wound. Rather, our task would be to 'remember' how embodied subjects come to be wounded in the first place, a memory that would require that we read that pain, as well as recognize that pain itself is already read in the intensity of how it comes to be felt. The task would not only be to read and interpret pain as overdetermined, but also to do the work of translation, whereby pain is moved into a public domain. Following from bell hooks, we could see our task as being 'not to forget the past but break its hold' (1989: 155). In order to break the seal of the past, in order to move away from attachments that are hurtful, we must first bring them into the realm of political action, an act which requires, at the very same time, that we do not universalize pain as the ground of such political action.

Thus, I would agree with Brown that a politics that assumes access to subaltern pain is possible, and that her pain constitutes her identity, is problematic. Indeed, this model of pain is problematic. We need to contest this model of pain, not in order to liberate politics from pain, or even to move beyond pain through politics, but in order to inter-

243

rogate how pain already enters the sphere of 'politics', how pain is already lived and felt differently by those subjects whose bodily survival may be at stake. Pain matters for a collective politics; it matters in so far as the experience of pain is precisely about the bodily life of the process of harm and being harmed (violence involves a relationship of both force and harm). Harm does not simply happen; it is overdetermined as well as contingent. In other words, harm has a history, even though that history is made up of a combination of often surprising elements that are unavailable in the form of a totality. Pain is not simply an effect of a history of harm; it is the bodily life of that history. So while injustice cannot be reduced to feeling bad, as Lauren Berlant (2000) argues, we can also say that injustice is unjust precisely in so far as it affects the bodies of individuals and communities, that is, in so far as pain impresses upon the surfaces of those bodies or creates the effect of the surface in the intensity of its affect.

So how does feminism respond to pain or how is feminism an affect of the response of pain? Of course, we are assuming at one level that it is my pain we are talking about and that feminism is about reading one's own pain as an aspect of a broader and structural violence. Clearly, to read the pain of being beaten by a man as domestic violence, and to read that as an exercise of power, is still to be implicated in the work of reading: and it is this reading of an affect that we often name as feminist theory. But it is not a necessary reading, and the difficulty for feminism is often that the affect of pain is read very differently by others, in a way that often privatizes pain, rather than seeing pain as an effect of the social and political distribution of power. While we are talking here about the contingency of feminist readings of pain as structural violence, it is nevertheless crucial to signify the relationship between such readings and the formation of attachments that are moving. While feminism may involve reading pain a certain way, it is also the affect of pain that often compels a movement into feminist consciousness, or that moves us to speak out against the forms of power we have read as already at stake in the experience of pain as such. In other words, what we read as well as what moves us is bound up with the formation of a feminist attachment.

It is important to remember here that feminism is not simply about the individual subject reading her own history in terms of the collective; it is about other bodies, whose pain is also part of the feminist attachment. When we talk of the experience of pain we assume it is 'my pain' because I cannot feel the other's pain. Much of the thinking on pain contrasts the ungraspability of the other's pain with the graspability of my own pain. Elaine Scarry makes this contrast in her analysis of pain and torture (1985: 4). But in some sense it is the ungraspability of the other's pain that compels us to approach others and that hence binds us with others (the ungraspability of the other's pain is attached then to the ungraspability of my own pain). As I respond to another's pain, I am responding to the urgency of that which cannot be grasped, an 'ungraspability' (rather than an identity) that is shared and that constitutes what we could call the sociality of pain. The sociality of pain requires an ethics and politics that begins with another's pain and moves towards others. In so far as an approach of pain begins here, then I must act about what I cannot know, rather than act in so far as I know. I am moved by what does not belong to me. If I act on her behalf only in so far as I knew how she felt (the fantasy of empathy), then I would act only in so far as I would appropriate her pain as my pain, that is, appropriate what I cannot feel. Such an approach would amount to violence.

Feminism does have a relationship to pain, a relationship that is mediated, as well as affective, intense as well as dependent on interpretation. But feminism does not come into being because pain offers an identity but because pain fails to offer an identity. Indeed, I have suggested that pain might be compelling precisely because it resists being transformed into an identity; it opens up oneself to others whose bodies one does not and cannot inhabit, even if they are near us, even if we approach them. Pain demands an urgent approach, an urgency that does not overcome the differences that require us to make an approach in the first place. Feminism's collective project becomes then a way of responding to the pain of others, as a pain that cannot be directly accessed but only ever approached. Crucially, responding to pain is dependent on speaking about pain and such speech acts are the condition for the formation of a 'we', made up of different stories of pain that cannot be reduced to a ground, identity or sameness. Stories of pain can be 'shared' only when we assume they are not the same story, even if they are connected and allow us to make connections. As bell hooks argues, naming one's own personal pain is insufficient, and, indeed, can easily be incorporated into the narcissistic agendas of neoliberal and therapeutic culture. For hooks, feminism can only move through and with pain into politics if that pain is linked to the 'overall education for critical consciousness of collective political resistance' (1989: 32). The politics of collectivity is about responding to the pain of others without assuming one can inhabit their bodies. This is not an attachment that assumes access to the truth of the other's feelings, nor is it an attachment that assumes that one's own feelings are the foundation for what compels us to connect with others.

Feminism and Anger

The relationship between pain and anger seems crucial to my argument in the previous section. It is not just that pain compels us to move into feminism – or compels feminism as a movement of social and political transformation. The response to pain, as a call for action, also seems to require anger: an interpretation that this pain is wrong, that it is an outrage, and that something must be done about it. But it is precisely the intimacy of pain and anger within feminism that Wendy Brown critiques as a form of *resentiment*. She argues that political claims made as claims of injury against something or somebody (society, the state, the middle classes, men, white people and so on) work as a form of reaction or negation (Brown 1995: 73). Brown argues that reactions to injury are inadequate as a basis for politics as such reactions make action impossible. That is, the over-investment in the wound 'comes into conflict with the need to give up these investments' (1995: 73). Brown sets up an opposition between reaction and negation as responses to injury and an action which she suggests earlier might wish to 'forget' the injury or, indeed, the history of that injury in the pursuit of a different kind of future (1995: 56). Hence, her argument implies that all forms of reaction lead to the fetishization of the wound. While Brown's critique is an important one, I would also suggest that there is no 'pure action' which is outside such a history of 'reaction', whereby bodies come to be 'impressed upon' by the surfaces of others. This is important as it suggests that if feminism is an emotional as well as ethical and political response to what it is against, then what feminism is against is not exterior to feminism and, indeed, may give that politics its edge. If anger is a form of 'against-ness', then it is precisely about the impossibility of moving beyond the history of injuries to a pure or innocent position. Anger then does not necessarily require an investment in revenge; 'being against something' is dependent not only on how one reads what one is against (for example, whether violence against women is read as dependent on male psychology or on structures of power), but also on what forms of action are felt to be possible given that reading.

More broadly within feminism, of course, the passion of anger has been seen as crucial. Nowhere is this clearer than in the work of Audre

Lorde, specifically in her critiques of racism against black women. As she writes so powerfully:

> My response to racism is anger. I have lived with that anger ignoring it, feeding it, learning to use it, before it laid my visions to waste for most of my life. Once I did it in silence, afraid of the weight. My fear of anger taught me nothing . . . Anger expressed and translated into action in the service of our vision and our future is a liberating and strengthening act of clarification . . . Anger is loaded with information and energy. (Lorde 1984: 127)

Here, anger is constructed in different ways: as a response to the injustice of racism; as a vision of the future; as a translation of pain into knowledge; as being 'loaded with information and energy'. Crucially, anger is not simply defined in relation to a past but as opening up the future. In other words, being against something does not end with 'what one is against' (it does not become 'stuck' on the object of either the emotion or the critique, though that object remains sticky and compelling). Being against something is also being for something but something that has yet to be articulated or is not yet. As Lorde shows us, anger is visionary and the fear of anger, or the transformation of anger into silence, is a turning away from the future (1989: 127). So, while anger is determined, it is not fully determined. It translates pain but also needs to be translated. As I pointed out earlier, the word emotion is linked to movement and translation: it is precisely a movement across and between, a movement that creates the very effect or surface of entities. So emotions of hate and pain are moving not because they have an inherent quality or meaning, but because they move us across and between different bodies, who surface as an effect of the movement. Feminism, as a response to pain and as a form of anger directed against that pain, is dependent then on acts of translation that are moving. For Lorde, anger involves the naming of various practices and experiences as racism, but it also involves imagining a different kind of world in its very 'energy' (1989: 127). If anger energizes feminist subjects, it also requires those subjects to 'read' and 'move' from anger into a different bodily world, not one that forgets what one is against (however much the 'what' cannot be assumed to be an object), but one that is moved by all that cannot be contained in the response of 'against-ness'. If anger pricks our skin, if it makes us shudder, sweat and tremble, then it might just shudder us into new ways of being; it might just enable us to inhabit a different kind of skin, even if that skin remains marked or scarred by what we are against.

Clearly anger involves a reading of pain (which also involves reading): we do not all respond with anger and to be angry is to assume that something is wrong. However, it is not necessarily the case that something is named or felt to be the cause of anger: there are moments of anger where it is unclear what one is angry about and all these moments do not necessarily gather together to form a coherent response. Or, as Carol Tauris puts it: 'There is no one-to-one correspondence between feeling angry and knowing why' (1982: 18). But feminism also involves a reading of the response of anger: it moves from anger into an interpretation of what one is against, whereby associations or connections are made between the object of anger and broader patterns or structures. This is what allows an object of knowledge to be delineated. The object is not then the ground of feminism (it does not come first, as it were) but is an effect of a feminist response. Anger is in this sense creative; it works to create a language with which to respond to what one is against, whereby 'the what' is re-named and brought into the feminist world.

This process is dynamic. We can see this by the different ways in which feminists have named what they are against (patriarchy, sexual difference, gender relations, gender hierarchy, phallocentrism). Indeed, different feminisms construct the 'object' of anger quite differently, in ways that are in tension, although they may share some connections. The attachment implicit in the response to anger is hence not simply about the creation of an object (and to create is not to create something out of nothing, but to produce a name out of a set of differential relations), as the object always fails to be secured. Not only have feminists created different names for what they are against, but they have also recognized that what they are against does not have the contours of an object that is given; it is not a positive entity. This is implicit in the very argument that gender permeates all aspects of social life and that it is in this sense 'worldly'. Anger moves us by moving us outwards; while it creates an object, it also is not directed simply against an object but becomes a response to the world, as such. In this way, feminist anger involves a reading of the world, a reading of how, for example, gender hierarchy permeates all aspects of sociality, is implicated in other forms of power relations, including race, class and sexuality and is bound up with the very construction as well as regulation of bodies and spaces. Anger against objects or events, directed against this or that, moves feminism into a bigger critique of what is. Feminism becomes a critique that loses an object and, hence, opens itself up to forms of possibility that cannot be simply located in what is. This allows us to recognize that it is when feminism is no longer directed towards a critique of patriarchy, or secured by the categories of 'women' or 'gender', that it is doing the most 'moving' work. The loss of such an object is not the failure of feminist activism but is indicative of its capacity to move or to become a movement. Feminism is still here compelled by what it is against but no longer is that 'againstness' de-limited as an object. So anger is a reading and is already read: it is an affect and it is affective; it energizes feminism precisely at the point of creating and losing an object. It is the loss of the object, rather than its creation, that binds or sticks feminism together as a movement no longer directed against an object that could be simply absent or present. This loss of the object is about opening up the possibility of trans/formation, of a change in all that has already taken form.

Wonder and Hope

In this final section, I want us to reflect on the intimacy of critique and affirmation in feminist attachments and in the forming of collectivity as an attachment. My relationship to feminism has never felt like one borne out of negation: it is never felt to be reducible to the pain, anger or rage that has nevertheless, at times, given my politics a sense of urgency. It has also felt like something creative, something that responds to the world with love and care, as well as an attention to details that are surprising. Luce Irigaray emphasizes this relation between wonder and movement: 'Wonder is the motivating force behind mobility in all its dimensions' (1993: 73). Sometimes how we feel and what we think are contained within the reproduction of the ordinary. Nothing noticeable happens and repetition, while it creates desire, sometimes just goes on and on. But then something happens which is out of the ordinary – and hence a relation to the ordinary – and that something surprises us. Surprise engenders new forms of movement, and hence new forms of attachment.

Certainly, when I first came into contact with feminism and began to read my own life and the life of others differently, everything became surprising. At the time, this felt like moving out of false consciousness, though now I see that I was not moving into the truth as such, but just towards a reading which explained things better. I felt as if I was seeing the world for the first time and that all that I took for granted as given – as a question of the way things were – was made, was particular and contingent. Wonder is about being moved by what is before us: it is about movement, but a movement that is made possible by being surprised by what is held still. It is through wonder that pain and anger come to life, as wonder allows us to notice what hurts, what causes pain and what we feel to be wrong, is not necessary, and can be unmade as well as made. Wonder is what energizes the very hope of transformation, the very will to politics.

For me, the politics of teaching women's studies, in which feminist pedagogy becomes a form of activism as a way of 'being moved', has been bound up with wonder, with engendering a sense of surprise about how it is that the world has come to take the shape that it has. Feminist teaching (rather than teaching feminism) begins with that opening, that pause or hesitation that refuses to allow the taken for granted to be granted. In the women's studies classroom, students might respond first with a sense of assurance (this is the way the world is), then with disbelief (how can the world by like this?) and towards a sense of wonder (how did the world come to take this shape?). The critical wonder that feminism has always involved for me is precisely about the troubling affect of certain questions: questions like 'how has the world taken the shape that it has?', but also 'why is it that power relations are so difficult to transform?', 'what does it mean to be invested in the conditions of subordination as well as dominance?', and so on. But what is striking about feminist wonder is that the critical gaze is not simply directed outwards, as it were; rather, feminist wonder becomes wonder about the very forms of feminism that have emerged here or there. So we might stop and think: 'how is it that feminism comes to take form the way that it does?', 'how is it that women's studies has taken this shape?', and 'how can feminism work to transform the world in this way or that?'. The wonder of women's studies hence must return to the teacher, who is also a student, who also must learn through unlearning what has been granted or given. This critical wonder is about recognizing that nothing in the world can be taken for granted, which includes the very political movements to which we are attached. It is this critical wonder about the forms of political struggle that made Black feminism such an important intervention, by showing that the categories we produce in knowledge (such as patriarchy, or even the category of 'women') can have political effects, in the sense that they can work to exclude others from the collective (Lorde 1984; hooks 1989). Black feminists show us the intimacy between the emotional response of wonder, critical thinking and forms of activism that try to break with old ways of doing and of inhabiting the world.

So wonder is also for me a question of hope, a hope that things can be different, and that the world can take different forms. Politics without hope is impossible and hope without politics is a reification of possibility (and becomes merely religious). Indeed, it is hope that makes involvement in direct forms of political activism enjoyable: the sense that 'gathering together' is about opening up the world, claiming some space through forms of 'affective bonding' (Roseneil 1995: 98). But hope is also implicit in the very attachment to protest: it suggests that what angers us is not inevitable, even if transformation can sometimes feel impossible. Indeed, anger without hope can lead to despair or a sense of tiredness produced by the 'inevitability' of the repetition of what one is against. But wonder and hope are not simply about the possibilities of the future implicit in the very failure of repetition – what Judith Butler (1993), amongst others, has called 'iterability', the structural possibility that things will be repeated with a difference. It would be tempting to say that it is in the failure of the past to repeat itself that the conditions for political hope might exist. But such an argument would empty politics of work and it would allow us to do nothing. Instead, I would argue that wonder and hope involve a relationship to the present and to the present as affected by its imperfect translation of the past. It is in the present that the bodies of subjects shudder with an expectation of what is otherwise; it is in the very unfolding of the past in the present. The moment of hope is when the 'not yet' impresses upon us in the present, such that we must act, politically, to make it our future. If hope impresses upon us in the present rather than being merely 'futural' (Benjamin 1997), then hope requires that we must act in the present, rather than simply wait for a future that is always before us.

The openness that gathers, even in the struggle against what is, involves the coming together of different bodies. It is here that the feminist 'we' becomes affective; it is here that such a 'we' is affected. For the opening up of what is possible takes time, work and love: a love for others, a connectedness to and with others, as well as work for and by others. One does not hope alone but for others, whose pain one does not feel but whose pain becomes a thread in the weave of the present, touched as it is by all that could be. Through the very work of listening to others, of hearing the force of their pain and the energy of their anger, of learning to be surprised by all that one feels

Sara Ahmed

oneself to be against, through all of this, a 'we' is formed, and an attachment is made. This is a feminist attachment, and attachment to feminism, and it is moving. I am moved by the 'we', as the 'we' is an affect of all the movements towards it. It is not an innocent 'we', or one that stands still. It is affected by the very 'against-ness' that calls it into being and so it is affected by what it is against, which cannot be reduced to an object, and hence also what it is for. Here, you might say, one moves towards others, others who are attached to feminism, as a movement away from all that we are against. Such movements create the surface of a feminist community. Here, in the very forming and deforming of attachments, in the writing, conversations, the doing, the work, feminism moves and is moved; it connects and is connected. More than anything, it is in the alignment of the 'we' with the 'I', the feminist collective with the feminist subject, an alignment which is imperfect and hence generative, that a new grammar of social existence might yet be possible. The 'we' of feminism is not its foundation; it is both an affect and an effect of the impressions of others.

So if feminism is an affect of everyday attachments – as a way of reading as well as responding to forms of pain and anger with a sense of wonder and hope – it can also become something that we are attached to. Of course, this is not to posit that feminism exists as if it were an object before us. Rather, one becomes stuck to the name 'feminism', not as that which refers to one thing in particular but as that which is associated with all that has moved us against what is. The word sticks and it sticks us together: not in a kind of 'happy sisterhood', but in a way that allows us to move through the world differently. And so, everyday, we might be compelled to declare 'I am/we are feminists', even when the meaning of the word is not decided in advance, indeed *because* it is not decided and because it has effects that are, as yet, not lived. So we say it, and we say it with a certain kind of love, a love that is impure, and not easy, but one that might give us life, a life that has all the vitality of the living, even if it is a life that has yet to take form.

References and Further Reading

Ahmed, S. (1998) *Differences that Matter: Feminist Theory and Postmodernism.* Cambridge: Cambridge University Press.

— (2000) *Strange Encounters: Embodied Others in Post-coloniality*. London: Routledge.

— and Stacey, J. (2001) *Thinking Through the Skin*. London: Routledge.

Bell, V. (1999) *Feminist Imagination*. London: Sage.

Benjamin, A. (1997) *Present Hope: Philosophy, Architecture, Judaism*. London: Routledge.

Berlant, L. (2000) The subject of true feeling: pain, privacy and politics. In S. Ahmed, J. Kilby, C. Lury, M. McNeil and B. Skeggs (eds), *Transformations: Thinking Through Feminism*, pp. 33–47. London: Routledge.

Brodribb, S. (1992) *Nothing Mat(t)ers: A Feminist Critique of Postmodernism*. Melbourne: Spinifex.

Brown, W. (1995) *States of Injury: Power and Freedom in Late Modernity*. Princeton, NJ: Princeton University Press.

Burstow, B. (1992) *Radical Feminist Therapy: Working in the Context of Violence*. Newbury Park, CA: Sage.

Butler, J. (1993) *Bodies that Matter: On the Discursive Limits of 'Sex'*. New York: Routledge.

— (1997) *The Psychic Life of Power: Theories in Subjection*. Stanford, CA: Stanford University Press.

Cvetkovich, A. (1992) *Mixed Feelings: Feminism, Mass Culture and Victorian Sensationalism*. New Brunswick, NJ: Rutgers University Press.

Freud, S. (1964) *The Standard Edition of the Complete Psychological Works of Sigmund Freud*, Vol. 19, trans. J. Strachey. London: The Hogarth Press (work first published 1911).

Griffin, G. (ed.) (1995) *Feminist Activism in the 1990s*. London: Taylor and Francis.

hooks, b. (1989) *Talking Back: Thinking Feminist – Thinking Black*. London: Sheba Feminist.

Irigaray, L. (1993) *The Ethics of Sexual Difference*. London: Athlone Press.

Jaggar, A. (1996) Love and knowledge: emotion in feminist epistemology. In A. Garry and M. Pearsall (eds), *Women, Knowledge and Reality: Explorations in Feminist Philosophy*, pp. 166–90. New York: Routledge.

Klein, R. D. (1991) Passion and politics in women's studies in the 1990s. In J. Aaron and S. Walby (eds), *Out of the Margins: Women's Studies in the 1990s*, pp. 75–89. London: The Falmer Press.

Lees, S. (1991) Feminist politics and women's studies: struggle, not incorporation. In J. Aaron and S. Walby (eds), *Out of the Margins: Women's Studies in the 1990s*, pp. 90–104. London: The Falmer Press.

Lorde, A. (1984) *Sister Outsider: Essays and Speeches*. Freedom, CA: The Crossing Press.

Lupton, D. (1998) *The Emotional Self: A SocioCultural Explanation*. London: Sage.

McNay, L. (2000) *Gender and Agency: Reconfiguring the Subject in Feminist and Social Theory*. Cambridge: Polity Press.

Probyn, E. (1996) *Outside Belongings*. London: Routledge.

Roseneil, S. (1995) *Disarming Patriarchy: Feminism and Political Action at Green-ham*. Milton Keynes: Open University Press.

Scarry, E. (1985) *The Body in Pain: The Making and Unmaking of the World*. New York: Oxford University Press.

Tauris, Carol (1982) *Anger: The Misunderstood Emotion*. New York: Touchstone Books.

West, T. C. (1999) *Wounds of the Spirit: Black Women, Violence and Resistance Ethics*. New York: State University of New York Press.

Select Bibliography

Ahmed, S., Kilby, J., Lury, C., McNeil, M. and Skeggs, B. (eds) (2000) *Transformations: Thinking Through Feminism*. London: Routledge.

Beauvoir, S. de (1953) *The Second Sex*. Harmondsworth: Penguin.

Bergvall, V., Bing, J. and Freed, A. (eds) (1996) *Rethinking Language and Gender Research: Theory and Practice*. London: Longman.

Butler, J. (1993) *Bodies that Matter: On the Discursive Limits of 'Sex'*. New York: Routledge.

Carson, F. and Pajaczkowska, C. (2001) *Feminist Visual Culture*. London: Routledge.

Collins, P. Hill (1990) *Black Feminist Thought: Knowledge, Consciousness and the Politics of Empowerment*. Boston, MA: Unwin and Hyman.

Foucault, M. (1978) *The History of Sexuality, Vol. 1: An Introduction*, trans. R. Hurley. Harmondsworth: Penguin.

Freud, S. (1975) *Three Essays on the Theory of Sexuality*, trans. J. Strachey (intro. by S. Marcus). New York: Basic Books.

Haraway, D. (1991) *Simians, Cyborgs, and Women: The Reinvention of Nature*. London: Free Association Press.

hooks, b. (1991) *Yearning: Race, Gender, and Cultural Politics*. London: Turnaround Press.

Jagger, A. and Young, I. M. (eds) (1998) *A Companion to Feminist Philosophy*. Oxford: Blackwell.

Kirkup, G. et al. (eds) (2000) *The Gendered Cyborg: A Reader*. London: Routledge.

de Lauretis, T. (1987) *Technologies of Gender: Essays on Theory, Film, and Fiction*. Bloomington, IN: Indiana University Press.

McDowell, L. (1999) *Gender, Identity and Place: Understanding Feminist Geographies*. Cambridge: Polity Press.

Marx, K. (1959) *Capital*, Vol. 1. Moscow: Progress.

Mulvey, L. (1989) *Visual and Other Pleasures*. London: Macmillan.

Nicholson, L. (ed.) (1997) *The Second Wave: A Reader in Feminist Theory*. London: Routledge.

Scott, J. W. (1988) *Gender and the Politics of History*. New York: Columbia University Press.

Spivak, G. Chakravorty (1987) *In Other Worlds: Essays in Cultural Politics*. London: Methuen.

Tong, R. (1998) *Feminist Thought: A Comprehensive Introduction*. Boulder, CO: Westview Press.

Woolf, V. (1993) *A Room of One's Own* (1929). In M. Barrett (ed.), *A Room of One's Own and Three Guineas*. Harmondsworth: Penguin.

Index